ALSO BY TOM COYNE

Fiction

A Gentleman's Game

Nonfiction

Paper Tiger

A Course Called Ireland

A COURSE CALLED SCOTLAND

Searching the Home of Golf

for the Secret to Its Game

Tom Coyne

SIMON & SCHUSTER

New York   London   Toronto   Sydney   New Delhi

Simon & Schuster
1230 Avenue of the Americas
New York, NY 10020

PHOTO INSERT CREDITS:
Insert p. 1—top photo (Open Dreaming); p. 6—bottom two photos
   (Fortrose & Rosemarkie GC and Castle Stuart); and p. 8—top photo
   (Highlands): Courtesy of Kevin Kirk/Recounter.
Insert p. 4—bottom photo (chute): Courtesy of Kevin Markham.
All other photos are courtesy of Tom Coyne.

First Simon & Schuster hardcover edition July 2018

SIMON & SCHUSTER and colophon are registered trademarks of Simon & Schuster, Inc.

For information about special discounts for bulk purchases,
please contact Simon & Schuster Special Sales at 1-866-506-1949
or business@simonandschuster.com.

The Simon & Schuster Speakers Bureau can bring authors to your live event.
For more information or to book an event, contact the
Simon & Schuster Speakers Bureau at 1-866-248-3049
or visit our website at www.simonspeakers.com.

Interior design by Ruth Lee-Mui
Maps on chapter openers by Jeffrey L. Ward

Manufactured in the United States of America

10   9   8   7   6   5   4   3   2   1

Library of Congress Cataloging-in-Publication Data is available.

ISBN 978-1-4767-5428-4
ISBN 978-1-4767-5430-7 (ebook)

To my girls,
of course

Alas! why plainen men so in commúne
Of purveyance of God or of Fortune,
That giveth them full oft in many a guise
Well better than they can themselves devise?

> —Geoffrey Chaucer,
> "The Knightes Tale,"
> *The Canterbury Tales*

Life is short. Golf very, very often. And dance naked!

> —Gramma Billy

ROUND

1. Littlestone Golf Club
2. Royal Cinque Ports
3. Prince's Golf Club
4. Royal St. George's Golf Club
5. Mullion Golf Club
6. Perranporth Golf Club
7. Trevose Golf & Country Club
8. Royal North Devon Golf Club
9. St. Enodoc Golf Club
10. Holyhead Golf Club
11. Bull Bay Golf Club
12. Conwy (Caernarvonshire) Golf Club
13. Wallasey Golf Club
14. Royal Liverpool Golf Club Hoylake
15. Royal Lytham & St. Annes Golf Club
16. Royal Birkdale Golf Club
17. Blackpool North Shore Golf Club
18. Eyemouth Golf Club
19. Dunbar Golf Club
20. Glen Golf Club
21. North Berwick Golf Club
22. Archerfield Dirleton Links
23. Muirfield
24. Gullane Golf Club, No. 2
25. Renaissance Club
26. Kilspindie Golf Club
27. Kingarrock Hickory Golf
28. Craigielaw Golf Club
29. St. Andrews Links, Eden Course
30. St. Andrews Links, Strathtyrum Course
31. Burntisland Golf House Club
32. Kinghorn Golf Club
33. Lundin Golf Club
34. Leven Links Golf Course
35. The Golf House Club, Elie
36. St. Andrews Links, Jubilee Course

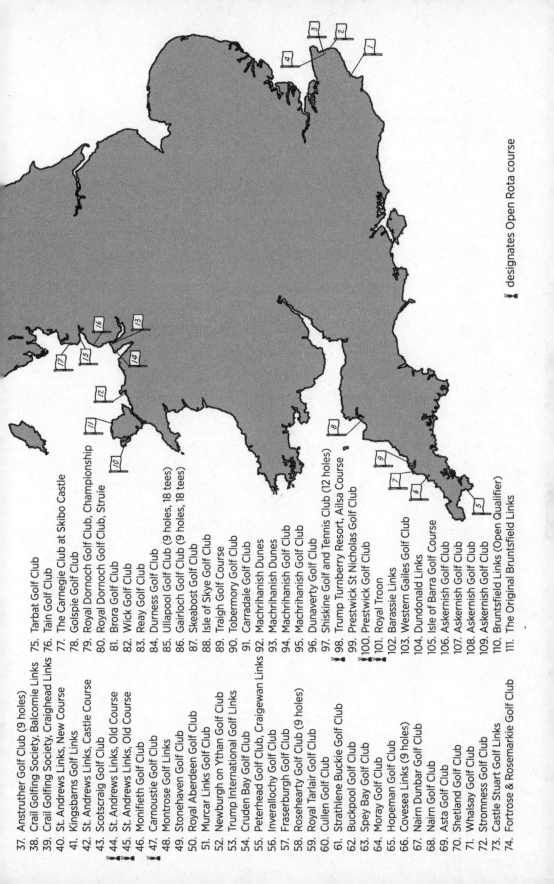

designates Open Rota course

37. Anstruther Golf Club (9 holes)
38. Crail Golfing Society, Balcomie Links
39. Crail Golfing Society, Craighead Links
40. St. Andrews Links, New Course
41. Kingsbarns Golf Links
42. St. Andrews Links, Castle Course
43. Scotscraig Golf Club
44. St. Andrews Links, Old Course
45. St. Andrews Links, Old Course
46. Monifieth Golf Club
47. Carnoustie Golf Club
48. Montrose Golf Links
49. Stonehaven Golf Club
50. Royal Aberdeen Golf Club
51. Murcar Links Golf Club
52. Newburgh on Ythan Golf Club
53. Trump International Golf Links
54. Cruden Bay Golf Club
55. Peterhead Golf Club, Craigewan Links
56. Inverallochy Golf Club
57. Fraserburgh Golf Club
58. Rosehearty Golf Club (9 holes)
59. Royal Tarlair Golf Club
60. Cullen Bay Golf Club
61. Strathlene Buckie Golf Club
62. Buckpool Golf Club
63. Spey Bay Golf Club
64. Moray Golf Club
65. Hopeman Golf Club
66. Covesea Links (9 holes)
67. Nairn Dunbar Golf Club
68. Nairn Golf Club
69. Asta Golf Club
70. Shetland Golf Club
71. Whalsay Golf Club
72. Stromness Golf Club
73. Castle Stuart Golf Links
74. Fortrose & Rosemarkie Golf Club

75. Tarbat Golf Club
76. Tain Golf Club
77. The Carnegie Club at Skibo Castle
78. Golspie Golf Club
79. Royal Dornoch Golf Club, Championship
80. Royal Dornoch Golf Club, Struie
81. Brora Golf Club
82. Wick Golf Club
83. Reay Golf Club
84. Durness Golf Club
85. Ullapool Golf Club (9 holes, 18 tees)
86. Gairloch Golf Club (9 holes, 18 tees)
87. Skeabost Golf Club
88. Isle of Skye Golf Club
89. Traigh Golf Course
90. Tobermory Golf Club
91. Carradale Golf Club
92. Machrihanish Dunes
93. Machrihanish Dunes
94. Machrihanish Golf Club
95. Machrihanish Golf Club
96. Dunaverty Golf Club
97. Shiskine Golf and Tennis Club (12 holes)
98. Trump Turnberry Resort, Ailsa Course
99. Prestwick St Nicholas Golf Club
100. Prestwick Golf Club
101. Royal Troon
102. Barassie Links
103. Western Gailes Golf Club
104. Dundonald Links
105. Isle of Barra Golf Course
106. Askernish Golf Club
107. Askernish Golf Club
108. Askernish Golf Club
109. Askernish Golf Club
110. Bruntsfield Links (Open Qualifier)
111. The Original Bruntsfield Links

A COURSE
CALLED
SCOTLAND

Spero

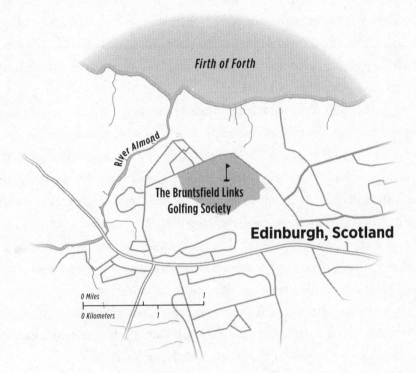

His bones arrived by shipwreck. In life he was a fisherman, but he did not die at sea. He persuaded his executioners to tie him to an × of wooden beams and expired after two days lashed to his crooked cross. He considered himself unworthy of being crucified by the same design as his savior.

Accounts describe his gratitude for martyrdom. As death approached, he proclaimed, "Receive me hanging from the wood of this sweet cross. . . . Do not permit them to loosen me." And history records the travels of a Greek monk, St. Rule, to whom God gave instructions to move the martyr's bones for safekeeping. Rule was to sail with the relics to the edge of the known world and build a church where the faithful would flock, finding health and hope.

Storms pushed the monk aground near a tiny fishing village that would be transformed just as Rule's visions foretold. A cathedral would be built, and a castle and a university, and it would become a place of learning and pilgrimage. A visionary cleric and a divine storm would turn a rocky bit of coastline at the fringe of civilization into a place that, eight centuries later, is still visited by six hundred thousand hopefuls every year. I'm one of them, though my route here was different than most. I designed my own shipwreck of a journey and prayed that my bones would land somewhere near the one-time resting place of St. Andrew.

Whether golf owes its origins to bored shepherds searching out diversions in the dunes or to itinerant wool traders who brought a Flemish game to Scotland, the home of golf would probably be a modest village today if a holy mission hadn't sent an apostle's remains ashore there. Maybe that's why the world's perfect town feels so divinely inspired, as if God wants you to be there. When you stroll the medieval streets of St. Andrews, with its mix of ancient history and college youth, its gentle bustle of golf and restaurants and golf and pubs and golf and museums, you walk with a sense of destination that St. Rule must also have felt. And since he could have simply sent the bones to Constantinople as the great emperor Constantine decreed instead of washing up on a stretch of sublimely golf-suited land, the saint's mission stands as proof that God is good—and that He's a golfer, too.

I want to believe all of that, just as I want to believe that one morning in the ninth century a Scottish king looked up and saw St. Andrew's diagonal cross in the sky above—white clouds against a blue sky—and took it as a sign to march outnumbered against the Angles. His vision and victory gave birth to the Scottish flag—white ✕ against a blue backdrop—and is too good a story to not be true. And I want to believe that the patron saint of golfers did actually utter St. Andrews' town motto as his final words, the Latin phrase now stitched into my putter cover and the only tattoo I might ever get: *Dum Spiro Spero*. While I breathe, I hope.

I'm not sure I actually believe any of that, but I do breathe, and I do hope. And maybe hope will be enough, or maybe it will be too much. When does hope become the dream that becomes a mistake? Do the clouds ever steer you wrong? Is your morning perspective sometimes slanted? What if you walk into battle while the miracles stay home? *Dum Spiro Spero*, but how many have hoped their way right out of breath?

I can't help but wonder these things as I stare at that blue and white flag stamped onto a dimpled ball at my feet, the plastic gleaming clean from my caddie's towel, struck three times this morning and still six feet from the hole. In these six feet there are three years, four hundred rounds, thousands of miles, and every dollar at my disposal. There are 107 British links courses played in less than two months. There are thirty-seven pounds of me lost among the dunes, spread over a million-yard walk in search of the secret to golf, and this par putt on hole one just outside of Edinburgh, Scotland, at a qualifying event for the Open Championship at St. Andrews—this meager distance—holds every ounce of it. A putt to prove it meant something, that I was right, that it was okay to think the wind held some providence, that we didn't crash into the shore by chance—rather, we arrived safely, and found happy destiny waiting for us.

Six feet to proof.

Who knows how a golf swing actually begins, how many neurons and synapses and small muscles have to get to *go*? That wasn't the mystery I was trying to answer on this odyssey—but maybe it should have been, because as I stare down at a silver putter head beside a white ball, I wonder which one is supposed to move first. Something terrifying and miraculous can happen over meaty par putts in competition: An infinite universe comes to fit neatly within the space of a golf ball. Time spins to a halt, and our bodies become inhabited by an unfamiliar presence. Too often that presence has shaky fingers and a grudge against God—*Go in, goddammit.* But the myriad rounds played in preparation for this one pay a dividend, because I suddenly feel an improbable movement in my shoulders; my body rocks, the clubhead comes unstuck and bumps the ball, sends it rolling, rolling.

I'm not breathing. But I am hoping.

Recall

London, England

BAYSWATER

WEST-END

River Thames

Green Park

0 Miles   1

0 Kilometers   1

When I was in college, I spent a semester studying literature in London. I spent most of my time getting lost in the West End and talking about books I hadn't read as though I had written them, waiting for the bartender to pull another pint of bitter. I was twenty years old with a handful of pounds knocking around in my pocket, roaming the city in search of bookshops and free museums and girls who fancied a Yankee accent. It was the time of my life. But I don't recall any part of that spring abroad as fondly as I remember the weekend my roommates and I hopped the train for Scotland.

I forged a passable handicap certificate for my flatmates, and my best friend Robert and I waited for my spikes to arrive in the mail from home.

We picked a bank holiday weekend and entered our names in a lottery for a Saturday foursome, and when we arrived at our destination Friday evening, our names were posted by the first tee, owners of a late-afternoon tee time—the last of the day—at the Old Course at St. Andrews. We ran off to rent golf clubs and find a bed for the night, then went to toast our good fortune, sure to ask the bartender for whisky, because as Robert had warned us during the train ride from London, when in Scotland, you don't call it Scotch.

I have chased a golf ball around much of the globe, but my college weekend in St. Andrews remains the standard against which all other golf getaways have been measured. We lost golf balls all over St. Andrews that weekend, soaked through to our skin after packing nothing but sweaters, smiles stuck to our faces as we walked fairways that we knew we would remember for the rest of our lives. We warmed our soggy bones with clubhouse brown and didn't talk very much, a little bit stunned by what we had just done. While our friends were backpacking around Barcelona and Bruges, we had lived our fathers' dreams. I called mine to tell him that I had just signed my card from the Old Course, and to warn him about the charges headed for his Amex. Nothing I might have learned or accomplished that semester could have made my dad any prouder.

It was a different life, and looking back, it seems a perfect one. I'm no longer in touch with the two flatmates who made up our foursome, but I know that every July when the Open Championship returns to our televisions at breakfast time, we each recall an erstwhile weekend and wish that we could go back. It's one of my rare fond memories in which I don't wish I'd had a greater appreciation of the experience as it was happening. I appreciated everything about my afternoon on the Old Course—every swing, every step.

Years later, as I watched Phil Mickelson lift the Claret Jug at Muirfield, that trip came back to me with not just nostalgia but also a bit of urgency. Breaking 80 with rented clubs, eating cheeseburgers instead of haggis, discovering a golf course that felt both accidental and ideal—I was in that weekend getaway again, shaping my shots off the sea breeze, billiarding my ball through rippled gorges, imagining grandstands of well-mannered mayhem as I tapped in on eighteen and cradled the Jug like a newborn.

I could play that golf. I *had* played that golf. Pure links golf was about playing with the landscape, not over it, and it didn't demand pretty or perfect golf shots; rather, links golf required guts. Perseverance. Creativity. Balls. It was a boxing match—stay on your feet and fight your way home—and I loved everything about it. Mickelson rope-a-doped the field that Sunday and turned me into a Phil fan, and as I watched the rest of the players pull up lame behind him, I got a text from a British friend who I expected was forlorn about his championship going to the grinning American.

Julian was a tall and easygoing Englishman who was always eager and ill-prepared for my golf adventures. He had joined me on my trip around Ireland with little more in his bag than designer sneakers and a comb, but if a journey offered the possibility of golf followed by a bright afternoon spent in a dark pub, Julian was up for it. He was born and raised in Manchester, found love in the States, and had recently relocated to Germany with a new baby in tow. Our chances of crossing paths seemed relegated to chance until Julian texted to suggest a get-together of my particular flavor:

Did u know there are only 14 brit open courses? Let's play them.

It might have seemed an absurd request for a golfing reunion, but Julian knew he had the right audience. Not only was I in a particularly wistful links mood, recalling the tall and wavy dunes of a former golfing life, but something had happened a few months before this Open that had my fingers itching for the oldest trophy in golf, the one Mickelson was holding to his lips at that very moment. Back in May, I had lived every bad player's dream and violated every good player's protocol—surely bringing me decades of bad luck on the course—for having hoisted the Claret Jug with my own hands and smiling for a picture.

I was revisiting Portrush in Northern Ireland as the host of a travel television show that involved me ad-libbing course commentary to the effect of "Amazing" and "*Really* amazing" a few dozen times per episode. When we finished filming at Royal Portrush, we met the club captain to thank him for giving us an interview and to assure him that our show had an Oprah-like following back in the States—among Mid-Atlantic golfers who watched cable television from 2:00 to 2:30 on Saturday afternoons, he was about to achieve rare celebrity. Pleased with our efforts, he mentioned that the Open trophy was there in the back and asked if we would like to see it. Portrush was hosting the Irish Open that year, so we said sure and thank you out of courtesy, about as interested in the Irish Open trophy as we were in another cup of tea. But when the manager brought out the trophy from her office, I believe I actually leapt—a little hop, and then I looked all around me: Who is here? Where's the security? Do they possibly know what that is?

"Here you go," she said. "Makes a great doorstop." And she handed over the greatest trophy in sports. I stood there in a hallway in the Portrush club-house, blushing a deep shade of crimson with my fingers wrapped around an Open champion's Claret Jug.

It had never occurred to me that they would be minding the Jug for Darren Clarke, who was a member at Royal Portrush, so this show-and-tell caught me dumbstruck. I remembered to ask for a picture, and I quickly looked at the list of names—true to legend, a giant *GARY PLAYER* stood out twice as tall as the rest, denoting the last year they allowed the winners to get their own engraving done. I was clutching a cup (albeit a winner's replica) that had been held by every golf immortal from Old Tom to Bobby Jones to Hogan and Palmer and Nicklaus and Tiger.

"Does my hair look all right?" I asked as I joined that list, with a big smile for the crew's cameraman. My hair did not look all right, but the Jug was in perfect focus.

Golfers who have any chance of ever competing for the Claret Jug avoid touching it until they earn it. The real players don't want to lift it, not yet, while the schlubs would wrestle each other for a quick feel. Somewhere in my golfing life, I had become one of them—a spectator. A schlub. I had once played professional golf and teed it up in a Tour qualifier with a lad named Sean from London, holding my own with a Brit who had just made the cut at the Open at Royal Troon, but now here I was, another blank face waiting along the ropes for an autograph. I hadn't even played a hole at Portrush that afternoon. My clubs were at home in the basement beneath too-small baby clothes, and I had not attempted a competitive round in seven years. I couldn't remember the last time I really needed to make a putt. I had no recollection of sincerely caring about a golf score, and had excused myself from golf ambition by believing that good golfers had to be bad dads or absentee husbands. The truth was, Mickelson was neither. So I had given a good chunk of my life to golf with little to show for it but a closet full of resentments and a photograph of one of the great phonies of the game hoisting a trophy he had no business touching, looking like a kid dressed up as the superhero he would never be.

In *A Course Called Ireland*, I played as many Irish links as any living person (that is to say, I played all of them). That links knowledge and passion had been shelved, an old manual for a car I no longer owned. In *Paper Tiger*, I learned the golf swing at the most micro of levels and took my life's shot at pro golf by way of a Tour coach, a personal trainer, and a professional shrink. I had learned what 68 felt like (it felt like it should have been 67), but as I approached forty, I hardly maintained a handicap. There was no joy in tracking my ballooning numbers, knowing their ascent was a trend I might slow but could no longer reverse.

As I watched the end of the Open at Muirfield, I wished for another shot while my three-year-old explained that we had watched enough Daddy shows and *Doc McStuffins* was coming on. My wife was about to have our second child, and my days of roaming the links with nothing ahead of me but another round and another pint and another story were long behind me.

Sorry, Julian, I thought, but I wouldn't be taking that trip. I could fantasize about a golf resurgence, but I would have to enjoy my fairway epiphanies from the living room. I couldn't summon the urgency to golf down another long road, not anymore. Life had changed, and as with millions of men, golf gluttony had gone the way of hair gel, two-seaters, and season tickets.

And then I got a phone call.

More

Philadelphia, Pennsylvania

N. Woodstock St.

Schuylkill River

Philadelphia Museum of Art

0 Miles   .25   .5
0 Kilometers   .5

We met at freshman orientation, though it felt like we had grown up trading secrets and insults. He was that acquaintance whose first handshake felt
familiar, who talked as if you had known each other all along, and who made
a faraway campus in cold, flat Indiana feel like home. He was a ginger as well,
but wore his red with confidence, brave enough to befriend another one. He
was better-looking, taller, smarter, a fearless golfer, and could chat up any
girl on campus and have them wondering whether he had a girlfriend by
his third sentence. He was also darkly insecure, and he subsisted upon and
propagated a banquet of bullshit. The fact that I could see that in him, and
that he knew I could, bonded us as brothers, two young men who needed

each other to know who they were—or who they were not. I wasn't Robert and he wasn't me, no matter how much we both wanted that to be otherwise.

Regardless of the time we spent apart, Robert was the friend who could quickly remind me how little people changed—most of all myself, as I still reacted to him with the same awe and acquiescence I did when we were nineteen. I hadn't spoken with him in a year. When my phone rang, I didn't recognize the number.

"I have an idea," Robert said.

"You're alive?"

"As far as I can tell," he said. "The dog seems to think so. He's licking my face. Dude needs a walk."

I could hear a late night in his voice. It was the nasal tenor of a horizontal talker, and I envisioned the mess in which he lay: takeout containers and torn-open boxes of wine and last month's mail. I worried for the dog's chances.

"You sound like you just woke up," I said.

"I'm sick. Brutal cold," he said.

"You had a cold last year. The last time you called."

"Can't shake it," he said. "When was that? Christmas?"

"I think so."

"I got your card. It's still here, up on the mantel. Looking at it right now."

I didn't doubt it, though I was surprised to hear that he had a mantel.

"I figured out where we need to go," he said, as if we had been collectively kicking around travel plans for months.

"*We're* going somewhere?" I said, and laughed. "*I'm* going somewhere: I'm going to pick up Maggie from ballet in ten minutes."

"Wow. Ballet. That's right out of the married suburban playbook, my man."

"We live in the city."

"Technically," Robert said, "but your soul is suburban."

This from the person I called my best friend. He said he had been watching reruns of the Open and was moved to epiphany by a memory. "You remember St. Andrews?"

I did, and somehow knew what he was after. Ever since college, when Robert had gone around St. Andrews at level par with borrowed clubs, he had been convinced of the divinity of the place. As we sipped spirits beside windows overlooking the links, Robert's eyes watched the sunset blaze across the dunes, and he said, "Whoever made this place knew something. They knew it. A very simple, very pure answer to this game. It's gotten buried under all the numbers and the bullshit, but you can feel it here. Golf has bones, and we just played them."

The rest of us smiled and twirled our tumblers and asked him what this answer was. He didn't have a clue, but promised us that one day he would know the secret, and when he did, "You can all say you knew me when. Brag to your friends about the day I kicked your ass at St. Andrews."

We didn't understand the part about bones and a secret, but as for us telling people we knew Robert when—we didn't doubt that for a sip.

"Remember Julian's text? The Open courses?" Robert said, his voice waking up on the other end of the line.

I said I did, regretting having forwarded the message his way.

"That was it," he said. "I see the future. And it's wearing a kilt."

"Is it? You're making a plan here?"

"It's not a plan. It's an inevitability," he said. "Scotland. All of it, searching for the secret. We go to golf Mecca, hunting for the Holy Grail."

I silently pardoned his mixed theological metaphors, and the line went quiet as I searched for holes in his argument. They were probably glaring to most, but to me, his case was irrationally compelling.

"Why not?" he said.

"For starters, I did that once, Robert. You were there."

"Exactly. And this is the upside-down opposite of that. No Tour coaches or headshrinkers. Forget the Golf Channel and the Rotella books. Yeah, you can get down to scratch. That's a real crowded monument. Scratch sucks. Scratch shoots seventy-eight in a qualifier for the Philly Open. I'm talking about skipping the pretenders and the guessers and going straight to the source."

He was wise to pilfer my own argument. For a decade, ever since I had attacked next-level golf via coaches and trainers and finely tuned technology, I'd wondered whether the decoder for golf was a simpler, more soulful strategy. I daydreamed of testing such a tack—less work, more play—and imagined a search for the soul of the game as a long-bearded seeker, a courier of fine hickory shafts, wandering in the Highlands and playing to the sounds of bagpipes and the smells of clan-stoked bonfires. Far from any driving range, I envisaged lost answers nestled at the bottom of ancient golf holes. My friend's words picked at my whims, but they would remain just that. I could barely find time to get a haircut anymore; chasing par around Scotland was pure Robertian fantasy.

But in case it wasn't, I asked, "And how long do you envision this trip taking? Weeks? Months?"

"Maybe a year," he said. "You've spent more time on golf chases, with less to show for them."

I admitted that I had. "But look at the Christmas card, Robert. I can't disappear for a year."

"Oh. Right," he said. In his pause, I could hear his mind trying to contemplate parenthood, a concept as baffling to him as breakfast. His bachelor's brain gave up, and he said, "Then I'll go find it, and you're welcome to join me."

I knew he meant it, and that he would go. He lived a life of uncommon feats and gestures, addicted to the next trip or task or unreachable frontier. Each promised to fix him; when it didn't, he planned larger. An episode three years ago in which he flatlined in an emergency room after a two-year happy hour seemed only to put more chase in his steps. Some people saw the white light and came back reborn, craving health and simple happiness. Robert saw the light and started looking around for something brighter.

"Won't be cheap," I said, wondering how a guy whose career had detoured back to carrying golf bags could afford such ambition. "Sounds like a lot of loops to pay for a trip like that."

"That's where your company would add a great deal to the itinerary."

Of course it would. "And you're well enough to do it?"

His laughter was interrupted by a cough. "Not at all," he said.

We were quiet for a moment. "You're crazy."

"You used to be," he said. "You were nuts. And people looked up to you for it. And you know it felt so goddamn good."

He was right; there was nothing more intoxicating than the look on someone's face when they listened to you tell a story they could not believe. *You did what?* Some people liked to feel special, but for Robert, special was the only thing worth feeling at all. And he knew my wires were twisted the same way.

"Listen," he said, "we do this, and you can go back home and weed your flower beds and go to ballet, and you will never have to wonder about what you didn't do."

"I like my life," I said. "I have a life. I love my life."

"I know you do, Tom," he said, his voice now lighter. "I believe that. But, Jesus Christ, don't you want to love it more?"

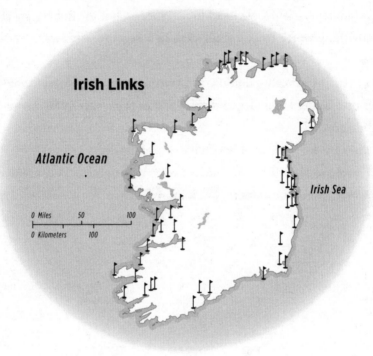

Planning great golf is easier than playing it. I find that arranging a golf journey—juggling dates and details and diving into a map—is the trip before the trip that stretches a week's fun into months. I'm an obsessive planner, perhaps because I suspect that my future is always going to be more compelling than my present, and I love to live there. I like to wade around in my past days, too—rearranging former conversations and imagining my past results improved. Maybe Scotland would give me some nows I could settle for, but until then, I relished the chance to spend a good year planning my and Robert's grand golfing tomorrows. I just had little idea where to start.

Robert's vision had us spending an entire season across the pond, digging golf balls out of the gorse and hanging on the whisky-warmed wisdom of caddies who knew where X lay on golf's map. His plan was to play every course to ever host an Open, plus every links in Scotland—"If we want to know what Old Tom Morris knew, then we have to out-golf him"—and then measure our summer of grand golf epiphanies at a qualifier for the Open Championship.

"If the answer to golf was easy to find, every investment banker who spent a week in St. Andrews would have it," Robert explained. Somewhere, in one of Scotland's yonder nooks or on one of its outer islands, there was a revelation waiting for us, a reward for golfers who braved the beyond. But before we roamed the UK in search of golfing miracles, the first divine intervention to secure would be a green light from a wife with a full-time corporate career and two wee ones at home.

The dream was a simple one. I expressed it to my wife, Allyson, as, "Do you think the girls are too young to travel to Scotland?" But what I was really saying was, *I want to go find the secret to golf and qualify for the greatest championship in sports.*

It was either that or paint the basement that summer. Seemed worth an ask.

The proper and peaceful arrangement of the married man's golf boondoggle requires decades of thoughtful practice. Golfing obsessively and remaining happily married demands preparations that predate a wedding, an engagement, and even a first kiss. One must bring one's love of the game into a partnership like a child from a former marriage: *I hope you like kids, because I already have one, and he golfs 278 times a year.*

If you have discovered your love of the game later in life, there is still hope for a golf binge, as long as you're confident that your partner condones obsession. This may require years of aloof or solipsistic episodes in order to ingratiate a spouse to your individualistic nature, warming them to a partner who sometimes—often for five hours a day during the summer—enjoys time alone. You must also be willing to put the time and work into establishing yourself as someone who is charismatically inconsistent, so that self-centered surprises become the charm of you being you.

Brokering a married golf boondoggle is also a craft best practiced upon a foundation of low spousal expectations. Ideally you have provided your partner past glimpses of what an asshole husband looks like, thus fostering a sort of hindsight gratitude—*At least he doesn't do that anymore*—for your future semi-asshole episodes. In my case, I had offered hard evidence of my asshole-husband potential when I wrote *Paper Tiger*, a smorgasbord of self-ishness that saw me moving to Florida and playing golf 542 days in a row. Such precedent made the four months needed for *A Course Called Ireland* an easy request—a 120-day retreat seemed magnanimous in comparison to that year and a half I spent on the driving range. This progression suggested that a summer in Scotland would seem status quo. That was my hope. But this was AK—After Kids—and kids blow the asshole metric to bits, to where ten extra minutes on the toilet spent staring at one's fantasy team lineup feels like a rare and heavenly indulgence.

Allyson—or, as my friends and family sometimes call her, St. Allyson—was well accustomed to my questing and migratory tendencies. We met in college, she a published poet and me a future mutual-fund salesman. But by graduation our paths had crisscrossed, and she headed for law school while I set off to write a novel. She became the adult in our relationship, with a buzzing work phone and a 401(k), while I dreamt up plot points and punch lines and took far too long to ask her to marry me. Tall and beautiful and selfless to a fault, Allyson was a steady anchor around which I orbited, often scared, sometimes broke, and always lucky as hell that the tether held tight. She never made me feel like she was putting up with me, even when I strug-gled to put up with myself. Somehow, I made her happy—happy enough that it felt as if she expected it when I told her about my plans for a summer in Scotland.

My previous golf-quest inspirations had been met with smiling head shakes and looks of amused surrender. But this request—my first attempted AK—was met with a look of genuine fear. Two little ones were tough to handle with both of us present and caffeinated. I could see the months of exhaustion and solo child-wrangling flashing before her eyes, and I said something I had never contemplated in such moments before, going off the boondoggle script I'd thought so cleverly written. I told her I didn't have to do it. I could stay here. It would really be fine if I didn't go, I told her, and I meant it.

Kids. They really do change everything.

For one of the first times in the life of teenage entitlement that I had managed to stretch into my fortieth year, it wasn't up to me. And I wasn't running something past her; I was asking her, and would have been content with a laugh and a request to go empty the recycling. Maybe that's why she said yes—or, rather, that I needed to go. I suspected I might have needed to go, but when I heard it from Allyson, I believed it. I believed it enough that this dream, in an instant, came to life and took over my days.

Needing to go wasn't about my needing more golf. There are only a handful of people on this planet whose résumés need more golf less than mine, and most of them play it for a living. I think she meant that I needed to go *now*, after so much had changed—whole oceans of life had transpired since I had last been this bold in my ambitions. It was as if she had a new husband with an untried bag of tools who wanted to see if he could make it, as if that former husband had passed away. A few years before, he actually had, but that was something we didn't need to talk about now, because life was moving forward in ways that neither of us dreamed it ever would again, and we had plans to make. Surely the kids were ready for Scotland. And I had already researched homes to rent in St. Andrews, finding one with room for a family and a long and blooming garden. She didn't even ask if Robert was coming. Approaching ten years of marriage, that was one of those questions upon which we no longer needed to spend our breath.

Whether I had gotten a green light or a red, my greatest boondoggle was marrying Allyson. She was full of joy, and had remained so through real darkness. She was still always up for the good, and what might be the grandest golf trip ever attempted—excavating the secret to golf and sharing it, taking my own stab at the tournament to top all others—was plenty good enough for her.

Provision

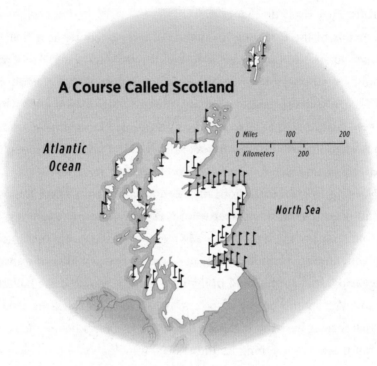

A Course Called Scotland

Atlantic Ocean

0 Miles 100 200

0 Kilometers 200

North Sea

I stared at a map of Scotland for months. The Michelin map was a little taller than my five-year-old, Maggie, and each course was marked with a tiny red golf club. There were loads of them. For each coastal golf course, I inserted a pin. Robert was unspecific about where the secret was residing, but we knew it had to be on a links. A true links is a seaside course set upon dunes—sacred, sandy altars on which the game of golf was born. After going through two packs of pins, I got a little nervous. I didn't mind when a curious Maggie pulled out one of the pins, as long as she didn't stick it in her sister. The more she pulled out, the less terrifying the trip appeared. She didn't pull out nearly enough.

I turned the board over and hung a new map, one sent to me by a friend. A trip of such ambition required help, so I opened up to assistance in ways I never had before. I didn't even know how to tell people I planned to play all of Scotland and find the secret to golf and qualify for the Open without it sounding like a joke, so I decided to trust the universe—surely it was smarter than I was, on most days—and listen to the people it put in front of me. And a woman named Gramma Billy stood front and center.

The emails started with Cruit Island. Pronounced *Critch*, it's a giddy nine-holer on the coast of Donegal in Ireland that I lovingly gushed about in my last book. Gramma Billy and her partner, Gene, sent me a warm email thanking me for the passages that had propelled them there. I was happy to write back to this kind lady who worked for an airline and who I might meet some day at check-in. More than a hundred email exchanges would grow from that first reply. It might be unwise to befriend strangers on the Internet who go from admiring your work to sending you gift packages with chocolate bars for you and teddy bears for your children, but as tricky as it can be to gauge a person's intentions and authenticity over the web, Gramma Billy from Canada transcended the murky paranoia of stranger-danger. If I was going to find anything life- and golf-changing in Europe that summer, I was going to have to accept the possibility that Gramma Billys are out there. They are real, they are here to help us, and they can be right, and the cosmos wants us to listen to them. So I did. And what could be the harm, anyway? Her emails always made me smile.

Self-described as a "crazy ginger-head senior who started golf just about the time I was sixty . . . started painting just about seventy . . . perhaps I might be an exotic dancer at eighty since I won't be known for my golf," Gramma Billy wrote bright emails that roller-coastered from frustrations with her golf ("Do you think red hair makes your head lighter and that tends to make it come up too soon?!") to inspirations and encouragement ("It's not the mountains that slow you down, it's the sand in your shoe. Enjoy the sunshine! YOU are a winner!") to blush-worthy stories of topless sunbathing in Australia or her dancing for Gene ("He always has a smile! Hint, hint, nudge, nudge."). And she sent me cards and notes; one that hangs above my desk reads: "Golf and yoga are a lot like life. Breathe deep, try to relax. And don't fart."

What she shared most were her and Gene's travel plans and experiences: they were hidden-gem hunters and had golfed much of the UK and Ireland, and she sent me scorecards from unknown courses that didn't have so much as a web page. Gramma Billy (or GB, as I would come to call her) was all energy and enthusiasm, and she boosted my book sales by pushing *A Course Called Ireland* on each passenger checking in at her counter with golf clubs. "I probably talk about you more than your own mum!" she wrote to me, and I believed her.

She sent me Scottish guidebooks and cheered me on with weekly check-ins, exhorting me to live fully, golf often, and dance naked. The poster Gene sent was a golf map of Scotland that he had seen in a Scottish B&B twenty years before, and he researched its origins and acquired a copy through the National Library of Scotland. This benevolent gesture rescued a rare Scottish chart that would be my spirit guide, a divine caddie, a golfing treasure map marking the path to the game's secrets. So I put pins in all its seaside courses, too, and suddenly my trip was twice as long. So many, many pins.

I consulted George Peper and Malcolm Campbell's definitive guide to links courses around the world, *True Links*, and discovered more required layouts born after my library map's printing. I checked out *Golf on the Rocks*, a book GB sent me that tells the story of an eighteen-course journey through the island holes of Scotland—some requiring daylong ferry rides or chartered prop planes, with courses seemingly reachable only by parachute, and soon there were tiny forests of pins sprouting up around my map's edges.

Scotland was beginning to look a lot different than Ireland. Ireland was a tidy little loop in comparison to Scotland's cracked and gnawed coastline, with links tucked into the deepest corners and holes hidden at the remote tips of unending peninsulas. Robert told me that the search for the soul of golf wasn't meant to be simple, so I ventured deep into the heart of Google Maps and crafted a tally of courses that included every layout to ever host an Open, plus every Scottish links I had ever heard of and about fifty of which I had not a clue. I tacked on every course Gene and GB had discovered on their UK travels—their picks, I decided, were musts on this mission, even though a handful were planted out in Wales and down in Cornwall on the southwestern coast of England. The trip had outgrown my map, covering three countries and stretching from the southernmost to the westernmost to the northernmost courses on both the Scottish mainland and its islands. If the secret to golf wasn't there somewhere, it simply did not exist. I could accept that result, but Robert was right—I couldn't accept the unknown possibility of a course unplayed.

Experience had shown that unexpected links would appear and alter my list, but after months of plotting, my pre-trip tally arrived at 107 destinations:

1. Littlestone
2. Royal Cinque Ports
3. Prince's
4. Royal St. George's
5. Mullion
6. Perranporth
7. Trevose
8. St. Enodoc
9. Holyhead
10. Bull Bay
11. Conwy
12. Wallasey
13. Royal Liverpool
14. Royal Lytham & St. Annes
15. Royal Birkdale
16. Blackpool North Shore
17. Eyemouth
18. Dunbar
19. Glen
20. North Berwick
21. Renaissance Club
22. Archerfield Dirleton Links
23. Archerfield Fidra Links
24. Muirfield
25. Gullane
26. Kilspindie
27. Luffness New
28. Craigielaw
29. Eden Course, St. Andrews
30. Old Course, St. Andrews
31. Jubilee Course, St. Andrews
32. New Course, St. Andrews
33. Castle Course, St. Andrews
34. Strathtyrum Course, St. Andrews
35. Burntisland
36. Kinghorn
37. Lundin
38. Leven
39. Elie
40. Anstruther
41. Crail Balcomie
42. Crail Craighead
43. Kingsbarns

44. Panmure
45. Scotscraig
46. Monifieth
47. Carnoustie
48. Montrose
49. Stonehaven
50. Royal Aberdeen
51. Murcar
52. Newburgh on Ythan
53. Trump International Golf Links, Scotland
54. Cruden Bay
55. Peterhead
56. Inverallochy
57. Fraserburgh
58. Rosehearty
59. Royal Tarlair
60. Cullen
61. Strathlene
62. Buckpool
63. Spey Bay
64. Moray
65. Hopeman
66. Covesea
67. Nairn Dunbar
68. Nairn
69. Asta
70. Shetland
71. Whalsay
72. Stromness
73. Castle Stuart
74. Fortrose & Rosemarkie
75. Tarbat
76. Tain
77. Skibo Castle
78. Golspie
79. Royal Dornoch Links
80. Royal Dornoch Struie
81. Brora
82. Wick
83. Reay
84. Durness
85. Ullapool
86. Gairloch
87. Isle of Skye
88. Traigh
89. Isle of Colonsay
90. Machrie
91. Machrihanish Old Course
92. Machrihanish Dunes Course
93. Dunaverty
94. Shiskine
95. Trump Turnberry Ailsa
96. Prestwick St. Nicholas
97. Prestwick
98. Royal Troon
99. Barassie
100. Glasgow Gailes
101. Western Gailes
102. Irvine
103. Barra
104. Askernish
105. Isle of Harris
106. Old Course, Musselburgh
107. The Open Qualifying Series—Bruntsfield Links

I didn't bother seeking Robert's approval of the final agenda. I knew our trip was really my trip the minute I silently said yes to it. As large as his presence loomed over the itinerary, I couldn't depend on his being there for a minute of it. Robert would come and go, commit and back out, show up and disappear; while he loathed unreliability in others, he relished his own. Robert would be with me throughout, but I could only guess at the days I would actually see him.

Complicating the arrangement of my Scottish splurge was the title on my business card, along with the fact that I carried such a card at all. It read *Assistant Professor of English, Saint Joseph's University.* I had somehow infiltrated academia in recent years, where I found that a professorship closely mimicked a round of golf: the bucolic serenity, the opportunities for growth and learning, the chance to feel like a genius and a moron in the same minute. In the interest of not blowing up my chances for tenure—as a professor, and as a husband—my proposed glacier of golf had to squeeze into a needle's-eye timeframe. If I left after my final class of the spring semester and teed it up the following morning, I would have less than two months till the Open qualifier. The absurdity was too gorgeous to resist. So I went and built a schedule of tee times, reservations, ferry rides, and flights, shoehorning 107 rounds of cross-UK golf into fifty-six days.

The itinerary sat on my desk for a few weeks, each date packed with two or three rounds without a single empty day to buffer for weather, shin splints, or pneumonia. At night, I dreamed gluttonous dreams—I was large and round, tobogganing hot dogs down my throat in the heat of a summer competition. I was running marathons with golf clubs on my back, a pale and waifish shadow of a man falling just short of the finish line, collapsing under the weight of a tour bag, dead and blistered. I had done crazy golf before, but at forty, a golf trip covering 107 courses seemed unhealthy in the kind of way that makes friends and forgotten siblings circle around you before a "family dinner" to tell you that they love you and want the old you back.

The list ended with the Bruntsfield qualifier as my final round, and I wavered on whether I should have stuck a return trip to St. Andrews for the 2015 Open there. Would it be a cocky and foolish tempting of golf's fates?

But if I didn't believe in my chances enough to plan for it—if *I* didn't trust that this plot pointed to St. Andrews—how was it supposed to come to life?

GB didn't doubt for one second where my round around Scotland was going to end: "We will be there! Pushing you on to St. Andrews! YOU WILL DO IT!" She was unafraid and stuffed with hope and so comfortable in her own skin, so carefree and convinced of the good in life. I didn't know whether she could break a hundred on the golf course, but it became clear that it wasn't Tom Morris I needed to become; it was Gramma Billy.

I would surely be joined by caddies and locals along the way, but in each cell of the spreadsheet I'd hatched (the first of my adult life), I began penciling in the names of friends and strangers who'd offered to walk a few holes with me. As a guest on the PGA Tour Radio Network one morning, I described the girth of my quest, and did something that this careful foursome-arranger had never done before—I left it up to chance, wadding up my best-laid plans and tossing them across the airwaves like dice. "If anyone listening wants to join me," I said, "I would love to have the company." And with that came the emails: *Were you serious when you said that? You got any spots left at St. Andrews?*

Robert told me I was an idiot.

"Do you know how many nutjobs are going to show up for this? Everyone's going to want you to entertain them and tell them stories about Ireland and shit. No thanks," he said.

His opinion mattered little in this case—he didn't need courting for the trip, and he excelled at inconspicuously avoiding the company of new acquaintances he wouldn't take the time to get to know. I explained that the open invitation came with a firm no-roommate policy, and that I could enjoy pretty much anyone's company on a golf course. I didn't tell him that a portion of the motivation for inviting all comers was to avoid two months on the road alone with my best friend.

Most of my potential companions inquired about St. Andrews, but I informed them that those two weeks of the trip—when I would be dropping anchor in town and day-tripping to courses all over Fife—were reserved for family. Those who were willing to hike out to farther-flung destinations included a couple from Rochester; a designer from Chicago; a pro from Florida; a consultant from Boston; the Women's World Speedgolf Champion, who was living in Amsterdam; and a character named Penn, from Georgia, whose emails were a blend of poetic links musings and first-day-of-school giddiness—*Holy cow, I'M PUMPED!!!*—that made it impossible to tell whether he was sixty or sixteen. When Penn forwarded along his Edinburgh flight times, with arrival and departure separated by eleven days, I felt my back sliding down my office chair. Maybe my laissez-faire approach had attracted not the sagest golfers but the loneliest and least balanced. Who decides they want to join a guy they've never met before in Scotland? For more than a week? It wasn't healthy thinking. Then again, neither was golfing Scotland for two months and trying to qualify for the Open. If they were unbalanced, this was the trip for them.

None of the partners I didn't know were as worrisome as the partner I did. Robert had nearly sunk my Ireland trip entirely, almost sending me home a month early after a run-in with Irish police. (When they showed up looking for him at our hotel, he was upstairs sleeping off a Jameson mugging while I begged forgiveness for an evening they seemed to recall far better than I did.) Robert had been with me for all my books, though I didn't write about him, per his request. Being reduced to a character in a story—like some sort of admirer or punch line—was, he felt, beneath him. So I promised I wouldn't write about him until he was dead. That would make him smile and say, "So, next year, then?"

"You've got nine lives and more," I would tell him.

Robert considered himself the spark behind the stories I had written and felt that my books were as much his as mine. I feared that he was right, which only added to my list of resentments about the friend I couldn't shake. He was still the twenty-year-old I wanted to be, and the golfer I never was. He would probably spend most of our Scotland trip drunk and under par. The dumb, lucky bastard.

Robert had been sick for the last three years—we both knew why but didn't talk about it—but any doubts I had about his showing up in Scotland were disproved when he messaged me a photo of his application for the Open qualifier at Bruntsfield. *GAME ON*, read the text. Suddenly, I didn't care about teeing it up at St. Andrews with Rory and Phil and the gang, nor was I worried about the travel habits of Penn and GB. I was after something bigger. The answer to golf took on a quiet and piercing focus: Beat Robert.

Posture

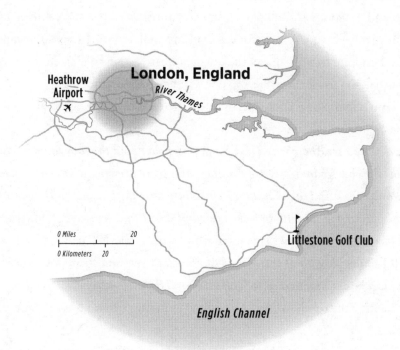

I took the biggest one they had. I hadn't considered whether the luggage I purchased was too large to check on a flight—who sells a travel-banned suitcase?—but mine passed only after the agent decided she could subtract two inches for the wheels. I had stuffed two months' worth of garb for golf in all seasons into one hard case. Hopping from one accommodation to another every morning meant I would have one hand for the sticks that would never sleep alone in the car and five fingers for everything else. Add a shoulder for my laptop, and my whole world would be able to travel sans luggage cart from hotel to tee box to car to B&B to ferry port to airport terminal, a snug one-man caravan.

I wheeled my life down the long hallways of Heathrow and arrived at a short line of Americans waiting for entry stamps on their passports. There were two officers stamping—a woman in a burka who smiled and breezed visitors through, and a large and bitter-looking lady who opened each passport like a nun opening a *Penthouse*. I prayed for the burka, as I knew the dates and locations scribbled on my entry form would raise eyebrows and might involve a supervisor while a tee time well south of London awaited me. When I got to the front of the queue, I heard a "NEXT!" from the angry agent that had me feeling like Oliver Twist begging for another bowl.

"You're here for a while," she said as she read my form without looking at me. "Can you tell me why?"

Well, you see, there was a text from my friend about the rota courses—rota means the courses on the Open rotation, and there are only fourteen, or really ten nowadays—and this was after I lifted the Claret Jug but shouldn't have, and once I played golf for 542 days in a row but didn't find the secret to the game, and there are a lot of links courses over here and I couldn't look Robert in the eye if I didn't play all of them, and Allyson said yes, and then Gramma Billy sent me a poster and told me to golf often and dance naked . . .

"Golf. I'm a golf writer. I'm going to write a book about your golf courses."

"You write *golf books*?" she said, as if I had told her I jumped unicorns over rainbows.

"I do," I said.

"That sounds boring." She turned back to my documents, her suspicions giving way to apathy. "What's this address in St. Andrews?"

"It's where I'm staying with my family . . ."

"Are they here?"

"Not yet."

She reached for her stamp, satisfied that someone willing to say they wrote about golf posed no possible danger to her homeland. But then she paused and looked at me. "Does your wife play golf?"

I said that she didn't, and the woman smiled, a point tallied for her side. "I don't blame her," she said as she handed back my passport. "Hey, he writes golf books!" she called to the woman in the burka, who looked up from her desk and smiled at me with tender confusion.

"Good luck," my friend said, and I grabbed my world by both hands and stepped forth into the now.

I inhaled deeply. I looked around me and told myself to remember this—all of it: a breeze knocking at my back, the pale green and yellow mounds, my cold feet settling into the turf. All the planning and predicting and hoping— it all led here, to this small patch of short grass, where I turned a golf club in my hand and waited for the group up ahead to clear the fairway.

A start. There were precious few moments in my life when I knew a beginning before it passed, when I could recognize a commencement, when I breathed deep and knew the jumping-off point. My first day of school, my wedding, the births of my girls—they all came with the fearful knowledge that only one thing ahead of me was certain: change. As I bent to stab my tee into the ground, I reminded myself that on this round, this two-month bout with my golf ball, I was responsible only for the effort, not the outcomes. There might be change for the better or for the worse, but all I could do was keep swinging. As few times as possible, I hoped.

It was time to make that strange and reluctant step from planning into living. Should I proclaim something? Raise a fist? Shed a few tears? I had plotted my golfing rebirth and now here I was, a new and braver and wiser golfing soul, alive and emboldened and committed to my cause. Yet there were no trumpets, no cannons, no rainbows—just rain. It all should have felt different here, but it was all too familiar as I watched my opening drive slide right off the wind and scurry into rumpled grass.

Stroke one of many happened on the links of Littlestone. Lesser-known than its neighboring Open venues in England's southeast corner, Littlestone held its own for history—both James Braid and Alister MacKenzie (the latter of Augusta National and Cypress Point fame) had their fingerprints on course updates after its inception in 1888, when it was laid out by Royal St. George's designer, William Laidlaw Purves. Charles Blair Macdonald, considered the father of American golf and one of the founders of the USGA, credited Littlestone as one of his design inspirations. And in a gesture of uncommon golfing bipartisanship, Littlestone once boasted the British prime minister as its club captain (H. H. Asquith, Liberals), while the leader of the opposition (Arthur Balfour, Conservatives) was its club president. Littlestone was no small player in the history of golf in England, and it greeted me on a Sunday morning with the wet breezes I had been missing. The old brick clubhouse had a British cottage feeling that told me I had arrived somewhere authentic, and a nearby water tower built to look like a castle turret seemed to follow me around the course as a target. The layout's undulations were subdued, a shortish but classic seaside track with sneaky sandpits dotting the holes to remind me I wasn't Stateside anymore.

Littlestone was a quick links refresher squeezed between marshlands and the English Channel, a morning that reeducated me on the basics of links golf—that is to say, the fundamentals of what I considered *real* golf, a game in which one's ball is meant to be played along and across a golf course, not just over it.

I had grown up learning to loft the golf ball, playing shots that avoided the course, hoisting irons over all that scary stuff to a benign island of short grass. But links wind forces you to observe and ponder and engage the ground ahead of you. You can't hide from the golf course when the wind is up, as it always seems to be on a seaside layout. For me, wind was a nuisance, a bad-luck impediment that denied me the golf to which I felt entitled, while the game's originators would have considered the breeze to be as essential to a course as the fairway and rough. It forced one to golf their ball, not just launch it.

By the end of my opening round, I had remembered: putt firmly, with a shorter stroke and a condensed follow-through. These were hearty greens—not glass but grass—and just because a ball was holding the ground didn't mean the wind would let it alone. Putts didn't drip into the hole over here; rather, they dove down to safety as if burrowing for cover.

I remembered to play approaches short of the greens—sometimes absurdly short—and think about roll and bounce and trajectory. True links are laid upon sandy soil—dunes, essentially—so that even in a downpour they drain like colanders, allowing players to runway their balls from all over. I gave myself license to putt from anywhere within fifty yards, and remembered that the flags are shorter over here, to keep them from snapping or dislodging in the wind. The diminutive pins play games with American golfers' eyes and add thirty perceived yards to each shot. My eyes would adjust and I would learn to punch shots and pop putts, I told myself, and forgave my pencil as it filled in an uninspiring 80, with a slightly more hopeful 36 on the back nine.

As a former Open qualifying venue, Littlestone was a good initial gauge of my game. I bogeyed the first hole but birdied the last; if the entire trip had that arc to it, I would finish in fine standing. Having left all my excuses back in the States, I felt bare in the breeze as I tucked my card into my bag. It was coming with me; that thin folded paper had a weight to it, its grams turned to pounds of new pressure. The shots all counted now.

Following my bogey-packed run at professional golf in 2004, the question I've heard more than any other is, "What was the difference between them and you?" Innate talent was an obvious delineator, but it wasn't the whole answer. I typically replied with something about tournament preparedness or their wedge game or their putting from inside ten feet, and that was all true. But I rarely shared the primary difference, because it's too weighty for grill-room banter. The real difference was fear. I let it play my golf ball, while they somehow kept it in the bag.

My itinerary was built to outlast and exhaust fear, to drain its muscles by way of repetition and render it limp. I'd read somewhere that the key to grappling with fear, to feeling real peace and security, was knowing who you were. I believed it, because on a golf course in a competition, I too often guessed at the player I was: Was I a good putter? Did I hit fairways? Was the sand really my strength? When I played well, I could stamp a yes on all the questions. When I played great, I didn't hear the questions at all. So maybe that was the secret: figuring out who I was. That seemed easy enough—a piece of shepherd's pie. I was a dad. A golfer. A writer, a teacher, a husband. I was a pretty good guy. But actually believing any of that? Not just saying it but knowing it? I suspected it would be easier to play 107 golf courses in fifty-six days.

In the meantime, it was one shot at a time, and the next one was at Royal Cinque Ports, host of the Open in 1909 and 1920. I drove with purpose and with pace; game on, round number one tallied and recorded. Round number one in the UK, that is—for the calendar year, it was round 132.

Not long after my Scotland conversation with Robert, I went googling for Open qualification procedures. I had donated an entry fee to the US Open a few times and knew the deal—you needed a 1.4 handicap and a check. The British Open's requirements seemed hidden on the Internet, as if their Open were actually a little less so, and I eventually found that to be the case. The handicap cutoff for entrants was 0, so if I was to embark on this quest for the secret to golf and test said secret in an Open tryout, it would take a large lump of faith to believe I could even qualify for the qualifier and get my handicap down to goose egg.

Not since 2005 had my handicap approached such a hollow sum. I did not belong to any club or course, and guessed my theoretical handicap hovered around 10. I played Chutes and Ladders more often than I played golf anymore, so before I bought any maps or pins or guidebooks, I spent a year gorging on golf improvement while trying to balance school and kids and the Golf Handicap and Information Network. Before the crazy kicked off in Littlestone, I had already been golf crazy for some time.

A swing coach was never part of the plan. My path to scratch was going to be built upon my new adult outlook—I had matured and earned perspective since I'd last given a damn about golf, and surely a mind now enlightened by a new family and some vague modicum of faith was worth a dozen strokes. I had been a drinking prodigy, an all-star handpicked from the crowd of aspiring drunks. Sober now, if I put the effort into chasing golf that I had put into chasing my next drink, the Grand Slam would not be out of the question. But no lessons or video work; no more launch monitors for me. I sought holistic and organic golf improvement based on healthy thinking and the lessons I had learned from *Paper Tiger*: beating balls is not playing golf, and there is no substitute for tournament experience.

I played eighteen holes each morning while the girls were home with a sitter, and I entered every tournament that would take my credit card. My daily scores crept downward, but my tournament results remained bloated: eighty-ish, oceans away from scratch. It was in the parking lot following a qualifier for the Pennsylvania Mid-Am during which I had blasted three balls out of bounds and finished DFL for the first time in my golfing career— I had played terribly the world over, but never before had I seen my name in that last box, just above the WDs and the DQs—that I decided to heed the new grown-up perspective of which I was so proud and ask for help.

We had lost touch over the years, but when I opened *Philadelphia* magazine to find that an old friend had been named Best of Philly Golf Instructor, it seemed to be another nudge from that cosmic caddie who had put Gramma Billy in my path, pushing me to give Dynda a call.

I had known Mike Dynda since I was a caddie and he was working his first assistant-pro job in the early 1990s, back when Dynda had a head of curly locks and could bash a 1-iron like a beefed-up Ben Hogan. Dynda had helped me through a case of the shanks when I was a teenager, and taught me firsthand the true heartbreak of the game when I was seventeen and carrying his bag, watching him three-putt the final green of a US Open qualifier and miss the cut by one stroke. He threw me his car keys and joined a case of beer in the backseat, where for the whole ride home to Philadelphia he hid his bottle inside a head cover and told me of the pain of giving one's life to something as fickle as a wobbly white ball. Twenty years later, it was me who sought to numb the golf angst when I called him to see if he could make me play like a teenager again.

The hair was gone, and he was now better known as a teacher than as a player, but Dynda had continued to be driven a bit barmy by the game as the years had passed—a fast talker, his insights moved at warp speed, but there was genius at work as we bounced from idea to idea, settling on a handful of swing flaws and remedies. In the warm months, we hit balls and played holes together, and he showed me how to read greens by feeling the slope with my feet and taught me the importance of a mental soundtrack: "I've got a little Foreigner in my head today so I can rock birdies. I had Michael Jackson last week, and I couldn't make a putt." In the winter, we hit balls in his studio with cardboard boxes leaning against my ass to help me hold my posture, and when we got bored on a rainy day, we watched Dynda's greatest hits on YouTube. He was the Weird Al Yankovic of golf, if Weird Al wore a Cobra Golf hat and spit into an empty water bottle behind the piano while he sang

> *Caddie, help me read this putt,*
> *'Cause I can't read putts anymore.*
> *It's getting hard, too hard to see.*
> *Feel like I'm knockin' on Dynda's door . . .*

He was the mad professor who seemed the ideal prefect for my eccentric ambitions, and with his texts and voice mails pushing me along, I was on the putting green before the kids were awake, playing eighteen and hitting a barrel of balls before it was time to pick Maggie up from camp.

Over the course of my year of handicap deflation, I fled the cold and visited Florida nine times, a feat for a golfing dad—even more impressive, I saw Mickey Mouse on only one of the trips. My in-laws' condo near Clearwater became a regular retreat where, at Belleair Country Club, the pro at Florida's oldest golf club allowed me to practice. On five such getaways, as my students wondered what kind of research their professor was doing that kept bringing him back to class with a sunburn, I made the drive from Clearwater to Naples, passing meekly through the gates to TwinEagles. I was always made bashful by the sprawling luxury of the place, until I felt at home on the back of the range in the studio of one of the great gentlemen of golf. Scotland had so many names that conjured golf distinction—Morris, Braid, Park, Robertson. Florida had one such name, too—Dr. Jim Suttie, or, as his friends called him, Doc. I felt fortunate that after a number of years out of touch, I could still shoot him an email asking for some of his time and begin it, *Hey, Doc . . .*

Tall, with an unsteady hip, Doc wore a wide-brim hat to protect the fair complexion of someone who, like myself, looked a little foreign in Florida. Doc was one of the first modern coaches in golf, a pioneer in utilizing technology and video at a time when you still needed a suitcase to lug the equipment around. I didn't expect that he would have changed much in ten years, and I was right. He greeted me with a hello and a handshake as if I had just been in to visit him last week. "Ready to go?" he said, the tripod that never seemed to leave his side in hand, a shepherd and his staff. His studio had changed a bit—more gadgets, from a TrackMan system to balance plates, with monitors embedded in the floor so students could watch their swings from any angle without having to look away from the ball. A new putting platform in the corner had more wires coming out of it than a polygraph, and everywhere on the walls hung photos of Doc with his Tour pros and his awards—top ten teacher in the US, best teacher in the state, PGA Teacher of the Year. Yet they hung in no particular order and were just crooked enough to suggest that Doc was not all that impressed, as if they all had to go somewhere, so, well, here they were.

During my last visit before leaving for Scotland, I had to wait for Doc to finish working with one of his students. When there was a spouse or a family waiting in the lawn chairs outside Doc's bunker, milling about like loved ones waiting for the jury to return, you knew a serious golfer was inside, someone who traveled with an entourage and on whose golf others depended. I could tell this was one of those players—his wife was walking laps around the range at an exercise pace, a routine that looked honed by years of waiting for her husband on a golf course. When Doc and his student walked out, he introduced us without an ounce of showboating or self-importance, simply saying, "Tom Coyne, meet Larry Mize." He had come to see Doc for a tune-up before the Masters. We shook hands and talked for a few minutes, two guys happy to be at one of the really good places in golf.

Both Doc and Dynda's cameras found the same bugs in my swing: an early release of my hands led to my standing up ever so slightly at impact, which sent my clubface outside the target line, causing me to wipe across the ball and sap pounds of power in the process. I couldn't help but feel useless as I sat in front of Doc's bank of monitors, watching him draw lines on my swing; I'd sat in this same chair and looked at these same lines ten years before. I recalled how an angry golfer once told me that our swings don't change, not under pressure. Our flaws are born into our golf. They will always make a comeback, especially when the golf matters—those anxious rounds when we most have to rely on our golfing DNA.

I had played hundreds of thousands of golf shots since I'd been here last, yet Doc might as well have been playing the tapes from 2004. So our golf swing was as unchangeable as our personality, as fixed as our lifetime habits and attitudes. That was fine. It was great, actually, because in the last three years, there was nothing about my habits and attitudes that had *not* changed. If my outlook on life could turn over and around, surely I could rejigger a golf swing.

After mornings on the range, Doc would take me out on the course with some of his minitour players, following us around in his golf cart with his Labrador, Bunker, by his side. I held my own with twentysomethings who were playing for their car payments. Our good shots were about the same, but their misses and subsequent recoveries were far fancier than mine, confirming what Dynda had been preaching over my yearlong race to scratch—that better scores weren't necessarily about better shots but better misses.

Doc and I never quite figured out whether it was my early release that caused me to stand up at impact or the other way around; but whether it was the chicken or the egg, he was sure I needed to loosen my hips and strengthen my core if I wanted any shot at a solid posture that would cover the ball at impact. Dynda had pointed to the same physical shortcomings, so with YouTube as my personal trainer, I spent much of the winter being that forty-year-old professor looking perfectly unnatural and potentially a bit creepy among the undergrads at the campus gym. I took cheap solace from remembering that none of the water-jug-toting teenagers were scratch golfers. Neither was I, but with each crunch and curl, I felt zero inching closer.

For eighteen months, I bombarded the clubhouse computer with scores. By sheer mass of golf played, I turned my misses from card-wrecking disasters into manageable quirks. On the final day of the season, the last day on which I could post a score in time for the Open application—October

31—I wore a Jordan Spieth Halloween costume on the course, not missing a putt inside ten feet and posting a score of four under par. With two hours of daylight to spare, I watched my handicap finally sink below the equator by .3 strokes.

I was scratch, a thing I never thought I would say again. I knew that for the players with a real shot at making it through Open qualifying in June, scratch was shit, but no matter; at least now I was shit enough to get started.

Robert would get to scratch without much effort. A disciplined regimen of pumping bogus scores into the handicap system would likely get him there, but the truth was, even though he only played on a semiannual basis, he could still fire 70 without so much as waving at the driving range. As hard as I knew his life had become, he still made it look painless and carefree, and the possibility that it might actually be that way for him at our age was flatly unfair. I suspected that he might go to Scotland and spend most of the trip in a pub in Glasgow while I hiked the Highlands in search of my one nugget of golf truth, only to find that Robert had it all along—care less, play better. And when it came to caring less, Robert was a downright ace.

No kids, no wife; his world was small, and he walked it untethered, a thin existence in which nothing mattered enough to qualify as a worry. It was tough to maintain such an unreality as your reality, unless you were mildly drunk most of the time; luckily for Robert, he was mostly drunk all of the time. You had to know Robert well to know if he was tight. It was probably a curse; if he had been a more pathetic load, he might have had to do something about it. But he was popular at his watering hole in the city, and when I visited him there (and that was the only place he ever suggested we meet), free drinks came his way from every corner of the bar. Everyone paid quick homage to Robert in his seat by the window, from the carpenters to the teachers to the bar backs, and he greeted each supplicant hello with a sincere smile and a question about a child or a mother or a new job on Market Street. He was still charming, and they could all see the same flawed contentedness in him that I saw—and envied, for some reason. I didn't crave drinks anymore, but I did covet one thing he had, the thing booze had given me more than anything else: a break from having to care. It gave me freedom from having to wonder about my life: *Am I doing it right? Is this enough?* Still, I wouldn't trade places with him for a shelf of Claret Jugs—the shakes, the panic, the hospitals, the self-hatred aren't worth it—but there were moments, quick but persuasive pangs, when I wanted what Robert had as badly as I had once wanted a crisp pint of Chardonnay: the dumb, numb, lovely smile of someone who doesn't give a damn.

The unfamiliar weight of giving a shit made my golf bag heavier, while Robert roamed unburdened, swinging his last and only club at the world. I couldn't always decide who was better off, so I just tried to keep moving forward—to stand up straight and find the next flag in front of me.

Heart

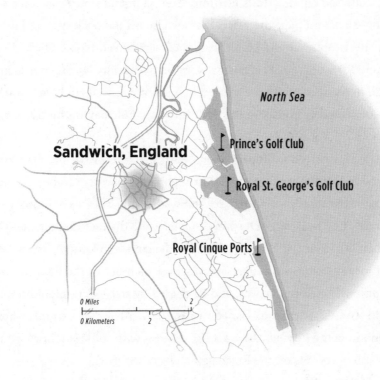

North Sea

Sandwich, England

𝗜 Prince's Golf Club

𝗜 Royal St. George's Golf Club

Royal Cinque Ports 𝗜

0 Miles   2

0 Kilometers   2

Duff was a friend who showed. He was a guy who was always up for it—up for moving his family to London, up for running the Paris Marathon with me, up for flying back to the States for twenty-four hours to catch a Notre Dame game, and up for playing four rounds of golf in thirty-two hours in the southeast of England. Our wives had worked together for years; we had bonded over our common alma mater and become friends. When it came to a big trip or a tall ask, Duff was a go-to guy, and I knew his why-not spirit would set the tone for my first days on the ground. I didn't want to be alone when the fears set in, as they did in the clubhouse in Royal Cinque Ports on day one, fifty-five days of unmitigated golf ahead of me, when I thought, *I'm not sure I want to play golf tomorrow.*

I would overcome, just as Duff pushed through on day one. Well over six feet tall, with the girth of an expat who had learned to love the British chipper, Duff had squeezed his feet into fresh golf shoes purchased for his upcoming spree and paid the price. Somewhere on the back nine at Littlestone his heel ruptured and bled through his socks, yet he still worked his way around Royal Cinque Ports that afternoon in the rain. Having not struck a golf ball in many a month, he overcame his name as well, and Duff golfed his ball courageously, finishing the first thirty-six-hole day in the UK at my side without grievance.

The locals referred to Royal Cinque Ports as Deal for the nearby town, and the course's rota heritage shone through in its narrow targets and obscured paths to safety, its contours replete with subtle hillocks and omnivorous rough. The Royal part of its proper name was a distinction that dated to 1900, when the Prince of Wales teed it up at the course in Deal. A Royal designation meant a club was judged worthy by a member of the British royal family somewhere along the way, and it's shared by sixty-some clubs around the world, from Australia to Canada to India to Africa to Ireland, where Royal Dublin in the Republic wears its Royal-ness with some stubborn irony. The sun still never sets on the Royal golf clubs of the world.

Royal Cinque Ports was heavy on history, and on golf shots; Duff and I flailed away in the rain, heads down, punching at the wind and screaming by way of our silence that we were having no fun at all. It was a round to get through, to survive and cross off and then get dry, and each passing minute in the clubhouse allowed our faulty golf memories to turn misery into fun. I was thankful that the local member who was scheduled to play with us was a no-show, allowing us to play quick and quiet golf. Duff was soldiering through a solid limp by this point, and I had carded a tear-soaked 44 on the front, the outward stretch playing directly down the coastline into needles of rain. If we hadn't been at the farthest point from the clubhouse as we turned from nine, I wonder whether we might have hung it up and hit the showers. Round number two, with my ass barely out of the starting gate, and I think I wanted to quit—and then here came our member, hiking across the dunes to find us, using his closed umbrella like a cane and smiling as if the sun were shining and he couldn't wait to teach us the intricacies of his course. And then I knew I wanted to quit.

My flooded earlobes weren't interested in hearing that the godfather of golf writers, Bernard Darwin, had been a member at Deal, or that he dubbed the alley on sixteen "a safe haven of insecurity," or that Harry Vardon, winner of a record six Opens, always laid back and played for the only flat spot on the fairway on seventeen. I wanted to know where the towels were and if the sun ever shined in the southeast of England, and why this member, Mark, didn't have his umbrella up. It turned out that Mark knew something I had forgotten about golf on a seaside links: Don't get too accustomed to the weather, because it will change soon. The wind turned to our backs and blew the water from the course; dry skies followed, and it felt as if we had lost half our clubs. Duff and I skipped along the closing holes of Cinque Ports, and Mark proved to be an extraordinary host and club historian; he explained that the thin concrete path along the grassy seawall was built there to allow soldiers to patrol on bicycles during the German threat, and that the course took its name from a medieval confederation of the five nearby port towns.

"You can see France from here on a clear day," Mark told us as we looked outward from the fourteenth green into a wall of English gray. "Today is not one of those days."

But it *was* a good day, thanks to Mark, who brought stories and shut off the spigots; yet we were still unsettled as Duff and I sat in the beautiful old clubhouse, a Victorian seaside manor, him trying to walk off his busted ankle and me feeling tired in a way I hadn't felt since that marathon in Paris. It was only thirty-six holes—I'd done that before—but I hadn't accounted for the exertion of walking into the wind, slugging through the gales as if tied to the earth. My game had bounced back with a birdie and a 37 on the back nine, but my spirit felt like the 81 on my scorecard—flat and uninspired. I knew these thoughts were coming, just as I knew the rain and wind were waiting for me, but on day one, I didn't expect to be looking out at a black sea and thinking, *I can't do this.*

It didn't help when I watched a black sedan drive along the thin road between the clubhouse and the golf course. It pulled into the empty parking lot, and out stepped a pale redhead in short sleeves. He walked across the lot as if it were a sunny day in Savannah, unmoved by his surroundings.

I hadn't seen him in years, but his first words were, "You played in this?" He picked my card up off the table and didn't say anything—just raised his eyebrows—then folded and creased it with his fingers. "Lot of golf ahead of you."

"Hey," I said. "It's you. How are you?"

Robert looked out at the wispy dunes in the windows. "Not bad. I got upgraded on the flight," he said. "The drive down here was eventful. I kept trying to convince the other cars that the right side was better. Nobody seemed to agree."

Robert sat down and ordered a Chardonnay in the land of gin and ale. Mark was chatting with other members at the bar, and Duff was still pacing the clubhouse; he pretended to be taking in all the history hanging from its walls, but I knew he was trying to work out the knots above his heels. Duff knew Robert. They had met on a dozen occasions, but as happened with most of the people I introduced Robert to, he would greet them as if they had never met—no matter that they'd spent five hours golfing together last September. There might have been a part of Robert that envied my having other friends, or a part of him that didn't believe they were real friends—they didn't really know me, or they didn't rise to the level of his peer. And in all the years of knowing Robert, I'd never done anything to make him think otherwise. I still let him walk into my life and become its focus whenever he decided to show up; no wonder he had the impression that he was more important. Because to me, for some reason, he was.

He wasn't going to play in this cold, and he had driven around Deal and Sandwich and decided to head back to London for the night. "When a man is tired of London, he is tired of life," he said, quoting Samuel Johnson in a voice that, to me, sounded very tired of life. He had a copy of my itinerary and planned to meet me down in Cornwall, or maybe just jump ahead to Manchester and take in a football match.

"I can hang around if you need me to," he said. "Or maybe you'd rather I not."

I didn't say anything. I didn't know what I wanted him to do.

"You okay?" he said.

"Yeah. I'm just tired. This is a lot, man. This is going to be a lot."

"There was never any doubt about that," he said. "Colder than I thought it was going to be. I should have packed more sweaters."

We talked about my impressions of the course, a definitive links, nine out and nine back that didn't feel forced or overdesigned. It didn't blow you away with drama, but in better weather, you could walk Cinque Ports every day without getting bored or abused.

"Sounds epic," he said. I don't think he was listening. "I'm going to roll. You should come back to London with me. You can't play in this. You get sick, and it's over."

"Thanks, Mom."

"You're welcome," he said, tipping his empty glass into his mouth. "Shit, nobody's going to know where you did and didn't play. Seriously."

"I would know," I said. "I've got day one under my belt. One day at a time."

Robert grinned. "Indeed." He picked up my scorecard and placed it on top of his glass. "Make sure you find a driving range. Do they have those over here? They must," he said, standing up. "You don't need me to stay?"

"I'm good," I told him. "Go to London. Say hi to the queen."

"I shall," Robert said, and after a ten-minute appearance—his first in three years—my best friend was gone.

Mark ran a top-rated B&B in Deal, where he had rooms waiting for us, transforming him from our host to our hero. We hobbled our way back out through the Cinque Ports lobby, and Mark stopped to show us Charl Schwartzel's name on the wall in commemoration of his winning the English Amateur Championship at Deal. More interesting was a mahogany board with gold numbers that memorialized the winners of Deal's annual Prince of Wales Challenge Cup, where in one of his final amateur events before ascending the pro rankings, Lee Westwood fired 83 and 77 to claim the title. An almost unplayable wind was blamed for scores that saw the best amateurs in England flirting with the century mark, and I noticed that the same had happened in 1972, when Walker Cupper P. J. Hedges won with a closing 86. These bloated tallies were the loveliest things I saw at Deal that day. I checked my back pocket for my card with its 81, and no longer felt compelled to toss it into the bin. Golf was hard; on a links, it was harder. And an 82 and an 86 were good enough to paint in gold on the clubhouse walls.

"One year, 162 wins it; the next, it's 138," Mark said as we left. "You can't conquer this game. You have to take what the course is giving and get on with it."

I walked the street along the beach in Deal that evening, still light at nearly ten o'clock, and found a glorious chip shop for my first fish and chips of what I hoped would be many—*Throw in one of those fried sausages, too, please.* Can't get those in Philly.

The town was quiet but charming, with pubs and hotels overlooking the waves. I thought that Robert had missed a true English town as I walked back to the Number One B&B, where I was staying (its street address was 1; serendipitous for Mark when it came to Internet searches), and I felt full and well. My legs were stiff in a hard-earned way, and the box of fried grease seemed to disappear before I even made it back to the Number One door. I slept a deep, thirty-six-hole sleep, knowing that when one has tired of the prospect of golf tomorrow, one has tired of life.

"You can tell people I was a pussy," were Duff's first words the next morning. He was not referring to an inability to finish the full English breakfast, as we both dispatched our allotment of eggs and sundry breakfast meats. Experience had taught me that I would eventually grow weary of the morning feasts of the British Isles and come to fear the too-yellow eggs, waking from sweaty nightmares of stubby sausages tangled with bacon the size of surfboards, so I enjoyed the full breakfast while there was joy to be had. Rather, Duff was explaining his decision to skip that morning's round at Prince's in Sandwich.

He planned on spending the morning shopping for bandages in town, then hoped to rally for Royal St. George's in the afternoon.

There was nothing weak about Duff's decision. I'd watched him battle his golf ball across much of southeastern England the day before, lashing it with the determined frustration of someone who really wished I were writing a book about British bar stools. We figured he'd hit enough shots yesterday to cover a third round without actually playing it, so his pass from Prince's had been earned.

Duff had picked me up at Heathrow and driven us down to Deal knowing that, in two days' time, he would fly back to Philadelphia to visit his terminally ill father for what he suspected was the last time. Duff was no pussy. He had grown-up guts—man guts—that I envied, handling his father's passing with courage and grace, and without complaint. He was no idiot, either. His heels were chewed up and bloody, though their ability to keep him off the golf course made them look beautiful to me.

I'd woken that morning with a body that felt as if it had been sewn into my mattress. The idea that I was going to drag these limbs around 105 more courses already had me feeling like a golfing Sisyphus, but I zombied my way down to breakfast and into Duff's front seat. He dropped me off at Prince's, where the golden dunes were soaked in sun, and the wind made me wonder whether I might spontaneously take flight behind my golf ball. If I were wearing a slightly larger shirt, I thought, I could coast my way over to France on this gentle morning tornado.

Prince's had a wide-open feeling about it, with three nines stretched across a broad swath of dunes that separated a pine forest from the ocean. The trees waved like grain in the wind while I enjoyed blasting a 380-yard drive downwind, then struggled to reach the end of the tee box when turned the other way. The breeze gave the golf a goofy quality, but for the first time during my short stint in the UK, I was finding the center of the clubface consistently, the travel cobwebs giving way to some focus born of my playing alone on an empty golf course. It would be a long two months if I had to play solo often, but a morning to think about nothing but the work I had done with Dynda and Doc made for a lovely walk 'round the home of the 1932 Open Championship, won by fellow countryman Gene Sarazen.

The breeze brought a steady stream of tears, and when I stopped on the tenth hole to wipe them, I noticed some redness on the fingers of my fresh white glove. I peeled it off and checked my hand—no cuts, just callouses—so I wiped my eyes again and discovered more red ooze. I made a mental note to be sure to clean my contacts every night if I was going to be playing in this sort of wind, and as I finished up at Prince's with a respectable 78, I took a strange confidence from having played until my eyes bled.

My expectations for the welcomes I would be receiving at the courses in England were modest. I anticipated a polite indifference bordering on condescension toward an unsophisticated American come to inspect their masterpieces. Deal had proven to be an open-arms club, and the welcome at Prince's was almost Irish in its warmth and overreaching hospitality. I was offered lunch and conversation and a tour of their small golf museum, where I learned of Prince's Golf Club's beloved Laddie Lucas, a future member of Parliament who was born in the Prince's clubhouse and would become known as the finest left-handed golfer in the world. He was a decorated RAF pilot, and when his Spitfire was hit over France in World War II, he used his knowledge of the Prince's links to crash-land by the fourth tee, allowing him to sneak in a quick nine before returning to the battlefront.

I had come to the UK with an idea that, when it came to links golf, the Brits might hold the classics but the Irish owned the welcome. I was finding, however, that club snobbery was a better-practiced art in my home country. Of course, I had yet to visit Muirfield, where exclusivity was the stuff of golf legend, but so far, it seemed that just because a club was old didn't make it curmudgeonly. Surely I would meet some of the stuffiness I had prepared myself for at Royal St. George's, host to fourteen Opens, most recently the 2011 installment, won by Darren Clarke. Yet while RSG wasn't necessarily a club where I would walk around the clubhouse in my pajamas, there was still a welcoming air about the place that I found refreshing, as if the members were happy for a visitor to have traveled so far to see what their piece of the golf map had to offer.

A friend of a friend of my parents had heard about my trip and emailed me an offer to join me at RSG, where he had been a member for years. Graham was a generous guide who knew every corner of the place and taught me the club's interesting membership arrangement. There were club members—a distinguished bunch for sure, including lords and prime ministers, as well as the likes of Ian Fleming, who took breaks from writing Bond novels to golf there. But RSG also had permit holders, locals who had purchased a reasonably priced pass to play the course according to a generous schedule. So one did not have to be anointed as a member to enjoy the course; it remained available to area golfers who, as permit holders, had their own tournaments and simple clubhouse next to the members' gorgeous Tudor mansion. They even challenged the members every year in a tournament, at which, I was told, the permit holders came out on top on a regular basis.

I expected RSG to be a bit plain from my memories of it on TV. Open courses were not built for television, and their kinks and curves tended to hide from cameras. A little brown, a lot of sand, some humps and some bumps—the old British links lacked the framing foliage that made Augusta's layout so distinctive, so my expectations of Royal St. George's were modest. I was sure it would be lovely and would feel as distinguished as its name suggested; well presented, but too subdued and polite for any real fun (my preconceived notion of most things British). Within four holes, I was reminded of how much I actually knew about links golf in the UK, which was hardly enough to fill the back of a scorecard.

Royal St. George's was a party. It was a hoot and a romp, as boring as a bullfight. Number four pointed me directly toward some sort of golf volcano, a massive dune with a bunker gashed into its side that hid the fairway from the tee box. The course seemed to toy with us, with blind shots over cresting dunes onto unlikely landing areas, but nothing about the knotty layout felt indulgent or unfair. There was plenty of safety behind or past the scary bits, as long as I listened to Graham; it was definitely a course to be enjoyed with a guide. You could feel the age and the time in the mounds, a rumpled topography that took generations of weather to sculpt. Sunshine only added to the joy of RSG, as Duff and I arrived at the last hole light-headed from the walk. He hadn't complained once about his foot or the drive back to London that was facing him, and I was unconcerned about the 42 I shot on the front nine. On the elevated eighteenth tee of this home to so many Opens, Graham turned to me and said, "Last hole. Let's say you need a par for the championship. A four for the Open."

Four for the Open. It would be—*should* be—my swing thought on every hole I played from here on out. *Four for the Open.* I cut a drive off the faraway bunkers that Graham had pointed out as my target, dropping the ball on the left side of the fairway. My links lessons were coming back quickly—just like riding a bike (into a fifty-mile-per-hour wind)—and I took two extra clubs and hit a punchy 6-iron, landing it twenty yards short of the green and rolling it up to fifteen feet. *Four for the Open*, and I watched my putt turn left in the breeze and drop for three. Never mind that they all added up to 80—I had bested a challenge at RSG, and I felt a tiny slice of what Darren Clarke and Greg Norman and Walter Hagen felt as they walked off this green having made their number and grabbed the Jug.

Duff won himself a par that day on the third hole. His total didn't break into double digits as we'd hoped, but he left Royal St. George's with enough souvenirs to remind him that it was well worth the Band-Aids. As we packed up our bags and lifted them into his car, I found a golf ball hiding in the pocket with my rain gloves—the one ball I had brought from home specifically for this round at Royal St. George's.

It was a Penfold golf ball, a brand dating to the 1920s, with a red heart above the name. It was the brand of ball James Bond used to defeat his cheating nemesis in *Goldfinger*, and the ball whose sales ballooned after Bond/Sean Connery declared, "Here's my Penfold Hearts." Though he renamed the course Royal St. Mark's in his novel, Ian Fleming's hole descriptions revealed that Bond was battling Auric Goldfinger across the links of St. George's.

The Penfold Heart had been rereleased in recent years, and a thoughtful reader, seeing on my blog that I was headed to RSG, sent me a sleeve. Trusting in the providence of such a gesture, I was careful to pack a Penfold for this round, a ball that had to be stuffed with birdies and the secret to my conquering the dunes of Sandwich with the cunning skill of a secret agent. And then I forgot the ball was in my bag.

I dropped the Penfold beside our car in the grass where we had parked and pulled a 7-iron out of the trunk. I watched the clean white ball with the small red mark soar from the parking lot out into the RSG practice grounds. It was my most effortless swing and best contact of the day, the heart springing off the meat of the clubface. *Tempo* and *Target* were my preferred swing thoughts when I remembered to think them, but swishing at that ball without a target—hitting it just to say I hit it at RSG—reminded me to swing easy, and that targets made that tougher. In finding a target, I found questions about my ability to hit it. Precision was everything in golf, but I had to find a focus that came without any fear: aim, and then accept. And I had to be more Bond: play fearless and hit away, because here's my Penfold Heart.

Lengths

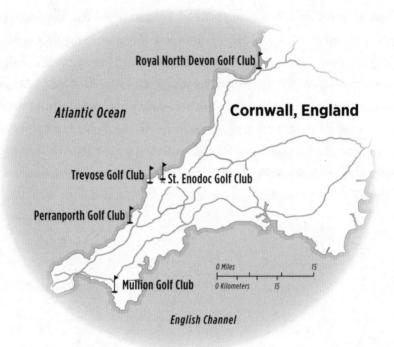

Royal North Devon Golf Club

Atlantic Ocean

Cornwall, England

Trevose Golf Club

St. Enodoc Golf Club

Perranporth Golf Club

Mullion Golf Club

0 Miles   15
0 Kilometers   15

English Channel

The bear in the train station wore a blue coat and a red hat. I snapped pictures of it for my children and texted my wife back home—*Tell the kids I'm in the real Paddington Station!* I dragged my suitcase and my golf bag to a spot on a bench next to the short sculpture and sat. It was 10:00 p.m. London time, though my body clock was still back in Philadelphia, and, with a ham-and-cheese baguette in my hand that I couldn't quite bring to my mouth, I caught my breath, feeling the sort of tired that makes one acutely aware of the weight of his head. On our drive back to London, I had seen the cliffs of Dover in the southeast corner of Britain (yup, they're white), and I was now headed to the southwest town of Penzance, three tee times awaiting me tomorrow on the opposite edge of England.

I was the only one hauling a golf travel case onto the sleeper train that evening. I shouldered it through the door and into my cabin, then looked at my golf bag as it took up every inch of space that wasn't bed, the tall black trunk mocking me: *This one's full, buddy.* I climbed over my clubs and hit my miniature pillow hard. Suddenly, there was a knock at my door—"Good morning, Mr. Coyne"—and a kind English gentleman passed me my breakfast tea over my luggage. I sipped it as the train rocked us through morning farmland, rushing by a blurry vignette of wire fences and moist green fields. I had to shake off the sleep to remember why I was there: I was headed to Cornwall to visit some of Gramma Billy's picks. I was there because I put a pin in a map. I sipped tea in golf shoes with my legs propped on a golf bag, with one solitary shred of knowledge to sustain me: I had no idea where the hell I was.

The lone rental car agency at the station in Penzance mercifully had one automatic car left in the lot, a purple hatchback of unknown brand that looked like a beefed-up Skittle. My clubs actually fit in the trunk, so I felt myself fortunate as I set my GPS for a place called Perranporth and pulled out of the lot into the wrong lane of traffic. I piloted the Skittle through the streets of Penzance like an old pirate, recalling that it isn't the driving on the left side that's tough; rather, it's the turning. I owe apologies to at least three drivers who were forced to examine the totality of their lives, reliving every regret and triumph, as they watched their end approach in a blur of purple. After each turn into the wrong lane, I embraced my ignorance: "Sorry! American!" I yelled at their closed windows, as if they didn't already know. It took me twenty minutes to get out of the small Cornish town, but once I did, I forgave myself for my novice piloting and wondered if, thanks to my morning jolt, someone would live their life just a little more fully that day.

The drive up to the north coast of Cornwall took an hour at my careful pace, and I hopped out of the car in Perranporth with a minute to spare before my 9:00 a.m. tee time. A quick glance from the parking lot revealed that I had a hike ahead of me; the simple clubhouse had the feeling of a lodge built halfway up a ski slope, with golf holes both cascading downward from it and stretching above it toward the clouds. The course looked like wild fun, and I hurried to check in at the pro shop, my travel fog finally blown clear by the promise and possibility of good golf.

The head pro met me with a warm welcome as I launched into what would become a well-practiced routine of introduction: "Hi, I'm Tom Coyne, an American golf writer here playing the links of the UK . . ."

"Mr. Coyne! Yes, we were expecting you today," he said as he looked at his tee sheet. "We've got you teeing off at 14:00." He read the confusion in my face and translated the time into American: "You're off at 2:00 p.m."

I understood twenty-four-hour time and appreciated its efficacy. It proved handy in keeping my itinerary clean, as the long days on this northern isle allowed for both 6:00 a.m. and 6:00 p.m. tee times. Being able to use 6:00 and 18:00 avoided confusion and landed the twenty-four-hour clock on the list I was compiling of things we should borrow from here and introduce back home. We had taken their language, so why not their clocks? Add to the list their ability to pay the dinner check instantly with tableside credit-card scanners (why must we see the bill first, awkwardly attesting to its existence?), their traffic lights that flashed yellow before changing to both red *and* green, and even their roadway roundabouts. They begin as the bane of any Brit-driving newbie, but after some white-knuckled practice, one finds there is nothing better than roundabouts for eschewing the brake pedal and getting there fast, particularly when one has to haul ass across Cornwall to the opposite coast for the first of three tee times I had somehow snafued.

I never did learn how the morning and afternoon rounds got flip-flopped on my ironclad, quadruple-checked, laminated-and-three-hole-punched-into-a-binder itinerary, but the folks down at Mullion were kind enough to allow me onto their course well past my allotted slot. So at roughly 10:30 on either clock, I set out on a coastal golfing binge I would forever recall as Cornwall Day.

This date had been circled on my now-suspect itinerary for months. Three rounds after an overnight journey on a sleeper train, on my first day driving a rental car on the opposite side of the road, with four hours of commuting among courses, seemed a recipe for foiling this Scottish journey before I even got to Scotland. Cornwall Day would require the help of a whole host of deities. I would need help on the weather, and I prayed for the courses to be friendly, flattish walks. The powers that be cooperated nicely on the forecast; the weather was windy but clear, cold but dry. As for the second prayer, the powers had a good laugh, tossed my ball off a cliff, and said, *Go get it.*

Mullion Golf Club had an angry glacier quality to it. It wasn't a very long course, but there were a handful of heart-stopping hikes on holes you wouldn't find on a golf course in my litigious homeland. The par 4 sixth dropped off a mountainside that I had to descend in a crisscrossing fashion like a child on skis, thinking to myself, *Holy shit, my car is up there—how do I get back?* That's what numbers eight and nine were for, I learned, as both played up a wall of green, the latter being a par 5 that Mullion's website refers to as "Cardiac Hill." I would have thought its layout an unreasonable anomaly if I didn't find even taller hikes along Perranporth in the afternoon. I scaled and scraped and wished I had gotten in better shape that winter. And from time to time, I stopped to enjoy the views at both courses that were not necessarily true links—they were more cliffside tracks—but each was full of deep-blue backdrops and quirks I cherished. Cornwall was known as England's cool corner, where folks were a little more open-minded and laid-back, and Perranporth and Mullion took on that character, two unfussy and funky vertical golf courses that made Cornwall Day a joyful calorie burn.

Somewhere between courses I stopped for a pasty (pronounced *pas-tee*) at a gas station (pronounced *petrol station*). I had failed to eat a sandwich in Sandwich, so I committed to sampling Cornwall's great culinary export, the Cornish pasty (forget a hen—there was no time). Awaiting me in a tinfoil robe beneath a heat lamp was a crusty boat of nonspecific beef bathed in onion and rosemary gravy. Edible with one non-steering hand, it was a tasty fix on a trip whose meals had been left off the itinerary. I would subsist on Snickers bars and gas-station sandwiches, which were quite nice in the UK if you fancied butter and bacon, which I did. The pasty was also a bite into the region's history, when the wives of Cornwall's miners invented for them a lunch they could eat with sooty hands. They packed pastry with stewed meat and vegetables, then folded up the dough into a sort of pouch with a thick crust along one edge that served as a handle. Miners could eat the good stuff and toss the dirty crust away, and the concoction also seemed an ideal snack for golfers at the turn. How many hot dogs had I gobbled with fingers glowing a pesticide blue? I didn't dispose of my pasty crust; I savored every crumb and calorie as I arrived at my third and final course of the day, the Trevose Golf & Country Club, where the view from the clubhouse made my full stomach leap.

I first checked to see if they would still be serving dinner at 22:00. They wouldn't, but they would send a burger to my room before the kitchen closed. My travels had taught me to always ask when meal service stopped; I had seen enough tourists enjoying peanuts from the bar for their suppers. Then I headed out into one of the loveliest clubhouse views of my golfing life. Beyond the leather couches pointed at a wide picture window was a fire pit softly glowing in the evening, and beyond the patio, a long first fairway reached out toward the ocean, tall cliffs and sea rocks sheltering a small harbor around the golf holes at Trevose. But more beautiful than the white spray on the black rocks or the warm orange flames was the path leading to the first tee: a gentle descent to what looked like a layout pimpled with mounds and gentle inclines, but still relatively compact and gloriously level.

Trevose was the most championship-caliber of the Cornwall Day courses. Designed by the legendary Harry Colt—who left his stamp on the likes of Royal County Down, Pine Valley, Royal Portrush, and Muirfield—Trevose had hosted the British Amateur, and at 7,112 yards wasn't the quick stroll I was hoping for at 6:00 p.m. But it was a meaty, pure links—not as eccentric as its partners that day, but true quality, with an opening nine that hugged the ocean and a back half that headed gently upward to the clubhouse. I played through in under three hours on an empty course and was pleased with a card that added up to 76. I had finally figured out how to avoid adding up my score as I played: become too brain-tired for simple addition. Along with a 74 at Mullion and a 75 at Perranporth, my scores were perking up, while my swing felt tired in a useful way. I made easy passes, with soft arms that let the clubhead lag like a bowling ball somewhere behind me. The contact, through much of Cornwall Day, was as good as I would need it to be at the end of this path I had laid out. Now to make some putts.

My legs had a wobbly jiggle to them as if I had hopped off a daylong treadmill, and I sank into the couch in my suite at Trevose, the ocean view in front of me faded to black. I chewed my burger like a cow mushing cud, and the stillness around me had a magical peace to it. The rush of the day settled into a keen sense of presence, and I felt a full awareness of where I was and the lengths I had traversed and how astonishing life was and how large and beautiful this world could be and how I was going to golf the UK and it was going to be the experience of a lifetime. I felt so much gratitude, and it tasted as easy as a well-done cheeseburger.

The golf today had been gorgeous, and my play was encouraging, but the real lesson of Cornwall was expectation. My assumption of what could be done in a day was far more modest than the reality; for all the time I had spent fretting over Cornwall Day, it just went ahead and happened, as all Tuesdays tend to do. My playing fifty-four holes was insignificant in the grand scheme around me, and I decided that my responsibilities henceforth would be simply showing up and getting on with it. Effort was mine; results belonged to somebody else. As for who that might be, I wasn't terribly concerned that I had no idea.

I'm not one for blending up God and golf. I don't think it does either of them much good. The idea that God ever really cared about a touchdown or a putt, as if the deity were some replay official in the sky, doling out victories and losses like Santa Claus, is a portrait of the Divine that I find unsatisfying. The truth is, I don't know enough about God to confidently offer Him or Her the capitalization, so I'm going to drop the tall *G* here, because to make god a proper noun means that I'm referring to a specific organization, place, or person, and god is as unspecific an idea as I can fathom. It doesn't say anything in my grammar guide about capitalizing mysteries, and the notion that there's a force behind all existence . . . for me, that needs to be the grand mystery, one that transcends our chases in the fields. So I'll stick to golf—unless golf gives me a glimpse of something unknown at work in my life, which it did in the southeastern corner of England. I don't think it was god I was feeling in my room at Trevose, but something about Cornwall Day had me wondering about the S-word, and if I now knew what it meant.

Spirituality always sounded to me like the stuff of oily gurus and self-help pulp and slow-talking converts desperate for a life of depth. It sounded like something lapsed Catholics used to cover their asses and stake some claim to salvation—*I'm not religious, but I am deeply spiritual.* I resented the term for its lofty aspirations, its vague promises, its application as an emotional panacea. It sounded like bullshit that I didn't have or want, which was what I called most things I didn't have but did actually want. And I don't think I have it, but I do have an idea of what it is now, and it isn't reserved for desert retreats or morning meditations. To me, it's the awareness of myself as part of something bigger. That's it; and it seems to fit with the flow and foibles of a game of golf. Few diversions will give you a better chance to see yourself as a small part of something vast than golf beside the ocean at sunset. Mountain climbing probably works, but I'm not that crazy.

So I don't know to whom or what I was grateful in Cornwall. I just know it wasn't me. There was some grace in my day, and that was enough. Not everyone would get it, and I wasn't sure I even did, but one person I knew for sure would not understand the peace I was feeling sent me a message, as if he were here specifically to interrupt it.

RND. Old Tom. First in England. Westward Ho!

I assumed that meant I would see Robert tomorrow.

Partner

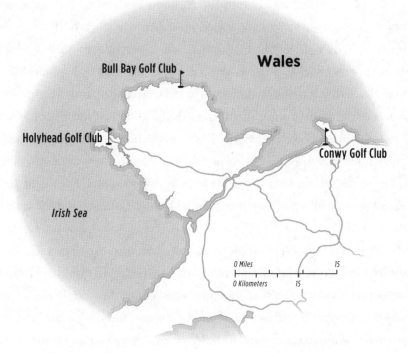

Bull Bay Golf Club

Wales

Holyhead Golf Club

Conwy Golf Club

Irish Sea

0 Miles   15
0 Kilometers   15

There were certain things Robert did not do before 10:00 a.m. Wake up was one of them, so I wasn't surprised that I teed off at St. Enodoc alone. A friend had called Enodoc the Ballybunion of England—high praise, comparing Enodoc to the jewel of Ireland's golfing crown. To me, Enodoc ended up being all that—and a bag of crisps.

Perhaps my affection for Enodoc was born of never having heard of it before Gramma Billy stuck it on my map, though I should have; the James Braid design has popped up on world top one hundred lists. Braid, born in Fife, Scotland, in 1870, surely lived to an age of 150—it had to have taken two lifetimes to design as many courses as are credited to his name, and to win five Opens along the way. Legendary golf scribe Bernard Darwin once called Royal County Down "the kind of golf that people play in their most ecstatic dreams," but for me, he was describing Enodoc. It was a golf dream from which one would wake in tears for its having to come to an end, a course stretched along a coastline that had literally been blessed by golf.

The club took its name from the eleventh-century St. Enodoc church, whose sturdy medieval steeple called me down the tenth fairway on what felt like the golf hole to which all other holes aspired, a long par 4 winding through a green valley, water snaking down its left side and spilling toward a blue sea on the horizon. I almost forgot that I'd made par as I hustled over to inspect the church set in the nucleus of the course, a sort of consecrated halfway house, curious about whether it might just be dressed-up ruins on display for visiting cameras. It turned out that St. Enodoc was a functioning parish, and mass was held there one Sunday every month. Time your round right and you could pop in at the turn and avoid skipping church again for golf.

Enodoc had cliffs and hulking dunes and bunkers with names like Himalaya (which makes an unofficial claim to being the largest bunker in Europe), with holes that played off launching pads and out to the water and then back along hillsides, protected by creeks and by the sea, and not an ounce of it felt designed: a gorgeous, immaculate, and, when I played it, empty slice of hallowed ground.

The place had a golfing poetry to it, so it was fitting to find that longtime Enodoc member and former UK poet laureate Sir John Betjeman lay buried in the church's small graveyard. The grave and chapel had me thinking of another English poet and his Tintern Abbey, and the inspiration he found in such bucolic surroundings. St. Enodoc was Wordsworthian in quality, and by playing it, I understood what Wordsworth meant when he said nature let him "see into the life of things." A round at St. Enodoc was life abundant.

I wouldn't tell any of this to Robert. For him, golf wasn't poetry; it was a means of producing a tally as evidence that he was still okay, and still worth one's envy. I made the two-hour drive up to Royal North Devon and found him sitting in his car in the parking lot, door open, sunglasses on, listening to country music just loud enough to give the impression that he did not give a damn that it was too loud. His bluster began before he even reached the clubhouse, his unimpressed attitude meant to impart an air of rare golfing skill. Robert's being unbothered by pretty much any setting was strangely intimidating, unless you knew him, in which case you suspected he was moving so slowly not out of arrogance but because he probably needed to throw up. Still, he could make a hangover look cool, or even admirable for the adventurous evening it suggested.

I had driven past the clubhouse before I knew I was there. It was tucked back behind a small agricultural or industrial park, a large sign on a building of metal siding announcing that Royal North Devon was around the corner and that it was England's oldest golf course. The busy farming machinery in the parking lot soon made sense as we were greeted by our first on-course livestock of the trip—a few bored sheep milling about the burn (a stream) in front of the first tee box. I was happy to find that RND showcased this marker of genuine links land, that it was shared with grazing animals the way golf's original layouts had split their space with farmers. Grazing land was too valuable to fence off from livestock, and golf began on such parcels for the same reason they were good for sheep. Because the sandy soil couldn't be farmed for crops, it was left to hunters, shepherds, and men in wool chasing leather balls as part of some strange new game. The sheep were more valuable than the ball-chasers, and I would guess that the farmers who shared Royal North Devon still felt that way.

Royal North Devon was a late addition to the itinerary, a course Robert insisted on after discovering it in Kevin Cook's *Tommy's Honor*. Cook's history recounts Old Tom Morris traveling from his post as designer/greenskeeper/head pro at Prestwick to lay out the links at North Devon in 1864, bringing Scotland's game to England like a great golf missionary. (Accounts tell of English golf having been played near London at Blackheath prior to Morris's trip, but his Royal North Devon design remains England's oldest established course.) Born and raised in St. Andrews, Morris relocated west to Prestwick when a gutta-percha golf ball got him fired from his hometown gig as a club maker. His boss, Allan Robertson, golf's first pro and a manufacturer of the old-school featherie ball, caught Morris playing the new ball and canned him for fraternizing with the competition. Off to Prestwick Morris went, where the Open Championship was born as an invitational to showcase their new and invincible pro's talents. A controversy over ball technology thus gave birth to golf's greatest championship.

In that first Open Championship, the fix was supposed to be in for Old Tom on a course he designed and looked after; it was a chance for Prestwick members to thumb their noses at the golf bullies up around Edinburgh and prove that they had the horse right here. But that didn't happen. Old Tom lost the first Open. Golf's will supplants the golfer's will—even Old Tom's—every time.

The Morris pedigree, combined with the fact that Royal North Devon was the home track of John Henry Taylor, winner of five Open Championships and a member of golf's great turn-of-the-century triumvirate alongside Braid and Harry Vardon—the three of them pretty much won everything for a while—made RND a must-play, yet I found it curious that the history section on its website made no mention of the Scotsman Tom Morris, giving the entire Royal North Devon spotlight to local boy Taylor. Was England's oldest golf course shading its Scottish debt? But even more interesting than the names in its archives was the name of the town in which it was located. Westward Ho! was named after Charles Kingsley's bestselling novel of 1855 as a strategy for drumming up tourism. A town named after a novel was irresistible to the writer in me, and to the grammarian in me, a town with an exclamation point in its name—the only such town in the UK—seemed a curiosity worth crossing off the list.

We threw our first drives into a vengeful wind, managing to miss the sheep munching grass beside the tee box. I thumped my second shot low along the par 5, while Robert ripped a towering hybrid that dropped out of the air like a shot goose. He slammed his clubhead into the hard fairway and muttered something angry that I couldn't hear through the breeze. We were both high-ball hitters—as Doc Suttie once told me, "You don't hit your ball under the wind, you hit your ball over it"—and Robert had yet to surrender to his surroundings. For all the golf we'd played together in Ireland, he had never worked to alter his trajectory there, either. If the air was still, he owned the course. If the wind was up, then he had 84 or so excuses to share in the clubhouse. He stubbornly lobbed two more wedges into the breeze and made an opening six to my simple five, and his love affair with RND came to a swift-blown conclusion.

The course required the lens of history to appreciate it. It was a forthright and authentic links of a minimalist flavor; its simplicity revealed its fine vintage, but it was not a postcard course for a golf thrill-seeker. The only standout design moment was on the fourth hole, where we teed off toward a wall of railroad ties that hoisted up the fairway like a dam. Railroad ties (or sleepers, as they were called here) on a golf course recalled modern tracks and Pete Dye, and I never liked them for the feeling that they brought something manufactured, something minigolf, into the game. But they were actually an Old Tom Morris innovation, and I would have to readjust my thoughts on so many Florida golf courses that made unintentional homages to golf's founding father.

We discovered other firsts at RND: A golfer playing with his terrier on a long leash was my first sighting of golf and dogs brought together in a way that made such undeniable sense, and that could certainly sell more tee times at home. Why do we leave our outdoor-loving friends at home when we go outdoors for five hours? If you find their unclaimed droppings a nonstarter, consider what the original golfers contended with on fairways shared with herds of livestock. Another first at RND was slow play. While the scorecard was stamped with the admonishment SLOW PLAY IS UNACCEPTABLE, on the eighth hole we found a foursome embroiled in a match for somebody's farm. We came upon them on the tee box, only to get a casual nod. They hit their shots and pulled their trolleys ahead without inviting us through to play an otherwise empty golf course. Such was certainly their prerogative, but I felt a worry in my gut as I watched each pause, chop, and missed gimme up ahead.

My playing pace so far had been below four hours, closer to three in most cases. Waiting to swing felt foreign, and on this day, it seemed a tad foreboding. I had already played eighteen, and there was no time for leaning on our clubs this afternoon, not with a six-hour drive up into Wales facing me at round's end. So I did something I normally tried to avoid: I followed Robert's impatient lead and hopped across the course to an open hole, skipping around and eventually filling up most of the scorecard. I hated to rush RND, but it was either that or listen to Robert complain, and when his mood went sour, it got dark, morphing from groaning about golf to doubting the worth of waking up at all. So we went fast and exited the RND property before the groups behind us could report the two golfers who were playing the course backward. I conceded myself two pars on holes we never quite found for a total of 74, while Robert refused to add his up because we hadn't played properly. I likely beat him by a dozen strokes that day. He said he would meet me in Wales, but as he pulled away I knew he was headed for a dark pub or hotel bar for an evening of conversation and crushed grapes, a setting where Robert was always scratch.

I gained an education in the English man as I motored north that afternoon, rolling the window down every few miles to blow the sleep out of my eyes. Walking thirty-six holes (well, thirty-four) was not the most prudent preparation for a cross-kingdom drive, but the promise of new country and more Open venues and another day closer to Scotland pulled me onward, even while my GPS confessed so many more miles to go.

The hours were put to use investigating something I had never encountered in Philadelphia—polite sports talk radio—as I learned that Liverpool had been a severe disappointment that season. There were Liverpool fans in every corner of the country, and they were all distraught. Chelsea was less popular, it seemed, even though they had just won the league, and when their fans called in, they struck me as Yankees and Cowboys types—smug front-runners. I learned that there were people who not only understood cricket but wanted to talk about it; England's best player had just been left off the national team for some sort of rules infraction. Cricket apparently had its own Allen Iverson, and outrage at his mistreatment was voiced in what I thought was anger, though I couldn't quite tell from its well-mannered delivery. A host called a guest a fool, then spent the next twenty minutes regretting his impertinence. The English man was angry, it seemed, and was ready to apologize for it.

I rode into the town of Conwy on the north coast of Wales in darkness, a castle at the town's entrance looming large and vigilant above a bank of yellow spotlights. Its ramparts and towers announced that I had arrived somewhere worth the drive. I took three unintended tours of the town before finding the Castle Hotel, where I stepped out of the car as if I were trying stilts for the first time. I attempted to stretch in the parking lot, but really just wiggled my arms at the air and then shuffled to the hotel entrance to find a room where I don't recall taking off my shoes, able to grasp only three simple ideas as I plunged into sleep: I was in Conwy, in Wales. I was playing fifty-four holes tomorrow. And Steven Gerrard was the greatest footballer in Liverpool history. He would never walk alone.

I had always thought of Wales as the Maine of the UK: sounds quaint, and I hear the scenery is lovely; if only I ever had a reason to visit. As part of the United Kingdom, it was overshadowed by mighty England and massive Scotland, and it lacked the cachet of Northern Ireland's contentiousness. It seemed like the cousin you forgot to invite to family dinner, and was probably best known for the title given to the heir to the Crown: Edward I was supposedly the first to call his scion the Prince of Wales in 1301, fulfilling a promise to the recently conquered Welsh that his son would be born in Wales and would be Welsh-speaking. Wales and golf had some history, but it was more of a rugby country; Ian Woosnam and the 2010 Ryder Cup weren't exactly Tom Morris and St. Andrews. But it was Gramma Billy who preordained my left turn into Wales to visit one of her and Gene's picks in Holyhead, and as with all things Gramma Billy, it made me smile.

I did not expect to see them for a few hours, but as I pulled up the slope into the parking lot at Holyhead and noted the short palm trees (I never got used to this botanical anomaly in Ireland, where the Gulf Stream pushed a temperate climate all the way from Mexico to the British Isles, allowing you to stand there shivering in three sweaters and wonder how the hell you were looking at Hawaii), but there was my tall friend from Manchester, the one who had played no small part in my being in Wales right now. Next to him was a newer, shorter friend on the putting green, both wearing stocking caps on a sunny Welsh morning.

At the age of fifty-five, Tom took his first golf trip to the southwest of Ireland and came home knowing what he wanted to do with his life. He hung up his corporate duds and decided to become an Irish and Scottish golf tour operator. Tom called his new company Old Sod Travel, and he contacted me for advice on navigating said sod. There began a friendship that would take us to golf clubs around America promoting golf in Ireland, all the way to a morning in Wales when he had been kind enough to pick up my friend Julian in Manchester and drive him out to the farthest edge of the UK. Julian had just arrived from Germany, and after a month's worth of email between two strangers about the precise location of Julian's mum's home and its distance from the Holyhead golf course, the two new travelmates had beat me to the first tee.

Holyhead was a special course, another James Braid brainchild built upon slopes that were filthy with gorse. The terrain was linksy if not true links, a windy seaside track where you seemed to be playing over, across, or around a treacherous mass of flowering yellow hillside. At Holyhead, the gorse bloomed along with our scores, as we were distracted by old stories and new news. Julian was now living in a sleepy suburb of Munich, where his German-language lessons were not going well—thus his eagerness for this trip back to his homeland. He was adjusting to full-time fatherhood, which had allowed zero time for golf. He confessed that his last round of real golf might have been with me in Ireland some eight years ago, so we let the gorse have the balls that morning (it's gorse if it has thorns; otherwise, the gold stuff is called broom—and this was gorse) and made it over to our second round of the day at Bull Bay, up across the Isle of Anglesey to its northern coast, with the pep of new company in our steps.

As one might have expected in a country that had been conquered and outshone by its noisier neighbor, Wales possessed a strong current of nationalism and pride in its Celtic roots, as evidenced by its use of the Welsh language on all its road signs. I'd never heard Welsh spoken aloud until we met the captain at Bull Bay, who was kind enough to join us for our round. In his fifties and of a sturdy, wind-resistant build, Trevor laughed when I asked him if he knew the secret to golf. Then he said something in Welsh. I think. It sounded like English spoken in reverse, and I wondered if he was transmitting the secret to me in code, like a backward message on a Led Zeppelin album. Golf's answer—at least, the Welsh version—would remain a mystery for now.

Trevor walked us around to the first tee, where two golf carts were awaiting our foursome. I eyed the two beautiful buggies with their soft vinyl seats. The temptation was mighty, but I declined, informing our host that my intention was to walk all my golf. Tom wisely acknowledged the futility of such a policy and opted to ride along with Trevor, leaving one lonely buggy beside the tee as my aching soles hit the turf, legs already seizing up from the thirty-minute drive to the course.

"You're not going to ride, Nigel?" Tom said from his cart, and Julian and I turned around to look for a fifth member of our party. There was nobody there.

"Nigel, you don't have to walk. Let Coyne do it."

While their two hours together in the car that morning had succeeded in bringing them to this remote corner of Wales, it had failed in acquainting Tom with Julian's actual name. Worse, Tom had slapped some generic Anglican label upon this Englishman—*Oh, they all look like Nigels*—and left Julian and me to cringe over who was going to correct him, and how. The fact that they had spent all morning together meant that we were well past any cordial window of name correction, and I lacked the energy for awkwardness. Besides, it was funny.

"You want to walk or ride, Nigel?" I said.

A wide smile spread across Julian-Nigel's face. "I think I'll walk."

Bull Bay offered a lumpy layout of long views and generous fairways, a course similar to Holyhead in its modest distances and cliffside setting, but with holes where the gorse was more of a backdrop than a participant. We didn't find a single sleepy hole as we golfed our way along the dark-blue bay. Two birdies and a handful of sloppy chips carded me a polite 76 that we didn't have a chance to toast in what looked like the top nineteenth hole in Wales, a second-floor bar where the glass doors slid open onto a wraparound patio, and where the members raised their pints to us on our way down eighteen. I was thankful Robert had disappeared for a few days. We would have been in that room for a week, and never would have made it to our third tee time around the corner from the Castle Hotel upon the links of Conwy.

Our other-side driving shortcomings multiplied when partnered in a caravan. Still wearing our spikes as we drove, we raced back toward town, the sun already low in the sky, forcing Tom to blow a red light behind me and take three extra spins around a Welsh roundabout. But we finally arrived at Conwy and hustled over to the pro shop, all of us limping from our hips, but Tom and Julian-Nigel excited by the prospect of completing fifty-four holes in one day. With rare resolve, we set our chins and hoisted our bags and pulled on the pro shop door, only to find it bolted shut.

We sniffed around the empty clubhouse, then came back out and knocked on the pro shop windows. The golf pro emerged from a back office, putting on his jacket to leave for the day. He let us in, and when we told him who we were, he explained that they were closing up and had expected us hours ago.

"We've had a busy day. We already played Holyhead and Bull Bay."

He looked at us for a moment. "Today?"

"Today."

"And you want to go out now?" There was doubt in his voice.

"We'll play fast and get in as many holes as we can before dark. If that's okay."

Apparently, our excuse amused him—I doubted that any other latecoming golfers had tried the Holyhead–Bull Bay defense before—and he smiled. "Of course it is," he said, handing us scorecards. "It's all yours. Shouldn't have anyone holding you up," he added, laughing. The pro locked the door behind us, and we were off to tee thirty-seven.

Built upon dunes where it was said the first golf ball in Wales was teed up, the Conwy links dated to 1875 and were laid out by Old Tom's nephew,

Jack Morris. In my heretofore brief experience with Morris courses, I would have to give the nephew the nod as course designer. There was plenty of Old Tom's handiwork left on the itinerary to sway my opinion, but Jack had done fine work in Wales. Founded by a handful of Royal Liverpool members, Conwy nestled into a corner of land between the Irish Sea and the River Conwy, and was an old gentleman of a track. The only Welsh course to ever hold an Open finals qualifier, its holes were confidently straightforward, and its drama was reserved and refined. It appeared an easy eighteen from afar, until you ventured forth and found its grabby bunkers and forced carries. We loved the distant Welsh hills and cliffs that framed our targets and provided an illusion of being on wild terrain without actually having to hike it.

The sun was setting over Wales as Julian-Nigel noted on the seventeenth hole that Conwy possessed a feature unique in golf. As he bent over to re-trieve his ball from the cup, his groan drowned out the crack and pop of his back. He looked like a giraffe trying to play marbles, and as he lifted his head back up he explained that the cups in Conwy must be a good yard deeper than any golf holes he had encountered before. The crick in my back had me imagining the same anomaly. My spine had ceased bending somewhere around the turn, and after tapping in on the last, I had to squat like a sumo wrestler to lower my fingers into the hole, dropping my ball back into my pocket for the fifty-fourth and final time that day.

It was dark again as we passed shadows of the Conwy Castle and squeezed our rental cars through the one-lane archway in its wall. The Castle was a World Heritage site that I would have to visit again. The golf would bring me back, certainly, and then I would be sure to leave time for this unexpected fortress that was in handsome shape for its age of eight hundred years, a hideout for the likes of Richard II and the followers of everybody's favorite holdout king, Charles I. Like the ruins I knew well from Ireland, the castle recalled the role that neighboring lands played in the tide-turning moments of the British monarchy. London got all the tourists, but it was in far-off corners like Conwy with its castle where the dustups went down and history was written. And the same could be said for golf in Wales—in my twenty-four-hour sampling, I found courses far from the links epicenters of St. Andrews, Inverness, Glasgow, and Liverpool that deserved their own Welsh golf vacation. Gramma Billy had sent me to a place that reminded me of something very simple about the game—that it was joyful. My morning started with fifty-four-hole panic and my evening ended with peace, so it was joy that I felt as I fell into bed and soaked in a hard-earned stillness of body and mind. I think I even prayed, if praying meant asking the powers that be to let the joy still be there come morning.

Folks who fret over the well-being of the game will tell you that today's golf faces three foes: It's too expensive. It takes too long to play. And it's too hard. Solving the third problem might serve as a tonic for the other two; if the game wasn't so difficult, we might be less inclined to regret the money we spend on it. And if we found the game less punitive, surely we would get around the course at a healthier clip.

Standing beside the door to the clubhouse at Wallasey Golf Club in the northwest of England, I learned how far golf hasn't come. A hundred years ago, golfers faced the same frustration over the severity of the game, and a doctor at Wallasey prescribed a cure. "The thought ran through my mind that many players in competitions got very little fun since they tore up their cards after playing only a few holes and I wondered if anything could be done about it," said the good doctor. We found these words on a plaque that commemorated one of Wallasey's members, a Dr. Frank Stableford, whose scoring innovation changed the game.

In the States, we prefer the hard math of tallying all our strokes, but club competitions in the British Isles are often played by Stableford format, in which you count points rather than swings. Ask a Scot or an Irishman what he shot in a tournament and he is apt to tell you 32 or 36, or "Ah, twenty-seven; didn't have it today." Stableford accounting can differ, but you receive points for birdies and pars and bogeys, and no points for double bogey or worse. The system is meant to reward you for good holes and to not irredeemably punish you for bad ones, and on links courses—places like Wallasey, where Stableford observed people abandoning their scorecards—the wind and weeds can turn average golf shots into round-killers. "I doubt whether any single man did more to increase the pleasure of the more humble club golfer," claimed British golf writer Henry Longhurst. Golf owed the doctor a huge debt as a man who grew the game, and in today's era of declining play, one wonders where Dr. Stableford is when we need him.

As Julian-Nigel, Tom, and I stood on the first tee at Wallasey and leaned into the breeze for balance, I wished for the care of a doctor, be it Stableford or Quinn or Jekyll. I was not actually sore, as I couldn't feel much below my waist and had to trust that my legs were there. We gazed out over a golf course that looked like morning delight. To our left, the eighteenth avalanched its way down to the clubhouse, its slope a mogul course landing at the green. Wallasey looked like another wild dune ride through the humps and bumps, though I wondered at our collective capacity to enjoy it as we grunted through our morning stretches, the three of us twisting on the tee box like great-grandparents dancing at a wedding.

I stepped up to the markers and bent over to jab my tee into the ground, and felt my head's ballast pulling me toward the earth. I caught myself. I'd watched Robert fall over on a first tee before, puke behind a golf cart, and then rip a driver down the middle, but I wasn't hungover—at least, not from pints. I was golf hungover. This was what I had been battling each morning—overconsumption that leads to physical and emotional distress. But as I had learned from Robert on so many golf trips, the hair of the dog that bit you was the only true hangover cure. Robert liked to recount the origin of the phrase as he enjoyed a morning cocktail, explaining that in medieval times, the cure for a dog bite was a potion concocted from the fur of the guilty canine. He thought such knowledge helped class up his cracking a Coors Light at the breakfast table. More of the offending substance was the only answer, so I steadied myself, leaned down again, and inserted my tee into the ground, letting out a moan as I stood back up.

"There's a lot of grunting when I bend over," I said, almost to myself.

"I'll try to be more quiet," said Julian-Nigel.

The best thing I could say about my opening drive was that it didn't suffer. Its time was ended with a decisive rightward bash, far and sure, deep off the property toward the morning traffic of Wallasey. Julian-Nigel's drive was not as resolute in its surrender. The bottom of his driver nicked a thin slice of his ball. The contact sounded like a jingle bell, followed by a wisp from the weeds directly in front of the tee box that swallowed his Pinnacle. We looked for his ball for a few minutes before we both lobbed one out onto the fairway and decided, as if there were ever any doubt that morning, that we were playing Stableford.

The hair of the dog gently worked its powers, and with each passing hole our heavy heads grew lighter as the thrill of Wallasey woke us, and we played a stunning links that lived up to its heritage. The course was originally laid out by Old Tom in 1891, then updated by the likes of James Braid, John Henry Taylor, and, recently, Donald Steel, a sort of gluttonous mix of first-team British course designers. Wallasey even added American Bobby Jones to its roll. It was a regular qualifying spot for the Open when held at Royal Liverpool (Hoylake), and Jones qualified for the Open at Wallasey in 1930 en route to golf's only Grand Slam. Jones was made an honorary Wallasey member and given a portrait painted by Wallasey member J. A. A. Berrie. Jones liked the picture so much that he asked for a second one, and today it hangs in the clubhouse at Augusta National.

We knew none of this history as we stepped up to the par 3 ninth tee and read a plaque commemorating Bobby Jones's connection to the club, on a hole named after him on the scorecard. This homage to a fellow countryman here in a corner of England caught me unawares and had me feeling oddly nostalgic, as if I hung out with Mr. Jones back home and would have to tell him when I returned—*Hey, they have a plaque for you on this really cool course in England*. Wallasey became an epiphany: Here I was, traveling far to find my way into Open qualifying, playing the course Bobby Jones had traveled to (in those days, his trip would have been a proper odyssey of steam liners and trains) to do the same. I was at Wallasey for a reason, brought here by providence to follow in the bold footsteps of an American hero. I wondered whether I had been carried to this rumpled path of sand and grass, 147 yards into the breeze, for my first ace abroad. Or I would settle for a birdie—a 2 here would be a bright-enough sign. Or a hard-earned par, a testament to Jones's steadiness. Or maybe just finding my ball after toe-knocking a 9-iron into the knee-high perdition, short and right of the green, would be a happy omen. I did find it, and I hacked it out for a four. A bogey still earned me a Stableford point, and I avoided the dreaded blob (what the Brits call an X—a hole unfinished or with no points scored). A point was proof enough that I was following Jones's path. Maybe he bogeyed this hole, too, though I doubt they would have named it after him if he had nearly blobbed the thing himself. I don't think Bobby Jones made a lot of blobs. Blobby Jones—probably not.

Wallasey snuck up on me, from its Stableford history to its golf-destination quality. As we ascended to the water views on the par 5 fourth (called Seaway, and site of one of my three-point birdies that morning), with the coast of Wales in the distance and a valley of turbulent fairway in the foreground, Wallasey earned certification as a "diamond in the dunes," as it had been described by a visiting writer prior to last year's Open down the coast. I knew there was great golf ahead at Hoylake in the afternoon, but on this trip, there would be nothing more uplifting than unexpectedly great golf, and that's what we found in the kinks and quirks of Wallasey. We left reinvigorated, remembering that no matter how much we planned and prepared, the charm of golf was that it would always surprise us. I too often took golf's capriciousness as its most maddening vice, but if I adjusted my stance and looked from another angle, its fickleness was the game's greatest gift.

Robert boycotted Wallasey and Royal Liverpool. He was silently protesting the fact that I'd told him I couldn't get him on Hoylake (as with Royal St. George's being called Sandwich, Royal Liverpool was known by the name of its town, Hoylake). My next rota course, and home to the previous year's Open Championship—atta boy, Rory—Hoylake was the only club of the 107 I planned to visit that wouldn't offer me a tee time. I hadn't even asked for a freebie, but their terse reply via an intermediary was that they "don't see any value in your playing the course."

My outrage quickly turned to agreement: What the hell would my playing there do for Hoylake? I dropped my resentment and turned to a friend of a friend who'd been a member at Hoylake for decades. Let's call my host Charles. Since Charles would have to play with us, and with Julian-Nigel and Tom along, there was no room for Robert. So he said he was going up to Royal Lytham & St. Annes (two names but one course), to hell with us, and would talk his way onto the course. I knew there was a tournament at Royal Lytham that week, but I didn't bother telling him. I didn't want to rob him of the dignity of his grudge.

Charles was an elderly gentleman and an enthusiastic host, and his welcome to Hoylake, as if it were his backyard playground that he was eager to share with visitors, dispelled our fears of Royal Liverpool stuffiness. He showed us around the clubhouse, each mahogany room chockablock with another chapter in the history of golf, with portraits of all the past Open winners at Hoylake—Tiger, Rory, Hagen, and Jones—hanging on dark walls. He explained to us that Hoylake, like so many of the great old courses in the British Isles, owed its start to the railroad. Where the railroads paused for itinerant Victorians, up went hotels and golf courses. Hoylake was built upon the grounds of the old Liverpool Hunt Club's racetrack, and Charles claimed it to be the oldest links in England. I took some silent satisfaction in having become enough of a UK links connoisseur to know he was wrong by a few years (see Royal North Devon). We stopped behind the famous clubhouse for a picture that Charles was kind enough to take, and for his age, he navigated our three iPhones well. As he eyed the screen and lined up his shot, Charles proclaimed, "Just trying to fit the big cock in!"

I turned to Julian-Nigel, and his wide eyeballs kicked off a fit of stifled giggles. Suddenly it was 1984 and I was an altar boy choking back laughs after Father Klinge farted during the Consecration. *Did he just say that? Hoylake wasn't so stuffy after all!* I would later learn as I perused the photos on my phone that Charles was referring to the timepiece on the clubhouse. The large *clock* was something of a Hoylake icon, its hands visible from much of the links.

My television memory of Hoylake was of a course long and relatively flat, a tidy, straightforward track unlike the jaw-droppers I expected up in the Highlands. Some of Hoylake fit that prejudice. Take away its name and history and you had an honest, hearty golf course in tremendous condition, a links you would enjoy but have a hard time recalling specific holes of that evening. It seemed a course built for an Open: roomy, long, and a challenge for pros who wanted to be tested but not tricked. *Come and get me*, the course seemed to suggest, with an unbothered, almost aristocratic air about it as if it well knew its own importance and didn't have to try too hard to impress.

Our bright day of Open golf was overshadowed by the quality of our accommodation. The Number Fifteen B&B took a few passes to locate, given that it lacked a sign (15 was the house number). Knowing that it was next to the fifteenth fairway only confused us, as the Open had swapped Hoylake's fifteenth and seventeenth holes for a more dramatic finish. It was worth a few roundabouts when we got there. My room was spacious and clean, but its finest feature was the wall of glass between my soft chair and the fairways of Hoylake, just a short chip over the fence. I imagined having booked this room a year earlier, watching Rory rumble down the stretch from my window. As I watched the thick, grassy mounds turn from green to black, I chopped away at my email in my warm room, and a text dinged in from Robert: *How was Hoylake?*

Top notch, I replied. I didn't bring up Wallasey, or the fact that I knew he didn't get onto Lytham that afternoon. *Where are you?*

It took a few minutes for Robert to respond. I imagined him mentally composing an answer that would suggest he was somewhere great that I didn't know about. Either that or he was searching Google images for a Liverpool strip club. I stared at my phone and waited for his reply—textpectation, I heard it called once—and thought about how much I missed my friend. The recent years had been distant and frustrating, watching Robert stand still as the world trotted past, unable to lift his eyes to see it.

It was not that long ago that Robert was out of college and trying to write a screenplay, living down the shore during the off-season with a beautiful girlfriend who visited him on the weekends and loved every flawed ounce of him. He was confident and always excited about the next project, the next trip, the next time we would be getting together for golf and wagers neither of us ever bothered collecting. He was everybody's best friend; if Robert was going to be there, a party or a foursome or a road trip filled up in a flash. He was kind to everyone; it made him feel valuable, the way he could glimpse someone and know their story, and then know how to make them feel good about it. There was a time when this made him the guy you wanted to be around—a hopeful face, empathetic in a genuine way. And in a few years, it had somehow turned and just made him sort of sad, as if the world was transparent to him, and what he had seen of it he found wanting.

I missed the time we spent in Ireland, Robert talking up the locals as though he had been born in their town, effortlessly adopting the tone of a place and showing me the joys of long conversation. When we checked out of B&Bs, it was Robert whom the lady of the house hugged. It was Robert whom the lads in the pub locked inside after closing, who sang songs he didn't know with a voice that turned the room silent. As I sat in my room in Hoylake, I realized that I had planned this trip for him, an adventure of such possibility that it couldn't help but bring back the hope in my friend's eyes. But so far I had seen very little of them.

I was half-asleep in my chair when my phone buzzed as Robert finally wrote back: *Chasing.*

Robert's awareness of his decline made it all the more pathetic. You could sympathize with someone who couldn't see his own condition, but Robert was lost and he knew it. I didn't know whether he meant he was chasing a woman or a buzz or the secret to golf, but as I went to sleep that night, I knew we wouldn't see him tomorrow. And that was probably for the best. The forecast was calling for something nasty.

British weather reports were about as useful as ashtrays on motorbikes—*Chance of sun with intermittent showers; chance of rain with clear spells*—but I begged tomorrow's to be wrong. Our upcoming day was crowded on my spreadsheet, and the clouds on the news seemed as if they had settled down over the town for which we were headed, ominous blobs of a hue appropriate for a place called Blackpool.

Approach

Blackpool North Shore Golf Club

Royal Lytham & St. Annes Golf Club

Royal Birkdale Golf Club

Irish Sea

0 Miles   15
0 Kilometers   15

Wallasey Golf Club

Liverpool, England

Royal Liverpool Golf Club Hoylake

River Mersey

The 120th-tallest freestanding tower in the world was everything I dreamed it would be. Rising high above the shore promenade, the dim Blackpool Tower stood like a beacon calling pale Englishmen to its beaches for sausages and a sunburn. The structure, inspired by the Eiffel Tower, opened to visitors in 1894, back in the days when summering in Blackpool was a Manchester ritual.

As we drove along Blackpool's long avenue of arcades and hotels and nightclubs, mermaid lampposts waving to us as we passed, Julian-Nigel recalled his childhood days in the back of an unair-conditioned car, face burnt beach red and covered in chip grease, as his family sat for hours on the one-lane road out of town. Listening to my English friend, I remembered my own day trips to Wildwood, New Jersey, a beach destination of tchotchkes and buzzy rides and free beaches, its boardwalk crowded with tank-topped man-bellies and moms sucking on cigarettes. It was a place draped in a thin film of joyless amusement, but time lends nostalgia to the sandy ice cream cones, and I liked something about Blackpool despite the half hour I spent in its soggy traffic. I liked that it wasn't hiding what it was, that it embraced its overt cheesiness and its rank as a second-choice destination, because people needed a second choice. Blackpool was charming more than it was sad, even in the downpour that morning. And its golf course was delightful.

The rainy commute had us well behind schedule as we hurried out of the parking lot for our tee time in the Saturday open at Blackpool North Shore. Saturdays were the hardest days to find tee times, as most clubs reserved them for member play, so in order to fit in a Saturday thirty-six, I had to either beg my way into a member's foursome or get invited to play in a competition. Fortunately, Saturday opens were abundant around the UK. Open fixtures were days when membership clubs invited outside golfers to play their courses at a reduced rate and vie for golf shirts in a tournament, and it seemed a practice worth imitating back home. Golfers got to play new courses and enjoy some competition, and clubs filled their tee sheets with paying players. Traveling Americans mostly overlooked open days, and that was a shame—opens were a great value, and getting mixed into a foursome of locals was a lot more fun than another round with three dudes you got sick of two days ago.

We held a handful of proper tournaments at my course back home, but in Great Britain, club calendars were crowded with trophy events. It made UK handicaps legitimate—their system only allowed for the posting of competition scores, and if you shot better or worse than your handicap, your index moved a whopping 0.1. Weekly no-gimme golf also made them better players. All over Britain, I witnessed golfers with antique bags and eBay clubs and covers on their irons, and with homemade swings that seemed a blend of cricket and karate, post admirable numbers. They knew how to golf their ball, and left golf vanity to Yanks like me.

It was dodgy enough that we were showing up to a tournament late, but it was downright embarrassing when we found that we were teamed with the club captain, Brian, a stocky man of middle age who was antsy to go and eyed us with disappointment as we approached, three limping Americans who probably just poured themselves out of a pub. I endeavored to make it up to him by unleashing my game upon this short and seemingly bare seaside track.

What I unleashed had Brian checking and re-checking my handicap— *Zero? What math are they doing in America?* Julian-Nigel hit every fairway on the front nine aside from the ones we were playing, and the stinging rain saw Tom retreating into a sad and contemplative space of quiet. It was a place I knew well, where you were surrounded by people but lost in your own head, realizing that your life as a golfer had been built upon a lie. We all felt a little bit of the golfers' blues on the front nine as we shot Brian out of contention in his home club's open.

Then, just like that, from the depths of golf depression, came one swing— a hybrid fired into a hillside, precisely where Brian pointed me, an approach that curled and hopped and rolled its way sideways to what seemed an inaccessible pin but magically yielded an eagle—and golf wasn't just a great game but my breath and my purpose. It was a lesson I had learned more than any other in golf, to stick around until the good happened. It wouldn't always be as dramatic as an ace or an eagle, but golf loves a grinder.

Two more birdies coming in had me under par for the back nine, and I was sure we would have to move the luggage around to make room for the trophy. Then we checked the scoresheets in the clubhouse and were reminded that this was a country of seasoned golf mudders. We wouldn't have to find space for anything but our egos, now reduced to travel-friendly sizes.

The clubhouse sat perched above Blackpool, overlooking the town and the coast and the fairways that ran up, down, and across a hillside. It lacked the subtle ripples of a links; rather, its drama was in its vast, thigh-burning slopes. Our footprints confirmed that we were playing a seaside course instead of a links. If water comes up around your shoes, you aren't playing on sand, and Brian explained that the grass was thin in spots because we were on clay atop rock, and clay took more time to warm and sprout grass after the winter. Blackpool North Shore looked plenty green to us, and it added a missing ingredient to my British mix—a genuine members' club off the beaten tourist track, where the gentlemen made a fuss over foreign visitors.

I had been giving a print of my journey to each of the courses I visited, a smart-looking dark-blue map designed by Ballpark Blueprints, on which all the participating clubs were noted and numbered, and Brian was the first recipient to get excited about his course making the list. The four of us stepped out of the rain to pose for a picture with the map, then made the hard decision to forgo the hot soup offered to us as we hurried off for lunch at Lytham.

I drove to Royal Lytham & St. Annes beneath clouds of shame. I approached its clubhouse, a bright-bricked Tudor manor in which I was sure a bell was ringing for a butler, with the regret of a phony. I had set off to do one thing above all others—complete the Open rota—and here I was at one of the mainstays of that rotation, where champions like Bobby Jones, Gary Player, Ernie Els, and Seve Ballesteros were crowned, knowing I had failed at arranging an itinerary that included it. I left my clubs in the car, and my dripping waterproofs, too. My search for the secret to golf would have to pause at Royal Lytham, where today's first tee was firmly off-limits.

The club was busy hosting the Lytham Trophy, a big-time amateur event with a global field, and a tournament at which Rory had finished third twice. My delicate Jenga of a schedule did not allow me to be in this part of the world on any other week, so I had to accept that my Open résumé would remain unfinished. The reservations folks at Lytham had graciously invited me to visit nonetheless and join them for lunch. I figured a poke around the clubhouse might soften the blow of rota failure, so Julian-Nigel, Tom, and I tiptoed into the locker room. The building was intimidating in its aged perfection, and in its dark-paneled changing room, the smoke of old ghosts seemed to linger, the specters of Victorians detaching their collars and checking their pocket watches all around us. The porter stopped us, and

I prepared for a reprimand for having stepped into a restricted space. But instead we met an ebullient smile and a hearty handshake.

"You've made it!" he said, as if the Lytham Trophy were a mere sideshow to our lunch reservation. "Welcome. This way, right upstairs. Settle in and get yourselves something warm to eat."

We did. On our way to the stairs, we took a quick look at the flatscreens in the locker room where that morning's scores were posted. A field from around the world was struggling in the wind and water, their numbers ballooning well into the 80s. Blackpool North Shore was no Royal Lytham, but my morning's 77 would have fit into the list quite nicely. I took some small encouragement from this, phony as it was.

The lunchroom was crowded with red-faced youngsters, wide-shouldered British teens with hair mussed from their battles on the course, and we each served ourselves a shepherd's pie and sat down among the elite. There were kids with TEAM ENGLAND jumpers (sweaters) on, lots of white belts and flat bellies on these Walker Cup hopefuls. You could tell their talent by their comfort, how they sat here in this temple of a clubhouse where nearly every golf great had sat before and could not seem less impressed. In all my chasing of golf at their level, this was the quality I lacked. On the course, we looked similar enough, but it was in the lunchroom where I felt the difference. They were comfortable among the best. It was their unbothered and regular game, their staid milieu. I felt my fakeness at Lytham, and also my age. I was sure some of these players needed their parents to drive them here.

We sat quietly, the pace of the last few days catching up with us in the soft leather chairs of the lunchroom, and I looked around at all the talent and the tiny-waisted bashers and thought to myself, *Who cares*. It struck me firmly, a revelation to knock me off my horse: Who the hell cares? Who cares what they shot or what their sweaters say? Who cares what they think of this threesome of sleepy-looking tourists over here? They didn't know me. They didn't know where I had been, and could never guess where I was headed. And the truth was, they weren't thinking about me at all. I had to stop playing the game in my head in which I not only knew what people were thinking about me but also thought that it mattered.

There was a time when I would have beaten Julian to the bar and figured out a way to feel peaceful here, but on this trip, I had to actually learn to get more comfortable in my own skin. They played golf. So did I. Sometimes they carded better than me, and sometimes they didn't. I didn't have to win their approval; I just had to put a ball into a hole. So I headed out to the putting green to do so.

Julian snapped a couple of pictures of me putting on the practice green with the Lytham clubhouse in the background. I went around, putting to eighteen holes and keeping score on the card (all 2s and a 1; I exploded Lytham's course record). It was as close as I was going to get to playing Royal Lytham that day, and that was fine. I had gathered what Royal Lytham & St. Annes had to offer.

As we pulled into Royal Birkdale after five o'clock on a rainy Wednesday, I could see it in Tom's eyes: he was golf-angry. Tom was as agreeable a gentleman as I had met in my travels; polite and positive, he had fallen in love with links golf later in life, so he had brought to the trip a sort of born-again enthusiasm for golf over here. He and Julian-Nigel (we had yet to correct Tom, and both silently accepted that Nigel—sometimes shortened to just Nige now—was sticking around) had hit it off as travelmates, but Tom had been scoping out British courses for his clients for two weeks before he met up with me, and at Birkdale he finally hit the wall. It was a mood I understood. Golf-angry was easy to spot—the bitterness, the regret, the childlike tantrum that, in adults, manifested itself as a silent face on a once un-silent man.

He was leaving tomorrow, so he was finding the wall at the right time. I wasn't entitled to surrender yet—far from it—so I had to nod and smile as he told us he wasn't playing Birkdale, not in this downpour. Judging by the parking lot, we all might be in for a surrender, I thought. There were two cars in the lot at Royal Birkdale, and they both belonged to us.

The young assistant pro behind the desk looked like the last shopkeeper in an abandoned town. He bolted upright at the sight of us: *Golfers? Today? Have you been outside?* The first tee was certainly open, he informed us, and as I hurried down a hallway to the bathroom before a round that I knew we would have to play in record time—a long drive to the airport awaited Tom and Julian—I took a moment to study the pictures of Birkdale's Open winners. It was easy to forget what had happened on a course when you were out there battling it, lost in your own numbers, but each Open clubhouse celebrated its champions with portraits and paintings, and it was at Birkdale where it hit me: By visiting the whole rota, I was sharing ground with every soul who ever meant anything to the game. It seemed an obvious epiphany, but I didn't realize the magnitude of such a gift until the pictures of Watson and Palmer caught my attention at Birkdale. I snapped a few pictures of Palmer's photograph, then thanked the pro again for still being there when we arrived and headed off into another land of legend.

You wouldn't know Birkdale's age and significance from its clubhouse. The modern white building looked like an ocean liner docked above the course, a clock stuck to the side of the vessel's lone smokestack. I was glad for that pause in the clubhouse, because outside, Birkdale was a watery blur. So many great golfers had stood here on this opening dogleg, studying its every blade of grass and envisioning their tack into golf's greatest stage. I just stepped up and whacked it. I think it went straight, but I wasn't really looking. I wiped the water from my eyes and lifted my bag onto my shoulder, its weight settling into a raw cradle beside my neck. It had been a long few days.

As I mustered the resolve to splash forth, I heard footprints behind us and turned to see a Boston Red Sox cap headed to the tee.

"Screw it. I'm playing," Tom said, and in doing so he put into words the abstract motivations that had guided most of my life. Why am I here? Where am I going? Screw it, and play on.

Even when played at a trot, Royal Birkdale easily topped the other Open venues I had visited, at least for challenge and intrigue. Very unlike Hoylake, each hole seemed to hide something from us—a green tucked around a corner, a bunker that seemed out of reach but wasn't, an elevated approach that required two extra clubs, not one. The variety of crafty holes energized us and lifted us out of our collective suck. There might be Open courses with more bunkers, but I doubt they're as hungry as the ones at Birkdale. Shot after shot, what looked like safe balls rolled their way into wet beds of sandy bogey.

The empty course seemed eager to punish us for waking it up on its day off, stealing balls and pushing putts away from the hole. Julian-Nigel got busy lightening his load for the upcoming flight. He emphatically fired balls into the gorse, hard and low rockets that none of us were tempted to look for. His swing hadn't progressed much during this trip, but he had mastered a new move where he was able to reach into the bottom of his bag and lob a ball twenty yards ahead of him in one fluid motion, back in play without breaking stride. His resolve was inspiring. He wasn't golf crazy like me, yet here he was, plodding his way through his ninth round in three days, suffering and spending his beer money on golf balls, with no reason to be out here other than to support a friend.

Julian-Nigel didn't know it, but his many strokes at Birkdale were an inspiration, as was the perseverance of Tom. In his late fifties, Tom had warned me that he wasn't going to join me for every round on my schedule, but as we hustled around Birkdale and all tapped in on the last, it turned out he had.

In the upcoming weeks, if I needed reason to carry on and keep searching, I would recall the time and the aches that my friends had given to my quest, and my complaints would quiet. Selfish twit that I was, I wondered whether I would have done the same for them. I aspired to be that sort of friend, to be like Julian-Nigel, who had gone so far as to write to the corporate office of William Hill, a British bookmaker, to prove his investment in my crusade. He sent me a picture of his special-order betting slip: *TOM COYNE TO MAKE THE CUT AT THE OPEN—£10 @ 1,000-1.*

It was hugs instead of handshakes as we said our good-byes and headed for the parking lot, where a truck with its lights on was parked beside the exit. A lone greenskeeper had stayed behind to make sure we made it around okay. With a wave good-bye as my car passed his, he closed up behind us, and my search through the southern half of the UK came to an end.

England and Wales had done their part. I had grasped the logistics of golf travel at full throttle and was hardening to the weather. My itinerary seemed like less of a question and more of a plan, and fear was giving way to process. The scores had declined slightly over the week, but upper 70s was a habit I would need to halt up north. My ball flight was somehow lowering; give me a year on the range and I don't think I could learn a knockdown, but point me into wind for a week and my body could figure it out. Links golf was changing my game without my thinking too much about it, and if this trend continued, if these great courses continued to lift my quality up to theirs, then my dream that golf's home could teach me how to play might actually play out.

And if it didn't? Screw it. I'm playing.

Home

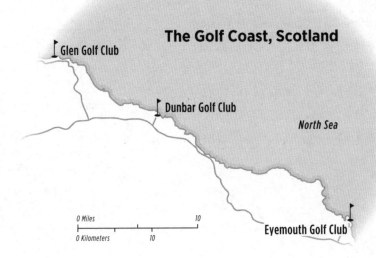

The Golf Coast, Scotland

Glen Golf Club

Dunbar Golf Club

North Sea

Eyemouth Golf Club

0 Miles   10

0 Kilometers   10

I landed in Scotland with plenty more baggage than my sticks and suitcase: I brought with me needs and nerves and assumptions. For someone who had hitched his life to golf, taking my first adult trip to its home was emotional and triumphant, and a wee bit worrisome. What if the place didn't live up? If Scotland wasn't my golf miracle, it wasn't as though I could hop over to Iceland to find my answers. This was golf's Mesopotamia, its Jerusalem, and its Cooperstown—either I found golf's soul here, or I was a fool for looking.

A rental snafu saw me handing over a royal flush of credit cards for the lone automatic transmission left in Edinburgh—a least, the only one they

didn't need back for fifty days—and exiting the airport in the accidental luxury of a BMW station wagon. I forgave myself for the splurge and embraced
the opulence as I zoomed down the A1. For a guy who had schlepped around
Ireland in one pair of soggy shoes, I felt as if I were cruising into the big
leagues, my backside toasty from the seat warmer. This was how the Tour
players arrived at their golfing destinations—in style—and maybe I could
pretend my way into their company.

I knew that learning Scotland's links after having sampled all of Ireland's
would peg me as an arbiter in the Scottish-versus-Irish golf-trip debate. I
wasn't ready to rank them yet, and surely would, over time, concoct a polite
rejoinder that would not offend friends on either side of the Irish Sea. I told
myself not to play at comparing them, but as I rode out to the first Scottish
golf course on my list, passing signs for Gullane, North Berwick, Archerfield,
and Dunbar, I already sensed a difference between an Irish and a Scottish
golf vacation.

When you golfed Ireland, if you wanted to fill your trip with top-
rated tracks, there was no way to get around long hauls to links scattered
around the island. The scenery comfortably consumed the time, but as I
passed a blue sign advertising this stretch of Scotland as EAST LOTHIAN—
SCOTLAND'S GOLF COAST, it became clear that this country promised the
ease of multiple links jammed within a tidy circumference. You could drop
your anchor in a dozen different Scottish towns and, within thirty minutes' drive, play a full itinerary without repacking your suitcase. Advantage
Scotland, it seemed, though you would need two months to play all the
courses, while with ten days and a bus driver in Ireland, you could cover
the country's greatest hits. There was no way to do Scotland's surplus of
links that way—not unless you had a rental car for fifty days and happened
to be married to my wife.

The East Lothian loop of courses was anchored by North Berwick, a
course I had heard more about than any other during my preparations. St.
Andrews, Muirfield, and Carnoustie were courses folks sounded like they
were happy to have played, but North Berwick was the course that emailers
recalled with the giddiness of prospectors who had unearthed a gold streak.

I would be there in a few days' time, but first I was headed farther down Scotland's Golf Coast to a place called Eyemouth. It was not a Gramma Billy pick, nor had I met any golfer who was familiar with it, but in the direction I would be traveling around Scotland (counterclockwise), it was the first coastal course on that path. It was the lone round on my calendar that afternoon, but what a round it would be—eighteen holes that would introduce me not just to golf in Scotland but, more important, to golf with Gramma Billy.

I had been too busy to think much about who was actually waiting for me in Eyemouth. After a year's worth of steady correspondence in which a woman named Phyllis (who called herself Gramma Billy) shared with me her love of golf and her uncommon joie de vivre, it finally hit me as I sat in my car beside a clubhouse overlooking the ocean: Who the hell was I about to meet? I had never partaken of Internet dating, but suddenly I knew the angst of John Doe standing outside a restaurant, wondering if the woman inside had cats, talked to them, and had possibly brought one with her.

We had built a nice little friendship via email server, and I wondered whether GB and I should have kept it that way. Meeting up was a chance worth taking, I told myself. I wanted to trust that the universe was putting the right people in my path, but as I walked into the Eyemouth clubhouse and headed up the stairs to where the pro told me a lady and a gentleman were waiting for me, not quite ready to meet a stranger who sent me chocolates and called me Sir Tom, I thought for a moment that the universe was out of its mind.

There was very little that was Gramma-like about Gramma Billy, who met me with big hugs and gifts: a white caddie bib with COYNE on the back for my looper in the Open, and teddy bears for my girls. She was thin, with bright-red hair and pink rain gear, sporting careful makeup and a coiffure that suggested she was here to golf, but not at the expense of looking her best. Gene was a tan and healthy-looking man in his sixties—nothing grandparently about his appearance, either—in a golf sweater from Carne, my favorite course in the world, that I immodestly assumed had been worn for our meeting. Our introduction held some of the awkwardness of meeting a complete stranger and an old friend at the same time, but any oddness was put to rest by the task at hand—golf. My itinerary was like having little kids; it could get me out of any awkward spot or save me from having to do anything I didn't want to do. *Sorry, can't make it—kids. Sorry, have to run—golf.*

Email Gramma Billy was a devil-may-care, carpe diem persona who feasted on life's marrow. Incarnate Gramma Billy was exuberant as well, but I sensed some anxiety about our afternoon. We had talked golf for a year, and now she had to go out and show her game to me, the big golf writer, so I felt her pain as the flops and flubs came along. I had been on her side of the twosome many times before and knew the feeling well—that sensation that you're playing through cement while the whole of the golfing world collectively judges, personally convinced you're holding up everybody's round and ruining their day, if not their lives. I kept telling GB that it was no bother, that we were out here for fun, but she continued to apologize for her misses. She had come to Scotland to help me on my Open quest and seemed quickly convinced she was interrupting it. Truth was, as I made par after birdie after par, Gramma Billy and Gene had brought some golf magic with them.

As we walked off the eighteenth hole that evening, it was clear that this quest had changed. The course was an adventurous surprise, and a track to be added to a Golf Coast itinerary for its sixth hole alone. After a snoozy opening stretch, I was sympathizing with the North Berwick golfers who skipped Eyemouth, until I arrived at a tee box that felt like a punch on the chin. I expected the drama to pick up as the holes worked their way down to the sea, but when I surveyed number six—167 yards over waves and into the face of a hulking cliff with a flagstick hoisted above the rocks like a candle perched atop a wedding cake—I was shocked, and I wondered if on day one I had found the best par 3 in Scotland. I was careful to abbreviate my follow-through to avoid tossing myself to a rocky death, pushing a 6-iron up beside the green and gladly accepting a four. It was one of only two bogeys I would make that afternoon, and alongside four birdies, I had finally broken the par barrier with a score of 70. The switch had been flipped, I told myself. No more begging for pars and settling for 78—in Scotland, the years and miles were going to converge in joyful destiny. No more hoping; it was time to get to the doing. And I had my good friend Gramma Billy to thank for coming along and turning my golfing tide.

Maybe it was the lightness I felt in my step for having to play only eighteen that day; maybe it was the forgiving rough or the short distances at Eyemouth (6,404 yards in total). But I think it was Gramma Billy being there to remind me of some things I'd forgotten in the hotel-golf-food-golf-hotel shuffle. Her presence recalled what I was after and how much it mattered, not just to me but to people like her and Gene; their caring made me care more, and I could feel that focus as I played. It seemed impossible to be the golfer I wanted to be, but when I saw myself through their eyes, I could play the part, the role of a guy who made two under look easy. I believed in my game at Eyemouth because I knew Gramma Billy and Gene did. Their presence reminded me that there was something more important than just getting on—and that was getting on well.

No more would I wake to mornings of traveler's doubt and bogey dread. The next dawn, I hurried out of the flat I'd rented by the sea in North Berwick and hustled off to the Dunbar links, where I was given a welcome as warm as Gramma Billy's. A Dunbar member named Graham had been following my blog, so he arranged for me to meet the club secretary and the pro in the shop, where I was given a book of course history and a Dunbar club tie. (Most Scottish golf clubs have an official necktie that's worn by members, and if you can buy one in the pro shop, it's a far cooler souvenir than another hat.)

Dunbar was a mainstay on the Golf Coast, where the game had been played since 1617. The course has been an Open qualifying venue, and its holes were engineered by both Tom Morris and James Braid, and if it were set any closer to the sea, you would have to play it in waders. The quaint white clubhouse seemed ready to fall into the ocean in a bad storm, and the holes hugged the water in a classic nine-out, nine-in routing. They were so tightly packed between the dunes and the sea that a few holes bottlenecked and crisscrossed as you worked your way out to the end of the property, careful to dodge oncoming shots as you hunted for your drive. It was a good course for a guide to tell you where to pause, and I had two excellent ones in

Graham and Eleanor, a married couple in their late forties, both with single-digit handicaps. I couldn't help but watch them and wonder if that would ever be me and Allyson someday. And then as I watched Eleanor beat her husband on most of the holes, I found myself pleased that my wife was a golf agnostic.

Along with steering me around the historic and exacting links of Dunbar (home to the first PGA Championship on the European Tour in 1968), Eleanor and Graham shared with me translations for Scottish lingo I was bound to soon encounter. I already understood that *wee* was the most versatile word in Scottish English—it could modify any noun in the dictionary, and might be invoked up to nineteen times in one sentence: *Take a wee left up at the wee shop where you can have a wee stop for a wee cup of tea and a wee bacon roll* . . . Less obvious were the expressions Eleanor decoded for me: *You're a long time deid* (Take it easy, you'll have plenty of time to worry when you're dead); *Lang may yer lum reek* (Long may your chimney smoke, or, I wish you well). The idioms only grew more complex as they turned regional, and Graham explained that up in Aberdeen, I might be greeted with *Foos your Doos?* (How are your pigeons?), to which I should reply *Still peckin!* I could have used their help in the Highlands, where I would hear *It's a sair ficht for half a loaf* (It's a sore fight for half a loaf, or, Life is hard), along with my favorite etymological enigma, *Is the cat deid?* (Your pants are short; they're at half-mast, for the dead cat).

My 76 wouldn't have gotten me into the Open, but with death to the left or right on every hole, I wouldn't have shot myself out of the tournament, either. Leaving Dunbar with some dialect and a decent scorecard, I stopped Eleanor in the parking lot to ask a question. She was one of the best players I had partnered with on my travels thus far, a powerful straight hitter who pushed around a Tour bag bejeweled with tags from courses in Florida and the Carolinas. Eleanor played as if she might know the secret to golf, so before I said good-bye, I asked her what it was.

"Keep smiling," she told me. And she was smiling when she said it.

•   •   •

On the east end of the town of North Berwick (pronounced *Bear-ick*, or just *Beark*), the Glen Golf Club was overshadowed by the celebrated North Berwick West Links down the street, but as Gramma Billy, Gene, and I hiked our way up to the first green after having launched hopeful approaches toward a hilltop, a thrill ride of cliffside golf came into view. Past the green of the golf course, I saw the dark-blue waters of the Firth of Forth, across which I could make out the coastline I would soon be golfing on my way around to St. Andrews. As we walked along greens planted atop rocky outcroppings and tees hanging over the ocean, it was hard to believe that such a small town harbored two such golf courses. Pundits said the West Links was the flagship of the pair, but it would take some real drama to prove that this Braid design was the lesser (for the record, the Glen claims golf was first played in North Berwick on their links land). As we played our way up and around the hills, out in the firth the Bass Rock seemed to rise out of the water like a giant granite soufflé. The volcanic plug was once home to a castle-turned-prison and was now a sanctuary for a million white seabirds and a lone lighthouse that we could see from most of the holes at Glen. The course had me thinking that golf upon sand might be its truest form, but as I'd found in places like Perranporth and Holyhead and Ardglass in Northern Ireland, golf upon rocks might be its most boisterous.

My assessment of golf courses and how I rank them for quality is an unscientific and emotional process in which I forgo all objective barometers and ignore any design diagnostics and instead rely on the flight factor: If you told me I could come back and play this course tomorrow, how willing would I be to change a flight and return? Would I feel a fervor and a zing in my bones? Would I pay the change fees and abandon my calendar? Was it worth alienating a spouse? Canceling a class? Or would the invitation be met with a passing jolt of excitement, or a fake smile, or a polite no-thank-you? I let my gut tell me how good a course is, and at Glen, it was telling me we had found something superb. The emotional ingredient of the flight factor meant that my estimation of a golf course was swayed by non-golf dynamics, ranging from the reception in the pro shop to the exaggeration of local history by the starter to the clubhouse views and the quality of the accompanying soup.

But nothing did more to heighten my appraisal of a golf day than the people with which I spent it, so no wonder I thought Glen was extraordinary after an afternoon with Alan McPherson.

I should have known who Alan was before the fifth hole, but it took me that long to put all the pieces from the previous year's emails and tee bookings together. He met me and Gramma Billy outside the pro shop and passed along a small goodie bag with brochures and Glen tees and golf balls. I was especially grateful for the tees—make sure to pack plenty, because in Scotland, you won't find any spares scattered around the tee boxes. Golfing Scots are a prudent lot. The locals I played with rarely abandoned a lost ball—you would expect the gorse to be ripe with Titleists, but I found strays only on tracks frequented by Americans—and they never surrendered their tees, chasing after the colored plastic sticks as if they were old family heirlooms. At one point, I was informed that the cure for seasickness in Scotland was to stand the vomiting bloke by the boat rail and put a 10p coin between his teeth. I didn't share this joke with Alan, who had a sturdy frame built for Scottish gales and spoke with a deep Lothian throat. With a white beard and rosy cheeks, he looked like a younger, fitter St. Nick, if Santa were only as friendly as Alan.

I neglected to read the business card he put in the goodie bag, or else I might have foreseen the revelation that was to come out on the links (the card advertised his blog: http://scottishgolfcourses-allofthem.blogspot.com). Alan was a longtime caddie who was currently looping over at a new, up-market Tom Doak course called Renaissance. I loved that caddies over here could not only make a living but also afford membership at their local clubs, yearly dues at most courses hovering around a few hundred pounds. As Alan offered his impressions of the links on my itinerary—it seemed as though he had played all of them—I was surprised when he asked me, "So you're at it again?"

The fact that Alan was familiar with my last book was enough to push Glen to the top of my world rankings, but I could have never guessed that this generous soul waiting for me by the clubhouse would turn out to be my kindred golfing spirit. He not only knew of my Irish trek but had read the book. More important, he *owned* the book, and had paid for it in hardcover. I loved him like my own father. Alan explained that if I had a chance to go back and read the first of his hundreds of blog posts, I would find mention of my book as an inspiration behind his life's own gonzo golf adventure. In *A Course Called Ireland*, he found a like-minded enabler for his own golf fantasy, and soon the walls of Alan's basement would be covered with over six hundred Scottish ball markers, one for each of the courses he'd played on his quest to play every single golf course in Scotland—nine-holers, island tracks, both links and parkland—and tell the tale of each one. When we met at the Glen, he had only twenty-some spaces left to fill.

Alan's whole persona seemed to glow as I watched his thick wrists muscle his ball across the Glen fairways, stringing together birdies and pars with a game that wasn't flashy but was well-seasoned. Forget Bagger Vance or Shivas Irons, I thought—here was my guide. Since the moment I first scratched *A Course Called Scotland?* into a journal, I had wondered whom I would ask to caddie for me in my Open qualifier. I expected to maybe find this imaginary wise man in a cave up in the Highlands, or falling out of a pub in Glasgow, or by a peat fire in a cottage on a remote Scottish isle. I didn't know how I would know who the right person was, but I would know. And I did.

I played most of the front nine under par, making the case for the request I planned to present to Alan at round's end. And Gramma Billy's game came into order as she knocked steady fairway woods toward the green and then hurried to putt out. She hit the ball often, but she played quickly—too quickly, I feared, and wished she wouldn't be so accommodating to her partners. As she made her way around the course, I noticed how Gene was often there to scoop the ball out of the hole for her, and how on most holes, he would toss her light bag over his shoulder and carry for the both of them, sometimes reaching over and holding her hand as they walked. It warmed my heart to see such chivalry and affection from my golfing grandparents, the sort of partners one looked at and thought, *Now, that there is the point.*

The fun of the Glen could not be diminished by our shockingly slow pace of play. Locals played quickly, ever racing the weather, but we were stuck behind two groups of visiting Scandinavians who finally stopped to smoke and let us through. I would run into Swedish golfers all over Scotland; as it was explained to me, the Swedes were golf crazy, but the game was prohibitively expensive over there. It was cheaper to fly to Scotland and play for the weekend than to book a Swedish tee time or join one of their pricey clubs. That was living, I thought—two weekends a month in North Berwick, traveling to Scotland's Golf Coast as though it were a trip down the shore.

Alan's caddie lexicon was well-primed with the encouragement and guidance one wanted from a pro jock. When I caught a drive on the seventh, he noted, "I don't go that far on my holidays"; and when it was time to it let it all hang out on a par 5, he exhorted me to "Let it rip. Don't spare the horses." He was a font of course history, explaining that Glen took its name from a small collection of trees near the first tee that Robert Louis Stevenson, a regular visitor from Edinburgh, walked and celebrated in his poetry. Tiny Fidra Island out in North Berwick's harbor was said to be Stevenson's inspiration for *Treasure Island*, its outline appearing in early editions of the novel. Alan explained how Fidra and Bass Rock and the lofted Glen fairways were the product of the curious green mountain behind us, its frozen black lava flows still visible beneath tee boxes at the water's edge.

On eight, when I went looking for the bell that a sign instructed us to ring as notice to other golfers that we had cleared, Alan laughed and said, "They're still looking for a replacement. The greenskeeper thought he had ordered a real beauty of a bell on eBay until it showed up and was about four inches tall. Makes a lovely Christmas ornament." The greenskeeper was otherwise on top of his game at Glen, where it seemed a lava base grew the greenest of grasses.

When I asked Alan a dumb question about the course down the road— "So if they call North Berwick the West Links, which is the East?"—he had a quick answer: "You're standing on it." Alan had played the Bruntsfield Links where I would be attempting to qualify at trip's end, cementing the far more important question I had for him. We had to rush the back nine and didn't finish the final four holes, a blasphemy I would not have allowed were it not for Gramma Billy's plans for dinner, at which I had been told the elixir for

Open qualifying was on the menu. But before we hurried off, I asked Alan if he might be willing to carry for me in six weeks' time at Bruntsfield.

"Of course I will," he said.

The qualifier had been looming like a judgment day, a cloud of dark insecurity for which I could only pretend to be prepared. But as I drove to dinner that evening, it no longer felt like a nemesis; it was a chance. I imagined Alan slapping my putter into my palm on eighteen, ahead of us a long walk to a green ringed with quiet faces. It felt real, and I felt ready. I wished we were in Bruntsfield in the morning. Still weeks away, but I was ready to change my flight and remain a little longer.

Standards

Firth of Forth

North Berwick Golf Club

Renaissance Club

Archerfield Dirleton Links

Muirfield

0 Miles 2

0 Kilometers 2

Gullane Golf Club

The Golf Coast, Scotland

Kilspindie Golf Club

They were magical meat, these lamb chops of legend. Back in 2013, Australian journeyman pro John Wade was staying at the Milleur House in North Berwick, hoping to qualify at Dunbar for the upcoming Open at Muirfield. The night before the tournament, the lady of the house, Moira, served John a plate of her secret-recipe lamb chops, and the next day, John went on to set the Dunbar course record, firing a 63 and earning himself a spot in the Open field. He credited his play to Moira's cooking, so it was with great hunger that I arrived at her home that evening, hoping that the secret to golf would be served with a side salad. Whether they were enchanted chops or not, the prospect of a home-cooked meal in lieu of another fried dinner set on a bath-towel tablecloth and eaten in bed seemed magical enough.

Leave it to Gramma Billy to find a B&B that had hosted and fed an Open qualifier. She and Gene had booked a room at the top-rated guesthouse, and through emailing with its magnanimous owners, Moira and Drew, discovered its qualifier legacy and arranged a special dinner where I could shovel golf redemption into my mouth. The house was immaculate and the hospitality humbling; dinner was served on fine china with the family silver, and each course arrived like a work of prosciutto and avocado art. The lamb chops lived up to their billing. I had wondered what my perfect pre-qualifier meal would be, and though that round was weeks away, I would recall this dinner and feel ready.

A golfing neighbor named Martin joined me and Gramma Billy and Gene, and along with Drew, he shared stories of the area's uncommon golf history, nearby Muirfield taking center stage. It seemed that most golfers in this part of the country had a story attesting to Muirfield's snobbery, and to its status as a bastion of expert imbibing. It was said a day at Muirfield meant a two-hour round of golf followed by a four-hour lunch. My hosts confirmed the mystique with their own tales of Muirfield haughtiness. Martin had been berated for entering the men's lavatory through the wrong door (the visitors' entrance was five paces away), and his elderly father-in-law once strolled down the long drive that leads to its famous black gate, emblazoned in gold with *The Honourable Company of Edinburgh Golfers*, where he stopped for a moment to gaze at the course beyond the gateway.

"What are you doing, sir?" asked an approaching member of the staff.

"Just having a look for two minutes," the old man replied.

"Make it one," he was told.

Even Ben Crenshaw and Tom Watson had been kicked off the course after sneaking out to play it with hickory-shafted clubs. Maybe they should have checked in at the pro shop, or maybe Watson was simply feeling entitled that Sunday—after all, he had just hoisted the Claret Jug on the eighteenth green a few hours before.

The stories of Muirfield's prickliness included Jack Nicklaus himself being turned down for a round of golf, and Tiger having to wait twenty minutes before being allowed to strike a ball during a practice round (golf before 7:00 a.m. is strictly forbidden). Tales of its men-only ethos are well documented. When the club made headlines for voting to remain a boys' club in 2016, the R&A revoked its rota card—no more Opens for Muirfield. An emergency re-vote the next year saw female membership winning the necessary two-thirds needed to pass, though 123 members still voted to keep women out, Open Championships be damned. *Forbes* called it "Scotland's snobbiest old-boy club" and told of a former Muirfield gatekeeper who enjoyed breaking the hearts of visiting Americans by picking up a pair of binoculars and surveying an empty golf course, only to tell them, "Sorry, the course is too busy to accommodate you today."

In a country where even private clubs warmly welcomed visitors with tee times and free run of the clubhouse, Muirfield remained a stalwart of traditionalism and exclusivity, at least in legend. And you almost couldn't blame them. Its Honourable Company of Edinburgh Golfers wrote the rules—literally. Golf's rules were first codified in Edinburgh by the Honourable Company (then called the Gentlemen Golfers of Edinburgh, and the oldest or second-oldest club in existence, depending on whose history you read) in 1744 for the world's first organized golf competition at the Leith Links, now a public park in the heart of the city. The winner was awarded a silver golf club and named "Captain of the Golf," giving birth to the position of club captain, an executive role still in use at every golf club in the British Isles. The Gentlemen Golfers wrote thirteen rules for that first competition, in stark contrast to the thousands of rules, subrules, sub-subrules, and decisions we lament today. Some of their regulations are still relevant; some decidedly less so. While I love a short walk from green to tee, I can't imagine following rule 1. And rule 4 conjures an eerie nostalgia for golf's feral past, when bones and broken clubs were notable obstructions:

Articles & Laws in Playing at Golf.

1. You must Tee your Ball within a Club's length of the Hole.
2. Your Tee must be upon the Ground.

3. You are not to change the Ball which you Strike off the Tee.

4. You are not to remove Stones, Bones or any Break Club, for the sake of playing your Ball, Except upon the fair Green and that only within a Club's length of your Ball.

5. If your Ball comes among watter, or any wattery filth, you are at liberty to take out your Ball & bringing it behind the hazard and Teeing it, you may play it with any Club and allow your Adversary a Stroke for so getting out your Ball.

6. If your Balls be found any where touching one another, You are to lift the first Ball, till you play the last.

7. At Holling, you are to play your Ball honestly for the Hole, and not to play upon your Adversary's Ball, not lying in your way to the Hole.

8. If you should lose your Ball, by its being taken up, or any other way, you are to go back to the Spot, where you struck last, & drop another Ball, And allow your adversary a Stroke for the misfortune.

9. No man at Holling his Ball, is to be allowed, to mark his way to the Hole with his Club, or anything else.

10. If a Ball be stopp'd by any Person, Horse, Dog or anything else, The Ball so stopp'd must be play'd where it lyes.

11. If you draw your Club in Order to Strike, & proceed so far in the Stroke as to be Accounted a Stroke.

12. He whose Ball lyes farthest from the Hole is obliged to play first.

13. Neither Trench, Ditch or Dyke, made for the preservation of the Links, nor the Scholar's Holes, or the Soldier's Lines, Shall be accounted a Hazard; But the Ball is to be taken out teed and play'd with any Iron Club.

So they enjoyed their traditions at Muirfield. I loathed golf snobbery, but I liked the idea of at least one place clinging to yesterday so snugly, almost like a sort of museum to golf's former pretensions. In fairness to the Honourable Company, they still allowed visitors two days every week—imagine that at Augusta or Pine Valley—and if they didn't want tourists jamming up their course, that preference was not necessarily born of golf isolationism. It was partly due to pace. Members at Muirfield exclusively played foursomes (alternate-shot in American). Drew explained that I would find tracks in the rough from where members pulled their trolleys down the sides of the fairways while their partners teed off behind them, a sort of rapid relay around the course that allowed for Muirfield rounds to be played in under three hours. It also meant that players had to have handicaps calculated from other golf clubs, as many longtime members would tell you they had never played their own ball at Muirfield. It was said that when you asked a member how they played that day, they wouldn't give you a score but rather would tell you, "Pretty well. Two and a half"—as in hours. The golf was something of a race to get back into the famed Muirfield lunch, which visitors could enjoy, but only if they brought a jacket and tie.

Muirfield was different, Drew explained, as I sopped up the last of my lamb-onion gravy with Moira's homemade bread. It was a gentlemen's club that happened to have a golf course, albeit a damn good one. Even referring to it as Muirfield was something of a misnomer. Muirfield was just the name of the course they were currently using; the Honourable Company of Edinburgh Golfers had called other tracks home during its history—courses at Leith and Musselburgh, the latter routed within a horse-racing course, as was the Muirfield property when it was first designed by Old Tom Morris. Club first, golf second; complementary, but distinct. They did not even have a pro shop in the clubhouse at Muirfield. Drew advised me to buy my souvenirs at nearby Gullane.

I appreciated the idea of this place continuing to do it in an old way that, from my perspective, was all new. That didn't mean I wanted to hang out there or experience its propensity for doling out golf shame. If I hadn't been wary enough about playing Muirfield already, my dinner in North Berwick persuaded me that I was going to be led off the property in seventeenth-century manacles, banned for my two-week stubble, or berated over the condition of the jacket and tie that were currently rolled up in my suitcase.

As if the meal Moira offered had not been benevolent enough, our conversation somehow took a providential turn toward the state of my laundry. My suitcase, stuffed with sock balls and twisted-up shirts, looked like a basket of old fruit, and was beginning to smell like one. Laundromats, or the hours required to visit one, had been elusive so far, but Moira bestowed tender sympathy upon me, insisting that I come back to the Milleur House with all my laundry. I had a brief moment of hesitation about turning over my stiff and ripened skivvies to this kind hostess I hardly knew. But the possibility of soft, perfumed underwear? John Wade had found his magic here, and as it turned out, so had I.

We ended our dinner with a toast by Martin that he attributed to Scotland's bard, the mighty Rabbie Burns:

> Here's tae us.
> Wha's like us?
> Damn few,
> And they're a'deid.

The flat I had rented in town was a hub of accidental luxury. North Berwick Holiday Homes had an owner who'd left on a last-minute holiday, so I was upgraded to the upper half of an old gray townhome overlooking the eighteenth fairway of the North Berwick links. For three evenings, I watched golfers finish in the ten o'clock twilight from my room, strolling down a wide final fairway to a stone clubhouse in the heart of town that looked like a smaller version of the Royal & Ancient's digs at St. Andrews. They were dry and happy as they finished, and I could hardly wait for the morning when I would step out my door, cross the thin street, and join them on what I had heard described as the most copied golf course in the world.

There is debate among golf-heads as to whether we have any true links courses back in the States. We have plenty of links-*style* courses (treeless and pot-bunkered), and we have courses set upon the sea. A genuine links demands a sandy bottom and a dune-lined top, and I choose to believe it requires links land born of the geographical phenomena of receding tides and sliding glaciers specific to the topographical record of Ireland and the UK; a flawed theory, surely, but I will contend that nowhere in the States will you find the magical intertwining of golf and town that you witness on the links of Scotland and Ireland, where in places like St. Andrews, Dornoch, La-hinch, and Newcastle, golf holes flow into the heart of bustling old villages, clubhouses reside next to pubs and B&Bs, and the course is public green space for the town's denizens, more of a people's park than a golf reserve.

Scots are deeply proud of their ancient "right to roam," which was for-mally set into law in 2003. In Scotland, you're entitled to stroll almost any-where, private land or not, in the name of exercise and the conviction that Scottish land belongs to all Scots. So on a sunny day, you'll find dog walkers and bird watchers—called twitchers in Scotland—on most courses. Imagine that at Cypress Point: *Morning gents, don't mind me, just stalking the stealthy brown pelican.* Pedestrians are respectful and mindful of the game going on around them, with the exception of St. Andrews, where caddies are accus-tomed to waving confused tourists off the opening fairway. So whether we have links courses or not, we do not have places like North Berwick, where the town hugs a golf course the way Chicago envelops Wrigley Field, and it gives golfers a feeling that these towns were built by and for the game they loved. The blond stone of the North Berwick clubhouse sat snugly up against the end of the Westgate Road (if you were looking for beach parking, you might run right into it), and for three days it had been calling me as I walked to the coffee shop or the chipper. Finally the day arrived when I would not walk past the clubhouse but head inside, and I did so quickly, because on this North Berwick morning, the wind was blowing as though the rapture was in town, propelling rain that felt like icy buckshot, and it had me saying my too-regular Scottish prayer: *Oh god, not today.*

Inside I found Gene and Gramma Billy, ever eager and early, along with a dozen or so Canadian golfers, everyone dressed in layers of bloated wa-terproofs that looked like their own personal tents. We stood there in the hallway wearing the same look of concern, as if we were all waiting outside a hospital room. *Is it going to be okay? Is this really happening?* Among us were many collective decades spent waiting for this round, yet we had arrived on the nastiest morning North Berwick had seen in years.

I wasn't expecting a reception by the club secretary (*secretary* is the UK title for general manager—i.e., the most important person you could meet at a golf club), but the large frame of Christopher Spencer appeared from out of the office, his North Berwick tie hardly long enough to reach his belt. He surveyed the crowd of waiting golfers with a dubious look, as if to say *You either play or you don't,* and he greeted me with an all-business voice and a Manchester accent that suggested I had arrived at a place of high standards. You expected—even appreciated—a little bit of lofted nose at North Berwick, which, having been founded in 1832, was the world's thirteenth-oldest golf club.

I was informed that North Berwick regularly received tee time requests from writers, and that they were rarely able to accommodate them. I wasn't sure whether I should be flattered or frightened for having scored one, but it seemed clear that I shouldn't waste my chance. Mr. Spencer asked if I would like for him to join me for my round, a question to which I opened my mouth without any words leaving it. *Not really,* I thought, *because I'm a little bit afraid of you, and I don't want to be the one responsible for subjecting you to the end times out there.* But he answered for me. "You've never played here?" I shook my head. "Then I should join you. A lot of history in those holes." And he was off to the locker room to locate his waterproofs, and we were off to the first tee to test ours.

At the opening tee box, which felt vaguely reminiscent of St. Andrews—a petite par 4, driver not required, the first and eighteenth fairways sharing the same short grass—Mr. Spencer informed us that we were going to be playing from the more forward blue tees, not the white markers that were reserved for members. All over Scotland, I would find this practice duplicated; member and visitor tees were kept separate, but often by only a few yards. "If the blue tees were good enough for Luke Donald and Bubba Watson," we were told, "I think you will find them good enough for yourselves."

I was beginning to hope the rain might make him reconsider his stewardship of my round, but Mr. Spencer—Chris—emerged as one of the best surprises at North Berwick, on a course that simmered with them. He didn't smile much (it's hard to smile with rain in your mouth), but I did manage to make him laugh when I learned of his transplanted status and asked him, "United or City?" It was like asking a Chicagoan "Cubs or Sox?" and potentially as inciting. He was Manchester United without a doubt, and a little football banter was a chance to forget the sport we were pretending to play. Misery loved company, and on this day, it required it, for I wouldn't have seen all eighteen holes of North Berwick without my friend Chris to pull me along.

Chris was a repository of North Berwick history, and he took the time to share stories when I could barely summon the resolve to nod and acknowledge them. He pointed out the home of John Imlay, god rest his soul, the part-owner of the Atlanta Falcons who was beloved around North Berwick. His stone manor had been refurbished with its own grand golf locker room, frequented by NFL players when they visited. And Chris told me about the time he met Tom Watson in his travels. Hearing that Chris was secretary at North Berwick, Mr. Watson said hello, and then, "I was once kicked off your golf course." Chris could laugh, because he knew the circumstances. Watson, in town for the Open at Muirfield, was staying at the Marine Hotel in North Berwick. He had been watching from his room as golfers struggled to play the short number fourteen, a hole called Perfection for the two perfect shots it required, when he headed out with a handful of clubs to attempt the hole himself. He was met by the superintendent, who told him, "I'm sorry, Mr. Watson, but you cannot be out here playing the course without a member." Taken aback, Watson wasn't sure what to say, until the superintendent told him, "But you can play it with me." With three clubs, they played the 358-yard fourteenth hole together three times, the super making three pars and Watson making three bogeys, tallies no doubt influenced by the effects of passing time and lager.

It was somewhere around the turn, so very far away from the clubhouse, that I recalled Martin's toast: I now understood why there were few like us and why they were all dead, and I suspected I might soon be among them. I envied them for being elsewhere. They couldn't have been this soaked in heaven, and at that moment, a toasty little campfire in hell sounded just fine. I did my best to keep my head up to see the holes I'd read so much about. There were courses with more acclaim and more championship history, but there may not have been another course with as many individual holes of fabled status.

Number thirteen, called Pit, was the hole I had been most warned about, a short par 4 with an ancient stone wall running along the front of the green. It seemed a merry touch of old-golf whimsy that we golfers were fortunate to see unchanged. *Don't argue with the wall*, they say at North Berwick; *it's older than you*. The par 3 fifteenth was called Redan for the way its outward-cropping green mimicked a redan fortification, where a V-shaped wall jutted out toward a point of attack. It was a hole whose name had become its own term in golf architecture and that had been copied on courses from Hawaii to Long Island. A redan hole has a sideways-running green with a portion extending outward and a deep dip in front; it asks a golfer to run the ball up to the green and use contours to turn his or her ball back to the pin, and on this original redan hole, I was pleased to card one of the very few pars that morning. I didn't fare as well at sixteen, where the thin green was divided by a gully so deep and severe that I could have ducked down into it and hidden from Chris. If I'd had an umbrella with me, I might have.

Chris told me how Nicklaus always stayed in the same room at the Marine overlooking this green when the Open was at Muirfield. He would watch golfers try to putt its contours in the evening and make dollar bets on their chances of getting down in two. He would have won money betting against me, it turned out, but putting through a five-foot dip was worth the bogey. North Berwick was quirky to such an extent that its quirks transcended the eccentric and approached a sort of organic brilliance. The fact that I could see this through sheets of water spoke to the place's greatness, and to the fact that I would have to came back someday, no matter that I ran from the eighteenth green that afternoon as though it were on fire.

After returning to my flat and quickly stripping off my layers, thick and damp as papier-mâché, I found a curious ball of pulp in my left pants pocket. It was a pink-and-white spongy sort of thing that fit in the palm of my hand, a weird little dumpling whose origin I could not understand. Was it an old piece of forgotten sandwich? Did it snow out there? I hesitantly peeled it apart to find some numbers written on it. It was my scorecard, turned into a glob of mush by the hurricane through which I had just attempted golf.

I was happy to see its state. There was no need to write those scores down, though I unfortunately remembered them. It was that kind of day, a character-builder, a test of golfing mettle during which my game regressed to a state of whack-and-chase but my mental toughness leapt forward several ranks. Nobody at Bruntsfield would have played through that, I was sure, and I had made it through, with this dripping marshmallow of a scorecard to prove it.

God bless Gramma Billy and Gene. They soldiered to the thirteenth hole, only to finally throw in the towel and make the long trek back to the clubhouse. She was so apologetic for quitting, insisting that she had never walked off a course before, and no matter how many times I told her that I understood and desperately wanted to follow her in myself, she felt as though she had let me down. Hers was a selflessness with which I was not familiar. I had had friends since childhood—Robert among them—who would be sitting in the clubhouse at a table of foam-lined pint glasses laughing at the sight of me tumbling down eighteen, but this woman and man to whom the game had introduced me wanted to cheer and support me through a golfing pneumonia. 'Twas a great game, and even on its worst days, I was so fortunate to play it.

My morning resolve was rewarded with an afternoon of sunshine, and I spent the second half of the day shooting a 73 on the Dirleton course at the nearby Archerfield Links, a new and luxurious complex with a membership list full of celebrity footballers. When I was finished, I stopped by Drew and Moira's to collect my laundry, which was not only washed and folded but also pressed and wrapped in paper. I almost wept at the sight of my lone pair of jeans.

"You ironed my jeans?" I asked Moira. I didn't know jeans could be ironed.

"We have our standards," she told me, refusing my money but accepting a hug. Standards—I remembered those. They'd been all but abandoned as I judged my days by numbers and miles. But as I dashed onward and forward, I had to remember to pause and play with standards in mind. I needed a tidier game, a golf defined by a criterion of quality to which I held myself accountable. I was good; I had to stop letting myself off the hook by settling for okay.

Four birdies at Dirleton showed that my game was tightening as I had hoped it would, my misses turning into potential pars instead of scrambling bogeys, and a good-enough swing had become engraved in my muscles. With time to go, I was further along than I had hoped, with so much more to be discovered. And yet, there was a part of me that felt as though Robert was doing it right, even as he did almost nothing at all.

Robert hadn't appeared in North Berwick yet, and I missed my friend who would have rued the golf but relished the chance to retell the day's despair through lips warmed by local malts. As I walked through the streets of North Berwick on my way to the chipper that evening (I embraced my right to hard-earned fried dinners, and was still shedding pounds by way of walking fifteen-plus miles per day), I saw the smokers congregated outside the pubs, taking long drags and hurrying back inside to where, through the doorways, I saw men in dark rooms leaning over bright glasses. I could hear the quiet conversation, the lovely sound of small friendships audible from the sidewalk. Robert would have had them all slapping his back by evening's end and would have a game set up for us the next morning, back in the days when I would have had few words to say about the town's golf course but whole chapters to share about its bars.

There was no comparison between life then and life now, no matter how I romanticized the thud of full pints landing on tavern wood or the repartee of like-minded strangers. Back then, I wouldn't have fought my way through North Berwick, and I wouldn't have headed back out in the afternoon. And I wouldn't have spared a moment's thought for anyone but myself.

There were children in the chip shop that evening, and while I'd been too golf distracted to miss my own kids as much as I had anticipated, it hit me in North Berwick as I watched a little girl beg her dad for change for an ice cream.

Parenthood was a peculiar business. When I was with my girls, I was too often searching for kid-occupiers that would allow me to return to truly important matters, like researching golf shoes online or scouring Trip-Advisor for the best B&B in Inverness. Kids were hard when you were with them. I would shuttle them around to the zoo and the kids' museum or the place with the dinosaurs rather than have to sit and wonder who these little people were, whether they were happy, and whether this parent was getting anything right.

I walked back to my flat with my bag of fry, missing every minute that I had been given with my girls and failed to really see them, unable to recognize that the stuff I was searching for was standing in front of me, asking me for another snack. I resolved to make every day away from them count, so that one day, when such things might matter to them, I could be doing nothing at all with my girls and say, *Let me tell you what Daddy did.*

Golf owes much to Morris, Jones, Palmer, and James Braid and the bunch, but its debt to *Ovis aries* can never be repaid. There is no golf today—not as we know it—without our fluffy friends in white. Next time you pass a field of grazing sheep at home or abroad, take a moment to smile and say thank you; our game's birth and evolution rests upon their delicious shoulders.

Golf wasn't invented by bored shepherds, as some stories might suggest, and as I would have told you before spending a summer in Scotland. It was played alongside them, certainly, as sheep were golf's first—and potentially future—keepers of the greens. *Links* comes from the Old English *hlinc*, meaning hill or ridge, or even lean, and it referred to the sand hills that were good for grazing and golf but not much else. In getting the unfarmable leftovers for their game, golfers were blessed with a wobbly dune topography that designers have labored to re-create ever since.

Without sheep to nibble the grasses to a tight playing height, golf's first courses would never have been spotted among the wild dune overgrowth, nor would it have been possible to maintain them. David Owen's *New Yorker* piece "The Ghost Course" gives credit to rabbits, too—sheep excelled at munching grasses to fairway height, but rabbits' smaller jawbones meant their flattened warrens were puttable, making for golf's first greens. But it was sheep and the role they played in bringing the game to Scotland that make them the patron quadrupeds of golf.

Robert loved to explain how the name *golf* was born of an aged acronym for *Gentlemen Only, Ladies Forbidden*, an etymological tale so stupidly false that I dared not mention it while in golf's homeland. The word's most likely origin is a guttural variation of the word *colf* or *kolf* (Dutch for club or bat). Colf was a Dutch game dating to the thirteenth century that involved clubbing a ball over and through towns and countryside until successfully sending it through a designated doorway—meaning that the windmill hole on your miniature golf course is a more accurate replica of golf's ancestry than the Old Course. Property damage eventually pushed colfers from the towns to fields and frozen rivers, where they struck their balls toward poles instead of windows, but the next time you hit a house with your ball, consider yourself a golf historian. And if you lose and have to buy drinks in the clubhouse, know that you're being faithful to the legacy of colf, where the losing side owed the winners a barrel of beer.

Early Dutch art shows club-holding figures playing colf all over Holland, portraits that far predate the first mention of golf in Scotland in the fifteenth century. And it was in one such painting that I witnessed proof of how colf/golf arrived in Scotia. In a small room attached to the clubhouse of the Gullane Golf Club, one of its longest-standing members pointed my eyes toward a print depicting colfers on ice *dressed in kilts*.

Mystery solved! Roaming Scots played colf before golf, and this was proof that the former had inspired the latter. This gentleman at Gullane had righted all my wrong notions about the origins of the game, and had even written about them in his lovely little book, *Golf on Gullane Hill*, a copy of which he signed for me: *Enjoy Every Shot! Archie Baird*.

A friend had told me to phone the club before my round at Gullane (pronounced *Gull-in*) and ask if a Mr. Archie Baird was available and if he could show me his golf museum. I did so, and the receptionist assured me that she would try to contact him and let him know about my interest in his collection of golf history. I went around Gullane's Course No. 2 with GB and Gene rather quickly, Gramma Billy bringing me more good karma as I played to the standard of a man wearing pressed boxer shorts (they actually were), carding six birdies and shooting a 69 on a sunny morning. There was no sign of any museum curator when we arrived back at the clubhouse, but as we waited outside, a short man with white hair stepped off the local bus and slowly made his way across the lawn to the entrance. He apologized for being late, but poor eyesight had recently lost him his driver's license, and I felt a wave of guilt—why had I bothered this gentle old soul to come down here on the bus and open up a locked door to see history I could find in a book somewhere? But when he did open the door, I understood that it was worth the trip for both of us. For me, the place held strange, beautiful treasures; and for Archie, it was a chance to show his life's collection to someone to whom it genuinely mattered.

The one-room museum was stuffed with leather-handled golf clubs and rusty club-making wrenches, with ancient brown golf balls scattered around the floor and walls covered with grainy photographs and headlines and course layouts. Archie walked us through the Dutch art of kilted colfers to Scots first playing golf here on this coastline (colf would die out in Holland, but its cousin would thrive in Scotland) to that seminal moment in golf history when the featherie ball was replaced by gutta-percha. Archie showed me a top hat full of goose feathers that would have had to be boiled down and packed into one expensive and labor-intensive featherie ball versus the iron press that could crank out dozens of cheap rubber pellets. Featheries were so dear that Archie showed me an old boot with a hole scooped out of the heel, a tool engineered for the stealthy stealing of golf balls. Pilfered featheries fetched a fine price in the pub, and their cost ensured that golf would remain a pastime of the moneyed gentry. The shift to gutties changed everything about the game, making golf affordable and accessible; right after sheep, golf owed its all to rubber.

Archie's compact collection of memorabilia was a windfall for a history buff, and he explained how he had married into golf treasure hunting. His wife was the great granddaughter of the legendary Willie Park; the Musselburgh father-son duo of Willie Park Senior and Junior won the Open six times between them and would be golf's greatest father and son if not for the Morrises. Archie's archives had begun as a handful of Park memorabilia collected to celebrate his wife's relative; after a lifetime of golf scavenging, he had amassed his gallery at Gullane. It was an appropriate venue for a museum, as golf had been played on the dunes of Gullane for 350 years, dating back to matches between rival weavers from nearby Dirleton and Aberlady. Weavers; again, golf was inextricably linked to wool. It was Scottish wool traders returning from Holland who brought a Dutch game to the dunes of places like St. Andrews, Dunbar, and North Berwick—their hometowns— and that game's descendant had brought me to Gullane to meet one of the great men of golf.

The four of us retired to the members' lounge, where Archie introduced me to more golf history by way of a beverage. John Panton was a beloved Scottish golf pro who won championships on both sides of the Atlantic, besting the likes of Sam Snead in the World Seniors Championship and representing Scotland in the Ryder Cup three times. He retired as an honorary pro to the Royal & Ancient, and the drink named after him—ginger beer and lime—was Scotland's version of the Arnold Palmer. The John Panton would become my go-to clubhouse beverage. Ginger beer, spicier and crisper than our ginger ale, had its own golf legacy: the fourth hole on the Old Course at St. Andrews was named Ginger Beer for the carts that would sell bottles of the stuff to thirsty golfers.

We talked long after our pints of John Panton were empty. Archie was impressed by my endeavor, and I was humbled when he said the poster I had given him would go up in his museum. He was pleasantly surprised to see a few Scottish links on my map that he didn't know. We said our good-byes and Archie refused a lift home, perhaps headed back to tidy up the museum for the next group of visitors who might be lucky enough to know to ask for Mr. Baird.

The Golf Coast offered all styles and ages of golf, from the prehistoric links on Gullane Hill that had been designed by god to newborn tracks by Tom Doak; from the dusty history of Archie's room to the modern luxury of the

Renaissance Club, where I ended my day. In selecting my courses, I had originally left Renaissance off the list for its youth. It had been built by a Florida businessman on the Archerfield estate, a parcel of one thousand acres located beside Muirfield that also held two other courses and took its name from King Edward I's archers, stationed there in the thirteenth century. Archerfield's latest resident, the Doak-designed Renaissance, had just opened in 2008. In a country where golf had been played before America existed, I thought I might save time by skipping a course that couldn't possibly hold the Scottish golfing soul I was trying to tap. But a friend insisted I play Doak's only design in Scotland and first in Europe. While I didn't get terribly excited about designer names, favoring courses that had me imagining a celestial creator versus a celebrity architect, I still wrote to Renaissance, and was glad that I did.

As well as the Scots did golf, Americans ruled when it came to accommodation. After weeks of Euro-sized hospitality, my sprawling room at the Renaissance Club looked like a banquet hall, my bed an acre of soft down, and my shower a vault of glass and tile. Replete with American electrical outlets, Renaissance was a nostalgic return to the largesse of home. The Mickelson burger in the bar that evening was a delicious tower of meat and chili, and I had to smile at Lefty getting pegged to the most caloric item on the menu. My room was upstairs in the clubhouse, and I was encouraged to treat the stunning new facility as my home. No worries about walking in through the members' door or not wearing a jacket in the dining room; wear your spikes wherever you wanted, come down to the locker room for a soak in the Jacuzzi, or hit the gym downstairs—just relax and partake. It was good to be home, if just for an evening.

The global reverence for Tom Doak's designs inspired unfair expectations as I imagined a stretch of pure golf Canaan, eighteen grand golfing landscapes that reimagined course architecture in the game's homeland. The opening three holes were tree-lined and sort of plain—good tests, but nothing this Tom couldn't have sketched out. As the course worked its way out to the water on holes eight, nine, and ten, I sampled some of the celebrated genius on designs that were inspired hikes around the ocean's edge, wide swaths of fairway that looked like a dreamy sea of wavy green, the sort of soulful golf expanse that Doak's name conjured.

Along with lofty expectations, designer cachet brings a temptation for golfers to play Monday-morning architect, as I did at Renaissance, wondering whether more could have been done with such remarkable property that might have led to a more consistent course. And it was difficult. Stretching to just over 7,300 yards, with bunkers placed for modern distances (versus Gullane, where I could pretend they weren't there), it was merciless in the wind. Severely shaped greens didn't add much to the playability, and while the stone wall running through the course was a nice homage to North Berwick, my knowing it had been built in the twenty-first century detracted from its character. Unlike the wall at North Berwick, this partition was not older than me, and I could argue with it. Renaissance was immaculate and dramatic (and covered with pheasants, I was amused to find). I wouldn't hurry to reschedule a flight if told I was coming back tomorrow, though if it meant another night in the clubhouse, I would skip the whole way there. The following morning, I woke refreshed in a room that made me feel like a proper member of the gentry, which seemed the appropriate mind-set when one was headed for golf at Muirfield.

There is some debate as to whether the Honourable Company of Edinburgh Golfers was the oldest club in the world. The Royal Burgess Golfing Society dated its origins to 1735, when it was mentioned in the Edinburgh Almanac, preceding the 1744 founding of the Honourable Company, whose club dates to those first rules of golf. I'm sure there are wood-paneled rooms full of men in red coats where the subject is still hotly discussed, but no matter who was oldest, what I found most interesting about those early days of golf companies was the separation of course and club. The Burgess golfers began playing their golf on the Bruntsfield Links, while the Honorouble Company was over at Leith, where some contend the warning call "Fore!" originated. With holes planted beside the battlements of the long-since-gone Ramsay's Fort, the cry may have warned golfers during artillery practice that cannon fire was coming overhead. Golf on Leith's five-hole layout had been recorded as far back as the time of Charles I, and if you think our presidents golf at inopportune times, consider the scene depicted on the Carnegie Shield at Royal Dornoch: It shows King Charles learning of the 1641 Irish rebellion midround at Leith. Whether the shock on his face was genuine or performed we'll never know; accounts claim the king was down in his match and used the bad news as a handy excuse for skipping out early.

There are few more decadent ways for a golf degenerate to pass a rainy afternoon than by clicking his way around Neil Laird's ScottishGolfHistory .org, an exhaustive golf encyclopedia in which Laird's chronicles shine with the intrigue of caddie-yard gossip. Though the circumstances of golf's first game are unknown, Laird details the first international match, a Scotland versus England dustup in 1681 at Leith. The Scotland-loving Duke of York had taken offense when two visiting Englishmen claimed golf was an English game, and he challenged them to a match. The Duke enlisted local stick John Paterson as his partner, and they swept the links with the Londoners. Paterson bought a house on the Royal Mile in Edinburgh with his winnings, calling the place "Golfers Land" and adorning the exterior with the motto "Far and Sure." It's a pub today, but worth a pilgrimage for any former caddie, and not just because caddies tend to thrive in pubs. A plaque commemorates the match, which also marked the first recorded use of a caddie in golf. The word came from the French *le cadet*, meaning boy or youngest; it had been borrowed in Scottish slang to denote a lackey or a porter, and the first one in golf was a boy named Andrew Dickson, who was hired to carry the Duke of York's clubs that day. By steering the Duke to victory, Dickson forever cemented the essential role of bag-toters in golf.

The Honourable Company and the Burgess golfers eventually left Leith and Bruntsfield as Edinburgh grew, both moving to a course set within the racetrack at Musselburgh. Without a clubhouse to call home, members stored their clubs under the grandstands and battled the crowds for tee times. The new and cheap guttie balls had turned golf into everybody's hobby, and upward of sixty golf societies shared the nine holes at Musselburgh. The two clubs tired of the golfing hordes and again moved on to quieter pastures, the

Honourable Company landing at Muirfield while Burgess built a parkland course near the city. This division of course and club persisted all over Scotland, where I would visit courses shared by three or more different golf clubs with four distinct clubhouses lining an eighteenth fairway.

I tried to imagine starting my own club wherein we borrowed the course at Augusta National and built our clubhouse across the street. I found this scenario unlikely, but it provided insight into why golf over here was open in a way I could only wish it was back home: in Scotland, the club was the precious thing, while the course was viewed as a sort of shared playing ground. The St. Andrews courses are associated with *five* different golf clubs (the R&A, the New Golf Club, the St. Andrews Golf Club, the St. Regulus Ladies Golf Club, and the St. Rule Club), yet half the tee times at the Old are reserved for visitors. The arrangement at Carnoustie is much the same, proving that member golf and daily fee play can coexist amicably, if we decide that golf is a game to be shared rather than a status symbol to be peacocked on hats and sweaters. There were plenty of things I would want to transplant from Scotland—ginger beer, brown sauce, Alan McPherson—but even more than their Right to Roam, it was the Scots' right to golf that I coveted most.

It struck me as strange that the game came from a place where class and exclusivity seemed so entrenched, yet it was in America, the everyman land of bootstraps, where golf became truly exclusive: We took the open game from the closed place and made it a closed game in the open place. Here was the oldest golf club in the world (probably), and I was walking right up to it, with clubs pulled from my trunk and every intention of playing it, almost positive they were about to let me do so. I stopped to quickly snap a picture of those famed black gates lettered in gold—*The Honourable Company of Edinburgh Golfers*—and then tucked my phone away, lest it be confiscated by that guy with the binoculars who enjoyed chasing Yanks away.

I was confused by the warmth of my greeting from the starter. *Mr. Coyne, we received your email, and I was able to reserve a good caddie for you.* If there was a course that did not need to be impressed by a writer's visit, this was it, but for the next six hours I would have to continually check my scorecard: *This is Muirfield, right?*

I played with two members and the club secretary, Stuart, a young and energetic manager who had recently been hired from Fife's Kingsbarns, a visitors-only course where hospitality reigned. Apparently Muirfield had become aware of its reputation (Google *Muirfield* and *snobbery* and you'll see why), and decided it needed to change. What was the point of being open to visitors if they didn't enjoy the experience? The place had so much to offer, Stuart explained, and they didn't want old stories to get in the way of people coming to experience it.

Muirfield still wasn't Disney World. I felt nervous tiptoeing around the clubhouse and walking the grounds, searching for my caddie. You want to feel a little nervous at the place that wrote the rules, but as we got out onto the golf course, the two Muirfield members in my foursome and my caddie were just a pack of tightly bundled cohorts fighting the wind. I was pretty sure my Italian playing partner owned most of Florence (he casually noted that he was in Scotland for his other club's annual meeting: *Which club?* I asked. *The R&A*, he explained. *Oh, yeah, I've heard of them*), while my other partner's thin English accent was so fine that I couldn't help but wonder when his family finally decided to give up the abbey. But the pursuit of par was the great leveler, and as I made back-to-back birdies in a breeze that had some North Berwick to it—sans the rain—I was just a golfer on a golf course, and a very good course at that.

Muirfield was an intricate links; not punishing or overly long from the members' tees but full of inexplicable bogeys. It was a target course where you eyed a hole and thought, *I can do this*, until your approach shot kept getting farther and farther away from the hole, finally settling into a subtle dip where par was still right there in front of you, if only you knew how to play this shot. Some rota courses seemed to reward wisdom, while others could be muscled into yielding birdies; Muirfield required both power and prudence, and it was no wonder it had crowned such a distinguished roll of Open champions, from Nicklaus and Player and Trevino and Watson to Faldo and Els and Mickelson. The ocean never quite came into view on the Old-Tom-then-Colt design, but its effects were omnipresent, and as the course worked in loops versus the links-typical coastal march, the direction of the breeze shifted with every shot.

My caddie, whose knowledge of the greens had gotten him hired by Dustin Johnson for practice rounds at the 2013 Open, gave me great directions that I struggled to follow in the gales. No matter; this was a round to not let bogeys get in the way of the experience or the access to such a seasoned looper. Since he had been around an Open, I was sure to ask him about the secret to getting into one.

"Short game," he said. "They get it up and down from everywhere. Their strikes are lovely, and Johnson hit it far, no doubt. But he would hit four different chips—high, low, spin it, bump it—and they'd all end up in a barrel. They can all hit it, but the most impressive thing is the wedges. They're lethal with a wedge in their hands."

And I was not. Mild-abrasion-dangerous, perhaps, but I had miles to go to get to lethal. Luckily, the miles awaited.

We'd started on the back nine, and having played like rabbits through the wind, we came around to find a backup at the first tee, so Stuart invited us into his office for a cup of tea while we waited. I soon found myself in a leather chair in the secretary of Muirfield's office, listening to him talk with the members about the upcoming Open at St. Andrews and who they would be inviting to play their course in the days leading up to it. Mickelson—Muirfield's most recent champion—for sure, but you can't invite Phil and not invite Rory, last year's winner, and then what about Tiger? It became an awkward business, like drawing up the A and B lists for a wedding.

I saw a pile of Muirfield member ties next to Stuart's desk and asked him if I could buy one. He laughed; this was still Muirfield. "*I* can't even get one of those," Stuart said, handing me a small picture frame. "Here you go. We're looking for a better place to hang that." I was looking at Mickelson's final-day scorecard from the 2013 Open, the actual competition card filled out in Francesco Molinari's handwriting, those four back-nine birdies so humbly written in small numbers. So the pros didn't circle their birdies. I, on the other hand, enshrined mine on the scorecard with circles or sketches of flowers and fireworks, highlighting them with a glitter pen. *Expect birdies*, I reminded myself. *Play to that standard.*

The standard was well over par on the back nine, and Muirfield proved why a modest three under was Mickelson's winning total. Even though we played from the boxes and not the Open tees, my 81 was no great disappointment. Today was about playing beside the honourable gentlemen, not my results on their golf course—the club was the thing. And I had learned something from my caddie and taken some confidence from playing such a venue with a minimum of nerves. Plus, I had finally learned what playing from the boxes actually meant.

I had heard the regular tees referred to as *the boxes* during my trip and imagined there was some legend behind the name, some tale of Old Tom teeing off atop a box in the Open, or Willie Park once eating a box of haggis and winning the champion's belt, but I understood the meaning when I saw actual red boxes on the Muirfield tees. I looked into the first one, expecting to find Old Tom's pipe or James Braid's ashes, but it turned out that the boxes, along with serving as tee markers, held things like banana peels and cigarette butts. They were trash boxes. But possibly, I mused, the oldest trash boxes in golf.

I soon understood why lunch at Muirfield could be a three-hour affair, even if you were drinking John Pantons instead of Churchill martinis. Dressed in our jackets and ties, we sat in a stately drawing room and talked quietly about things I pretended to know of. Stuart told me about the club calendar's highlight, the twice-a-year members' dinner at which the gentlemen dressed in their red coats and arranged all their foursome matches for the upcoming season. He showed me around the trophy cases stuffed with ancient silver. Cooler than the trophies, though, was the old voting box he pointed out, a wooden case with a hole in the front. You would take a black ball in your hand and stick it into the box—to vote yes, you dropped the ball into the chamber on the left; for no, you dropped it into the right. One noball could deny someone membership—thus the origin of the term *blackballed*. I would find similar voting boxes at other Scottish clubs, lest I give Muirfield credit for inventing everything.

Stuart could tell I was antsy to get on with our meal. I had more golf ahead of me that afternoon, so he finally asked our members if they would like to "go through," which seemed a smart way to ask if you wanted to get some grub. The buffet lunch eaten at long tables had a boarding-school vibe to it, the members distinguished by their club ties as we paraded along a protein-laden smorgasbord. Stuart said the menu did not change, and why would it? I piled my plate with beef and fowl and potato and pasta, a manly feast built to provide ballast in the wind outside, or to soak up the gin served next door.

I thought I would be racing my way out of Muirfield that day, yearning to roam free and breathe twenty-first-century air again, but I was actually disappointed to go, having made a few unexpected friends. Once again, my conviction prior to investigation was well off the mark. But I did have to hurry my exit and skip dessert, leaving my partners mid-banquet. I had thirty-six holes left in my afternoon, and I wasn't playing foursomes.

I would recall Kilspindie as a charming links fit for any skill level, a locals' course with scenic vistas that you could go around twice a day without risking boredom. And I would remember Craigielaw as a young but solid track at the ocean's edge, with a sublimely located lodge where my bed waited a few hundred steps from the final hole. Kilspindie was a shorter, more compact course and Craigielaw a roomier links, but I finished three over at both of them, fair scores in an uncommon wind that I needed to start accepting as common.

I recalled seals on the beach at Kilspindie—I'd played among foxes, sheep, and, on a trip Down Under, a spread of lounging kangaroos, but gray seals were an exciting first. Yet clearer than any memory from that afternoon is a distant call of *FORE!* I can still hear it, probably louder now than I heard it then, and I see myself standing in a fairway, stiff with confusion, wondering if a better name for Kilspindie might have been Kilgolfer.

We'd been shepherded around Kilspindie by a member named Chris, who shared a friend in common and had come out to battle the breezes with me, Gramma Billy, and Gene. With a white beard and a tartan cap, Chris was a twinkle-in-his-eye sort of Scotsman whose thin, blue sweater contrasted our layers of wind-breaking armor. His full frame took the buffeting of the air unbothered, and his was a look I saw all over Scotland and recalled from my Irish afternoons—that mien of sincerity and peace that seemed so elusive to a Yank. As someone who hailed from a land of unsettled aspirers, I sensed a brilliance in the Scottish countenance; it seemed one-layered—not in a simple way but in a wise, you-get-what-you-see sort of candor. Good people or bad, angry or elated, Scots were genuine in a way I envied and admired. Chris was not only sage about the quirky little links of Kilspindie, he educated me on some more Scottish slang as he pointed across the water at two soft hills that the Scots called the Paps of Fife.

"Paps—that means hills?" I asked.

"It means tits," Chris said.

We were happy to have a guide, as Kilspindie's snug layout made for intertwined golf holes and a peculiar routing that squeezed eighteen holes into a space better suited for fifteen. I didn't know whether it was the turkey from lunch or the emotional hangover of visiting Muirfield, but I dragged myself across Kilspindie's short back nine. As we headed down sixteen, a downwind par 4 where my ball had come to rest a short distance from the green, we paused in the fairway for Gene to play his ball. Gramma Billy and Gene were golfing well, and I had grown accustomed to GB's hustle and self-critiques and Gene's golf chivalry. We made a good little group, and as the scorecards had shown, they brought out my best golf.

As Gene played his shot, I heard a faraway *Fore!*, barely audible in the wind. Too tired to move very fast, I turned my head and mumbled, "Heads up," then turned back around to watch Gene hit. But there in the grass in front of me I saw a sparkly hoop earring. And next to it on the ground—were those sunglasses? I looked up and saw Gramma Billy holding her face.

She wasn't speaking or moving. None of us were.

"Did that . . . hit you?"

"My god," was all she could say as Gene tended to her, peeling back her hands to show a bright red spot on the upper corner of her cheekbone. The drive had come from over two hundred yards away, and it missed Billy's eye by the width of a tee. The impact was one ball away from her temple, where contact could have been far more dire. Gene waved his arms at the golfers on a distant tee, calling "What the hell?" He looked as though he was ready to grab a club and head after them, but one of them was already sprinting toward us.

I stood there, not knowing what to do, tired in a way that made the circumstances feel somewhat unreal. I surveyed my options—do I run for help? Call an ambulance? Say paps? I'd seen people get hit by balls before, but it was always in the leg or ass, and it was always somewhat funny. I had a sick impulse to laugh—*Wow, that ball hit you in the face, how about that!* But this was serious, so I tried to comfort my friend and show genuine concern, because I *was* genuinely concerned, though a small part of me wondered how close my ball was to the green and if I could get it up and down for birdie.

I had been told good golf required a certain amount of selfishness. I possessed it by the pallet.

The offending long-ball slicer apologized frantically as we stood there waiting to see if the injury grew more severe, if there would be blood or a collapse, which seemed well possible. Gene and GB accepted his apologies as politely as they could, given the situation. Only in golf do you get beaned in the face by a stranger's rocketing projectile and tell him *No worries, keep playing your little game.* And in a moment, Gramma Billy reached for her chipping wedge and moved ahead, telling us she was fine, that we should play on. She finished that hole and the next two without complaint, all of us quiet and uneasy from this strange dose of danger dropped into our carefree afternoon.

I made par on sixteen. Damn it.

After we loaded our bags in the parking lot, we hugged our good-byes and promised we would tee it up again someday. Gene and GB's trip had come to a close, but they said they would be following my progress all the way around, and that the email check-ins would be abundant. It was not until that evening as I lay in bed that I realized what had happened at

Kilspindie, and grasped the disaster with which we had flirted. Aside from some swelling, GB would be okay, but today had reminded me that injury was a possibility—now a reality—on this trip, and that if I made it through without a car wreck or a busted ankle or influenza or a golf ball to the face, I would have been granted my golfing miracle.

I would later get an email from Gene that read, "Thank you for your friendship to Billy. It makes a difference in her life," and as I read it, I felt a strange sensation squeezing my eyes and tickling the top of my nose—I think some people call it crying—because Gene had it the wrong way around. Gramma Billy's kindness made the difference. It gave me something to strive for that, unlike all these goddamn golf scores, I could maybe figure out. Her life was about much more than her own living. Maybe by the time someone called me Grandpa, mine would be, too.

From the Golf Coast of East Lothian, I was headed through Edinburgh and up around the coast to the next pocket of storied links in Scotland, the courses of East Fife. The plan was to meet my girls up in St. Andrews; we had rented a home with a history that I hoped would seep into my game through our two weeks living there. Called Cowpers Close, its front door sat on South Street in the heart of town, where nearly a century and a half before it had been the birthplace and family home of James Foulis Jr., winner of the second US Open, whose father was a club maker alongside Old Tom. The girls were excited for the flowery yard out back, while I was eager for the rare chance to stay in the home of a major winner, as I didn't envision Tiger or Rory renting out their places anytime soon.

At the airport, I stood around the customs exit as families poured through the sliding doors, travelers hugging loved ones and searching out their drivers among the crowd of sign-holders. I waited twenty minutes, then thirty, until the doors weren't sliding open anymore. The flight from Newark had deplaned, I was told, as the wait approached an hour. I paced inside and outside, checking my phone and looking for a good place to throw up, until the doors finally slid open one more time, and out rode a yawning two-year-old with curly red hair. She looked confused to see me until her five-year-old sister ran around from behind the stroller and jumped into my arms.

As we drove to St. Andrews, I listened to Allyson tell me about the flight—it had taken forever to get the car seats off the plane—and I looked in the mirror at my two girls watching Scotland rush past them. I wondered if this was really my life. I was taking my small children to the home of golf. *My* girls are going to walk *those* fairways. This was so much better than that trip to Hershey Park. Maybe they wouldn't agree, but my gratitude for what I was going to share with them was overwhelming.

I wasn't even there yet, but I so badly wanted to return to St. Andrews for the Open in July. When I finally got home from Scotland, I wanted to be able to tell them we were all headed right back. I already knew the town's motto—*Dum Spiro Spero*—and as we pulled up to our new Scottish home, I was breathing hope deeply.

Perfect

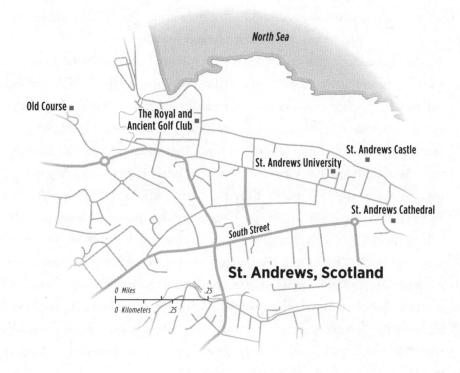

North Sea

Old Course ■

The Royal and Ancient Golf Club ■

St. Andrews Castle ■

St. Andrews University ■

St. Andrews Cathedral ■

South Street

St. Andrews, Scotland

0 Miles   .25

0 Kilometers   .25

Scotland abounds with great golf towns and great castle towns and great cathedral towns that overwhelm you with history. There are whisky villages and foodie retreats near college hubs and ancient burgs where yesteryear drips from the sooty walls. There are hamlets for hunting gravestones, districts for queuing up at museums, and enclaves of family-friendly fun. But there is only one town that is all of the above, a veritable utopia nestled into an elbow of Fife's coastline.

Any proper search should start at the beginning, and Archie Baird had taken me to golf's back in Holland, then moved me forward to the time of Old Tom Morris, keeper of the greens at St. Andrews for forty years, and a figure I had always considered a grandfather and patron saint of golf. Truth was, some of those laurels belonged to his boss, the formidable Allan Robertson, resident club maker in St. Andrews and the man who broke golf's gentility boundary. The game had been left mostly to nobility who could afford the equipment and time until Robertson became golf's first pro and earner, making cash as a featherie stuffer and perhaps more as a gambler on the links—it's said he never once lost a money match.

At St. Andrews, you could reach even further back than Robertson, to Mary, Queen of Scots, the mother of golf who kept a cottage at St. Andrews and played the course incognito. After her husband was strangled to death in 1567, Mary was spotted golfing at St. Andrews a few days later; her enemies claimed her golfing mood was proof that she was in on the murder plot. She would lose her crown and spend the rest of her life in prison for what might be history's most costly round of golf. But even before Mary and her devotion to St. Andrews, there was King James II, who banned golf in the village in 1457 because it was distracting his archers. The ban was lifted in 1552 by Archbishop Hamilton in a decree that guaranteed the people of St. Andrews would forever be allowed to use their links land for golf. And before James, there was St. Rule, who shipwrecked here with the bones of the apostle Andrew, and then there was Andrew on his crooked cross. One could go back as far as history tempted at St. Andrews, and with the ancient ruins of its castle and cathedral looming behind the Royal & Ancient clubhouse—both far predating the town's golf courses—the temptation was everywhere.

I had struck up a correspondence with our landlord, who had grown up in our rental, the home that had previously belonged to Henry Foulis and turned out to be, in my mind, the Internet's prime achievement to date. We could not have dreamt up a more dreamlike accommodation, with copious clean bedrooms and book-lined sitting chambers, a playroom in the basement with a closet full of toys for the girls, and a long garden crowded with flowers and butterflies that, for my city kids, was a storybook in their own backyard. She described for me what growing up in the idyllic town of St. Andrews was like, and how today it perfectly prepared one for life in the

1950s. We would come to agree, to the point where Allyson was inquiring about whether the house might be for sale (sadly, it wasn't) and insisting that we come back every year on vacation. For this miracle of spousal conversion, I would forever be indebted to the magical perfection of this town.

When my mother arrived at our temporary home, she walked through the hallways with her mouth agape, saying, "This is so *nice*," as if she were on a design show where her dream makeover had just been revealed. Mom and Dad arrived shortly after Allyson and the kids, and at eighty years of age, they confessed that they had a very different expectation of Scotland. They had recently watched a travel show on which the host went on an epic Scottish pub crawl, replete with booze and brawls. "I thought everyone was going to be drunk from whisky and fighting in the streets," my mother said. I laughed and assured her that was just Glasgow. (I kid, my Weegie friends.)

You would expect the home of golf might be only that—golf pubs, golf shops, golf museums. St. Andrews had plenty of those, but it also had culture and history and learning, with golfers blending into packs of undergrads from St. Andrews University as they hustled to and from classes in academic robes. You stay here and feel like you've done more than chase a ball around, and that your travels are better for it.

When it came to the golf, there is no stage as revered and as accessible as the Old Course at St. Andrews, and driving into town for the first time is a breathtaking epiphany: *That's a golf course?* And then: *That's THE golf course!* There's the R&A clubhouse, the first tee, and that shot-bending hotel—you don't have to go hunting for them; they call for you to step right up and touch them. The golf pours into the heart of town, and the course is treated by locals as their public park. In fact, the Old Course is closed every Sunday to maintain its status as a public green space. Come walk your dog or stand in line with tourists for pictures on the Swilcan Bridge. The picture we took of my girls atop the famed stone overpass on eighteen, smiling in their yellow rain boots—if there were someday a picture of the two of them standing on the moon, it would not make this golf dad any prouder.

It was a joy to walk from my front door down to one of the first tees, leaving the car parked on South Street and bounding past the pubs and the golf shops and the tall windows of the Royal & Ancient, feeling as though I'd lost several pounds. I actually was lighter by at least a stone (fourteen pounds) already, and Allyson wondered where in the UK I had left my jowls. Golfers came for the Old Course and often bundled it with the New (the second course at St. Andrews, with an 1895 birthdate that rendered it not terribly new), but it was on the less-crowded Eden, Strathtyrum, and Jubilee, each with their own histories and signature holes, where I felt a welcome break from the rush and was able to retune my turn and rethink my habits on challenging but generous links.

The Balgove was a wee course, ideal for a round with kids or the golf-timid, as the challenge of St. Andrews's courses ascended from Balgove to Strathtyrum to Eden to Jubilee, then to the New and Old, and finally up to a wild storm of a course newly built above the town.

As rich with lore as St. Andrews was, its courses were not the most theatrical in Scotland. The links land was relatively flat, and the magnitude of the town's layouts, particularly the Old, hid from players looking for framed wows. Opened in 2008, the Castle course felt as if it had been built in response to this void of conspicuous drama; it was a big, ballsy routing of collapses and climbs and wild greens. As massive as the greens were on St. Andrews Old, with sixteen double greens making for putting surfaces the size of hockey rinks, they were relatively flat. Not so at the Castle. The 75 I shot there might have been my best round yet, given the punishing topography, with green complexes that I was told had already been redesigned to make them more playable. I shuddered to think what they were like in 2008, because their current state was like putting across a potato chip.

Locals complained about the Castle as something of a circus course, and Tom Doak had blasted the design in one of his books, giving it a zero rating and dismissing it as a maelstrom of design excess. I wondered about his impartiality; the Castle course was designed by David McLay Kidd, a sort-of rival who had gotten the nod over Doak to design the first course at Oregon's acclaimed Bandon Dunes. Surely there was an ax to grind in a zero rating; the course deserved critique for its severity, but I found the Castle to be a mighty spectacle, and a yin to the other St. Andrews courses' yang. While the New and Old Courses might feel a bit reserved on a windless day, the Castle would test all your golf muscles on any afternoon.

My love for St. Andrews was certainly nurtured by the amount of golf I could play without lifting my suitcase. It wasn't just the courses in St. Andrews; there were links all over the Fife coastline. Some of the closest were at Crail, the seventh-oldest club in Scotland and home to a pair of contrary links. The new Craighead course was a longer track set back from the sea and had been designed by Gil Hanse, a favorite of mine for his ties to Philadelphia; his Craighead layout made Hanse the first professional American architect to design a Scottish golf course. It offered golf of genuine quality and intrigue, but I found it to be entirely empty of players. Members preferred its shorter, quirkier, and aged sister course, the Balcomie Links, where the layout ducked into sea caves and twisted around dunes, with its final four holes seemingly squeezed into the space of a football field. Hanse had done his best, but he couldn't compete with history, and at Balcomie, the history was rare.

As I crept along the path from fourteen to fifteen at Balcomie, with waves on my left threatening to crash me into the stone wall on my right, I found a dark pocket in the rocks that was marked by a plaque. I'd read plaques commemorating Bobby Jones, Arnold Palmer, and Old Tom, but a golf sign for Constantine was a first. His plaque beat Old Tom's by centuries. I had stumbled upon Constantine's Cave, where Constantine I, king of the Picts, had been killed by invading Danes after being abandoned by his army in 874 AD. I didn't see an X, but no matter; I'd found the spot—a prehistoric waterside cave on a golf course by St. Andrews, and the tomb of a king. Surely, the secret lay within.

I stepped inside, out of the rain, and breathed cold, ancient air that smelled of Viking blood and stale beer from the crumpled-up cans at my feet. I waited there like Linus in his pumpkin patch, expecting golf's spirit to show itself to me in the form of Old Tom's ghost or an angel wearing knickers or a gray apparition of the unknown Scotsman who first brought golf to these hills and had been waiting here a thousand years to whisper golf's secret into my ear, but all I heard was my buddy Rich: "Anything good in here? Wow. Smells like piss."

Rich, from New York, was taking a break from his Irish golf holiday and had joined me for a day at Crail with his golf-devoted wife. He was in his fifties, but it was his younger and fitter partner, Kim, who dragged him around the golfing world, pulling him out of bed at dawn for tee times. He'd discovered that their tee times on the two courses at Crail would amount to a price that wasn't much cheaper than an international membership, so he decided to just go ahead and join the place. So it was with two members from New York that I enjoyed one of my favorite thirty-six-hole days, where two first tees were a 9-iron apart.

On the Craighead links, I was laboring through my worst front nine of the trip (I opened with a double, then chased it with a smattering of bogeys to prove it was no fluke) when a golf cart approached us. Perhaps they'd gotten word of my play and had arrived with more golf balls.

Out of the cart stepped Martin Dempster, a tall and serious-looking Scottish golf reporter who had finally tracked me down to detail my quest, and who I wished had arrived on any morning but this one, when I was begging my clubs for contact.

"Tom?" Martin said, extending his hand. I looked around for a moment—*Tom? No Toms here.* We walked the fairway and talked of my quest and my impressions of Scotland. It had all been magical, I assured him, and our conversation turned to my chances for qualifying for the Open.

I told him I was hopeful, and as I stepped up and ripped a drive down the fourth fairway with a reporter looking on, I thought, *Why shouldn't I be?*

"There will be nobody there who's more prepared," I said. "One hundred seven courses—this is sort of the world's longest practice round." I waggled my wedge and posed confidently over my ball, ready to knife a knockdown through the air and make it dance by a pin that was looking vulnerable on the front of the green. *Pity he didn't bring a photographer,* I thought, *or a film crew to witness what this Yank was doing to Scotland.*

The ball danced, but it was a drunken peg-leg sort of boogie, my Titleist gently kissing the hosel of my wedge and pirouetting hard to the right. I held my follow-through, postured and deliberate, as if my pitchout into the cabbage had been perpetrated with purpose and skill. If I stood there long enough, maybe time would freeze and then reverse to that moment right before I fisted a shank in front of a reporter who had come here to bear witness to my British Open ambitions. I wanted to tell him about the time I saw Steve Stricker shank one at Merion—*It happens!*—but instead I did the only thing more embarrassing than hitting a shank: I reached into my bag for another ball without bothering to look for the first, like some careless Sunday chop.

The article would be generous in talking about my journey around Scotland. I desperately wanted to text Martin that evening and tell him of my afternoon round at the Balcomie: *Stop the presses! I made four birds and was two under through fifteen!* I would leave out the part about finishing with three bogeys to close with a 70. But Martin was kind to me, even though he did work in a mention of my shank. I was a writer; I knew I had granted him copy gold. He said that my game was otherwise in good form and that he would be there at the Open qualifier to update readers on my final progress. I bought a half dozen editions of the *Scotsman* in which, on a page in the sports section, my face was smiling beside a Crail flag. When I showed it to my two-year-old, Caroline, as she sat in her high chair eating a crumpet from the bakery across the street, she looked at the newspaper and pointed at my picture. She smiled and said, "Daddy."

I so wished this place were for sale.

During lunch in the Crail clubhouse between rounds, Rich dispatched three quick pints and turned wistful in the way links golf and pints could make a man. He gazed through tall glass windows onto a world that, from our chairs, looked like it was all fairways and cliffs and ocean.

"Look at the people here," he said as we watched the locals finish up a competition on the Balcomie links, the members pulling their trolleys and going about their glorious morning routine. "They look content. They've got their friends and their families and they're out playing some golf. Good enough. You think they give a damn if they have a BMW or not? They're not trying to keep up with anything. They're happy. Life looks pretty good from here."

I was sure that not everyone in Scotland was happy, and I imagined Rich would concede as much, but his generalizing possessed a useful insight: There did seem to be a contentment to life here that looked foreign to this table of Americans. There was something about the mood in old countries that felt distant for a person from a young one, like the people here weren't so hell-bent on rearranging the world, as if they understood that it had been around for a very long time and that their place in it was modest and should be accepted with an ounce of humility. I was from a land where one's place in life was malleable by law, where accepting one's station was in some way a failure; over here, knowing one's place seemed a source of peace, and perhaps enjoyment. It was hard to really enjoy yourself when you weren't sure who you were, and it seemed the people here did know, at least from our view through the glass.

Even as I cherished my weeks in St. Andrews, I knew they were my halcyon days. Each morning began with a walk to the baker for crumpets (fancy pancakes) and pastries in the shop that had been frequented by the Royals when they visited Prince William during his studies at St. Andrews University. William had met Kate at a coffee shop down the street—I knew this because a banner shouting *WHERE WILLS MET KATE!* covered the shop windows. Next to the bakery, I would buy that afternoon's lunch at a place called Munch that I imagined the Royals skipped, lining up with a gang of guys in yellow construction vests for my sack of bacon rolls (I had learned to follow the hard hats for a good, quick bite).

The bacon roll seemed to be the ubiquitous belly-filler in Scotland, proffered with a frequency matched only by tea and biscuits: *Time for a bacon roll? Can we get you a bacon roll? Stop into the bar, they have bacon rolls.* And tee times were often advertised as including a bacon roll at the turn. I'd yet to sample a bacon roll until I visited Munch. Having been offered one on a daily basis, my expectations were high for what I was sure was a national culinary treasure, a fine pastry of pork and elaborate fixings with a secret sauce whose recipe had been handed down through the generations. It turned out that the bacon roll was a piece of bacon. On a roll. And it was good. Add some brown sauce (the best thing to come out of the UK since Sir Francis Bacon himself) and it was a traveler's lunch perfected.

As the seat of higher learning in Scotland, home to the third-oldest university in the English-speaking world, with alums like King James II and the reformer John Knox, St. Andrews boasted a food scene more vibrant and ambitious than one would expect for a coastal golf town. We loved dinner at Forgan's gastropub, which had once been the 1-iron factory of Robert Forgan. A trove of cleeks had been found under the floorboards during restoration, buried in dark purgatory as all 1-irons should be. Around the corner from our front door, white boxes of fried fish couched in vinegar chips from the Tailend takeaway saved us money, enough to splurge at Rocca in the course-side Rusacks Hotel, where our table in the window allowed us to judge players' swings on the Old Course while forking foie gras. For lunch, the pepper bread from the Old Cheese Shop or the scones that spilled out the windows at the Gorgeous café were Allyson's favorites. St. Andrews had us wondering whether we came to golf or eat, while its bevy of pubs could have a visitor forgetting to do either. The Jigger Inn, beside the seventeenth, was a staple for golfers; our caddies told us that you "jigger in and stumble out"; these were the same guys who referred to the storm shelter on the golf course as the Fairway Hotel, where one could grab a few hours' rest between the Jigger Inn and a loop at dawn. While the Jigger had its devotees, it was the pub a few paces from the final green on the Old that captured golfers from around the globe, a hotel lounge harder to escape than Hell Bunker.

The Dunvegan was sacred drinking ground for hackers and Open champions alike, where you could barely make out the wallpaper between all the hanging history and photographs of its catalog of celebrity guests, from Tiger to Neil Armstrong to Ben Roethlisberger (who, legend tells, signed his crew's record-setting number of emptied Grey Goose bottles as though they were footballs bound for the Hall of Fame) to the Claret Jug itself. It was both a scene and a hangout, the rare combination of tourist stop and local haunt. Before Robert even suggested a place, I knew it was where I would be meeting him.

The bar was uncharacteristically quiet when I found him seated in a back corner of the lounge, and his thin frame looked as if it hadn't moved in a week, like he was stitched into the crimson upholstery. You could have mistaken him for one of the characters in the still portraits hanging above him—he moved about as much as they did, and had taken on a similar gray pallor. But he was smiling when I arrived, as if he had something he was eager to share. First, he ordered a new bottle of Chardonnay to replace the empty one in front of him. I declined the fresh glass and asked for a John Panton as Robert got to telling me that he had it all figured out.

"I love . . . this place," he said, and I could tell by the slow turn of his head as he surveyed the room that he was well marinated, even though nobody here would notice it or cut him off. I had been the same way, able to remain inconspicuously sozzled through almost any occasion. Inside, his body was a pickled mess, but he could still talk to you as if he had been nursing a shandy, clear and clever and engaged. And on this evening, he was even excited. His wet eyes were alive as he told me, "This place is it."

"This pub?"

"St. Andrews," he said. "It's just . . . everything. So obvious, too. St. Andrews. Not exactly a clandestine destination. I knew it, when we were here in college, and being here now—I get it. It's overwhelming. The peace, it's like a giant womb of golf and goodness, and feeling settled—actually feeling settled." He exhaled a long breath. "So guess what, Tommy boy?" He didn't wait for me to guess. "I'm staying."

So much for the Coynes buying that house and relocating to St. Andrews. Robert finally had his plan—move to St. Andrews, join one of the clubs, and golf and caddie permanently. There were enough new faces passing through every day so that the place would never get stale, and enough old faces to meet and make the place home.

"You're going to live here? For good?" I said.

I watched him swallow a deep mouthful, and though it had been years, I could still feel the warm bite in the back of my throat. "Home of Morris. Home of golf. Home of me," he said. "You don't see it?"

Of course I did.

"Golf courses," he continued. "Co-eds. Loops for days, and a library right over there. And this place, right here. Anybody who's anywhere else right now is a sucker. They're losing at life, TC."

I sipped my ginger beer and nodded, and for a moment I forgot that Robert was anything other than my hero.

"Old Tom's buried around the corner," he said. "Did you know that?" I did. "Have you seen it yet?" I had. "He fell down the steps, right over there, in the New Club, and he died. Old Tom—he took a header, and poof. *Sic transit gloria.*" From the distant look in his eyes, I could tell he was imagining such an end for himself, and finding it beautiful.

A foursome of American golfers entered the lounge, their cheeks red from the wind. They inspected the room with wide eyes, a look on their faces like they'd been searching for these chairs all afternoon.

"More pilgrims, come to see the holy blissful martyr," Robert said. "Look at them. Their promised land. But they'll abandon it in a week, because their dental practices are thriving."

Robert waved down a waitress and sent the foursome a round. "Tell them it's on him," Robert said, pointing across the table at me. "He lives here."

I smiled at the young woman. "That's fine. Thanks."

Robert was in such high spirits that he even asked about Allyson and the family. He had never met Caroline, and he'd seen Maggie only during a brief visit for her baptism. That night in St. Andrews, I'd told the kids I was going out to visit Uncle Robert, but they had no idea who that was. It was a sad circumstance, but in that moment it made me grateful, because it meant they didn't know who I was then, back when Robert wasn't such a stranger.

"It's incredible when you think about it—the coincidences, all the trips, and how it all brought us right here," he said. "It's so clear I could cry. Think about where I was—you remember where I was?"

I nodded. Five years before, I had visited Robert in the hospital after he died. It wasn't enough for him to die once—he had to flatline three times in the emergency room while docs paddled him to try to reboot his heart. It had stopped pumping after a week spent drinking in a hotel room in Philadelphia where he'd said he was holed up to work out a new business plan.

They pulled him out of his room on a stretcher after he managed to call 911. I quit drinking a short time after seeing Robert that morning, my friend hooked up to bags and a bank of blinking machines. Robert did not. A little reboot was all he needed, he said, and so St. Andrews would be his next one. A new plan in a new place.

"I used to wonder, why the hell am I still alive? What's the point?" He looked out the windows, his eyes damp and strangely sober. "It makes sense. It actually makes sense to be alive. All along, there was a point. What a fucking relief."

Robert said he would come by that week to see the family, which we both knew was an untrue but polite way to end our evening—when false courtesies overtook the conversation, it was a sign that our time was up. I wished him well and genuinely meant it, though I wondered if it might be the last time I would see Robert. I knew that the thing he loved most about St. Andrews was the chance to expire in the town where Old Tom and his sons had passed, some drunken romantic notion that he would be laid to rest next to them. *Sic transit gloria.* An end that finally fit him was the point my friend had found.

Or maybe I would see Robert in a week or a month or a year. Some people lived, danced, cried, worked, died. But Robert—he lingered. Even when he wasn't, he was there.

If Robert did find his way out of the pub and remain in St. Andrews, he would have a lifetime's worth of golf surrounding him in Fife. He would love the quirkiness of the Kingarrock course on the Hill of Tarvit estate, where you played a restored parkland nine-holer with hickory-shafted clubs and balls designed to fly turn-of-the-century distances. Before your golf, the hospitable head pro, Andrew, gave you a short primer on golf and the estate and the history of the game, then rewarded you with snacks and ginger beer after your round, a day of back-in-time golf worth the short drive from St. Andrews. The Leven and Lundin links, two side-by-side courses, shared a lofty and intertwined history: As chronicler Neil Laird points out, golf at

Leven dated to the eighteenth century, and it was likely the first golf course with eighteen distinct greens. Old Tom added his touches to its design, and Tom Jr. won the first invitational there in 1868. As the course became too crowded for the four clubs using it, Lundin and Leven eventually split the links, and each developed their own courses, the former seeking out James Braid to bolster their half of the holes. The annual MacDonald Trophy is still contested over the original layout, combining holes from both eighteens, and yellow flags on each course identify holes that comprised the old Leven layout. And there are people who care about which flags are yellow; design wonks get giggly at the mention of Leven, as the name denotes one of the hole "templates" utilized by American golf's founding father, Charles Blair MacDonald, who borrowed his hole plans from Scottish designs. His "Leven Hole" was a short, risk-reward par 4 inspired by Leven's original seventh, and you've probably played one—MacDonald's templates, including the North Berwick–inspired "Redan Hole," have been copied the golf world over.

While they were both fun tracks, I found Lundin to be the more special of the pair. The Braid pedigree showed through in the course's meticulously lumpy layout, busy with burns and gorse and green-hiding hillocks, and its condition had me guessing that Lundin's greenskeeper's budget was envied by his colleague next door. The hybrid I cut into the wind on the closing par 4 was the best shot I'd hit in years, and as I stood there watching the ball follow a path even better than the one I had intended, working against the breeze toward the Lundin clubhouse, I hoped that the windows were crowded with golfers to see my ball cozy up to the hole. As I tapped in for birdie I saw that they weren't, but a 73 on a first visit felt like my scores were settling into a proper latitude.

Elie was harder to find but worth the confusion, and the embarrassment of asking for directions to Elie as I stood, unknowingly, in the Elie pro shop. My car's GPS was outfitted with an inspired feature for finding golf courses, so each morning I simply punched up the next links on the list and followed the gentle British accent to my destination. But Elie was not on its course register, even though, as the childhood course of James Braid, it owned one of the more prominent reputations among the East Fife clubs. I eventually found a place called the Golf House Club near the village of Elie (the division between club and course would continue to confuse me, and my GPS), and when I entered the starter's hut—don't enter the clubhouse at the Golf House Club, I was told, which was a separate entity from the course—I knew I had found Elie when I saw the periscope.

Alan McPherson had foretold that I would be visiting a club with a working submarine periscope near the first tee; and after I met the starter at Elie, he invited me to come grab the handles and survey the course. The periscope had been salvaged from the HMS *Excalibur* submarine and presented to the club, and from what I could tell through its viewfinder, I was in for a giddy morning of golf played down to the water's edge, waves breaking against the bulwarks of dark cliffs and tall sand that bookended the course. I had Elie to myself on a cold, clear day, when I discovered the ocean run from holes ten through twelve to be Fife's Pebble Beach, and the most obvious of epiphanies continued to come into focus—that Scotland was stuffed with great golf courses large and small. Nearby Anstruther (called Anster by locals), a town better known for its fish and chips than its golf course, was a wee oasis of golfing bliss. Having to walk only nine holes over the compact routing inspired my enthusiasm, but Anster's fifth hole (called the Rockies) was rated the hardest par 3 in the UK, and at 245 yards off the top of a precipice and across a wasteland of sea-soaked rocks to a green tucked behind a cliff without an inch of safety between the tee and the hole—it was a tough shot. I took my five without complaining, because the nine-hole course at Anstruther was, yard for yard, as much fun as I had had with my golf clubs in a while.

My scores continued to contract across the links at Monifieth, a worthy locals' course where I drove a par 4 and made the putt for eagle, uncovering another Scottish secret to golf: hit your drive onto the green. It's easier. And my dad and I had a good day at Scotscraig, a tight links-ish course that regular Fife golfers revered. Designed by Morris and Braid and founded by R&A members who wanted an extra venue, Scotscraig was void of ocean views but boasted two or three holes that you could put up against any in Fife—particularly the fourth, called Plateau, where you drove to a landing pad hovering above wasteland with eager OB down the left, as hard as any Scottish par 4 that I had seen or played.

On the Saturday we visited Scotscraig, the course was congested with a tournament, and in all the waiting, a member struck up a conversation with my dad. The member was a round, gray-haired man whose twosome kept riding up on us in their cart. When we met on the sixth tee, I expected him to ask to play through or to complain about the pace, but he was jolly and untroubled, pleased to hear we had come to Scotscraig from the States. Often overlooked by travelers on a St. Andrews binge, the course had its own history, where David Robertson, the father of Allan, was once the official ball-maker. Scotscraig called itself the thirteenth-oldest club in the world, no matter that I was confident I had already played the thirteenth-oldest club in the world. Twice. (The ordering of Scottish clubs' origins was no small matter, it seemed, with clubs defending and trumpeting their rankings with vigor.) Scotscraig was one of the original red-coat clubs, à la the R&A and the Honourable Company, where gentlemen played in crimson jackets as if riding horseback on a hunt. The original penalty at Scotscraig for playing in less suitable attire was two bottles of port, to be donated to the membership.

As we waited on the tee box, my father explained my trip to our new friend in Fife—over one hundred courses in eight weeks—to which he replied, "I used to do that. But then the doctor gave me something and it went away." Such wit was the Scottish demeanor to me, polite and droll and proud—more Irish than English, but with a British polish and a touch of mannerly restraint, and with considerably fewer *fuck*s sprinkled into their daily dialect than their Gaelic cousins. Theirs was a curious national identity, particularly at the time of my visit, fresh off the heels of a tight national referendum in which the country (barely) voted to remain tied to England as a part of the United Kingdom. What seemed strangest about the recent vote was how few people were talking about it, as if the winners didn't want to gloat about remaining linked to their onetime adversary, and I sensed a collective, quiet unease about the way the whole thing went down.

Leading up to the vote, the independence-promoting Scottish National Party had been rerunning *Braveheart* on TV, but I was told the move for independence had less to do with William Wallace and more to do with the oil up in Aberdeen. You were far more likely to see Ferraris cruising the Granite City than Edinburgh or Glasgow (I counted three during my Aberdeen pass-through), as the oil from the North Sea off Aberdeen had made Scots wealthy and eager to keep that bounty Scottish. But it was tough for some—the majority, it turned out—to bind their fortunes to the fickle price of oil and to abandon the comforts of an ancient and reliable commonwealth. I had imagined the move for independence as a kilt-and-bagpipe affair, a Celts-versus-Angles dustup about long-fingered landlords and pure Scottish blood, but it seemed, as did most things, to come down to dollars, or pounds. What would the Euro mean for Scotland? Who would run the health system? What if oil prices took a dump (which they would soon thereafter)?

I was accustomed to the Irish birthright of resentment toward all things English, a cut-and-dried grudge between occupied and occupier. It was more complicated in Scotland, where it was great being Scottish, but not all that bad being British, too. It was convenient to reduce Scottish history to painted faces versus English armor, but Scotland's history was a jagged saga of those face-painters (the Picts, Scotland's Highland natives) clashing with the Irish-rooted Gaels, who kept their distance from the Britons, who all feared the Vikings but joined forces with them—for a while—against the Angles, until the Normans came along. It was a country born of a half dozen peoples sharing three distinct languages (English, Scottish Gaelic, and Scots, a near-extinct derivative of Old English), each with a myriad of regional dialects. It all forged a uniquely Scottish strength and identity, but perhaps an unsettled one as well, in which the meaning of Scotland for the Scottish was not so obvious to every Scot.

We didn't broach politics with our new friend at Scotscraig—it was a subject I avoided on any golf course—and what would be the point, as I knew that golf compromised the sample. Golfers skewed conservative, and in Scotland, that meant there would be more Union Jack wavers than separatists on the links. I suspected that I had inched closer to a nationalist pocket when, at Anstruther, I saw a blue-and-white flag planted on an outcropping along the coast, the Scottish banner wind-torn but untouchable on a tiny isle of rock.

It was isolated but conspicuous in a poignant way. And on the remains of a World War II–era bunker down the coast was spray-painted *Soirse Alba*— Free Scotland, in the native Gaelic tongue—a billboard aimed toward where the royalists might be walking: namely, the town golf course.

Trying to explain all this independence business to my dad would have passed some time, but instead we shared a few polite jokes and told the Scottish gentleman that we would see him on the next tee, where we would surely be waiting again. At home we would have joined up and made a foursome, but foursomes with four balls in play were relatively rare in the Scotland I had seen. Twos and threesomes seemed the regular game, and it led to a better pace, aside from today.

I was bubbling with golf rage by the time we turned at nine. Accustomed to three-hour rounds, I had lost touch with golf patience, and instead of enjoying a few extra minutes with Dad, I was convinced that this course was full of fumbling hackers who'd arrived at particularly this time to thwart my journey, a golfing conspiracy set against my having dinner with my kids. How dare they, these chops, these twitchers, wandering the links land as if the holes were there for their diversion, when there was serious business at hand?

It wasn't good when the golf slowed down; the days then presented me empty spaces that I might fill with doubt or delusion. Go was working, but pause was tired and hungry and prone to self-pity. I wasn't good enough. Golf should be easy, but some days—this day—it was a mystery, and the last thing I needed was more time to wonder how all these people could fail at it and still smile, could live and golf effortlessly when to me it was all grind.

Somewhere on the back nine we passed a tee box we had already played, where a twosome was waiting on a bench. They nodded and said hello, not a bit of bother or rush anywhere on their faces. They were bundled up comfortably and sat there waiting as if they might soon get to golf or they might not, but it would hardly matter either way. They were outdoors on a sunny afternoon in this setting of craggy earth and quiet trees, where someone had been brilliant enough to forge them a path to play a game. I walked past them to where my ball waited on the fairway, and some advice a friend once shared occurred to me: If you find yourself in a room full of assholes and you can't find one redeeming face in the crowd, then there's a good chance that you, in fact, are the asshole. This course wasn't filled with chops and rubes and morons; there was only one here, actually, and it was the guy who couldn't enjoy himself on a bright afternoon of golf with his dad.

I tried to slow my pace and notice my footsteps. I considered the air and the shapes of the holes, and the ancient seabed on which I was now standing, the waters having pressed these ripples into the soil. I summoned a little bit of gratitude for my circumstances, and the rest of the back nine went peacefully, even as I pulled my drive on eighteen so far to the left that getting home in two required a cut 6-iron off an adjacent fairway and over a cluster of trees to a deep pin I couldn't see through the branches. I didn't see my ball land on the green, and I had to guess from the ball mark that it hit long and reversed its way back to the cup, where I tapped in for the best birdie I had yet made in Scotland. There were no demands or requirements or grind in that three; there was just hit and follow and tally. And once again, the less I demanded, the kinder the sum.

Found

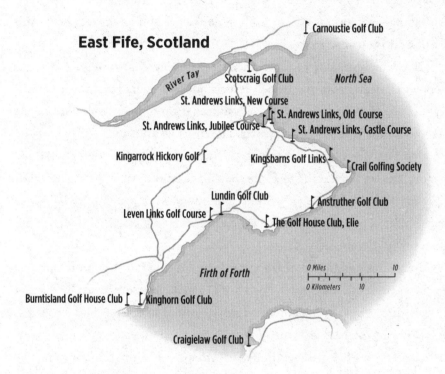

East Fife, Scotland

[Carnoustie Golf Club

River Tay

Scotscraig Golf Club

North Sea

St. Andrews Links, New Course

[St. Andrews Links, Old Course

St. Andrews Links, Jubilee Course

[St. Andrews Links, Castle Course

Kingarrock Hickory Golf [

Kingsbarns Golf Links

[Crail Golfing Society

Lundin Golf Club

[Anstruther Golf Club

Leven Links Golf Course [

[The Golf House Club, Elie

Firth of Forth

0 Miles   10

0 Kilometers   10

Burntisland Golf House Club [[Kinghorn Golf Club

Craigielaw Golf Club [

Overlooking the seaside village that shared its name, Kinghorn was a sneaky little liar of a golf course. At just over five thousand yards, it had me teeing off in expectation of a quick waltz across the dunes; I got Kinghorned instead. Back in 1850-some, Old Tom discovered a way to design a course in which every hole played uphill, a course whose scorecard flaunted junior distances like some sort of pernicious lure, pulling in linksmen unprepared for the battle ahead. But I cherished my afternoon on a surprising and somewhat forgotten Morris gem for its zany par 3 holes and endless ascents, for the extraordinary company, and for the fact that the starter could not have given two sheep about who I was and why I was there.

I'd grown accustomed to feigned recognition in the pro shop—*Ah, yes, the wandering golf-writing person*—followed by directions to the first tee. But at Kinghorn, the gentleman in the starter's office listened to my spiel about my cross-UK endeavor and my prearranged tee time via the tourism office as if I were reciting obscure French poetry. When I finished, he responded with Philadelphian frankness: "Right. I don't have you on the tee sheet. And we don't do courtesy greens fees."

The Kinghorn rate of fourteen quid was generous enough, and I was happy to pay and play as a true visitor on a locals' course that was operated by the Fife Golf Trust, an organization keener on selling tee times to Scots than to busloads of my countrymen. The club's website and scorecard made no mention of its Morris heritage, so I felt as if I were playing a bit of hidden history known only to the locals in the village below. And after a serendipitous meeting with the man who became my playing partner, I would love everything about this curious little course that was worth so much more than my twenty bucks.

I was chasing my scorecard toward the parking lot—upon my opening the door from the clubhouse, it had been ripped out of my hands by the sort of gale that people in my country chased around in vans but here was dismissed as a fresh breeze—when I literally bumped into a foursome of members coming off the eighteenth green. Perhaps it was my fumbling, apelike gait that revealed I hailed from yonder, but whatever the tell, one of them asked where I was from and whether I was heading out to play alone. John was in his retirement years but was fit, and he was determined that I not play Kinghorn for the first time without a chaperone.

John proudly navigated me through a clifftop amusement park of crisscrossing fairways and vistas of cold, dark water. He pointed out two tiny islands in the Firth of Forth that, when I zoomed in with my camera, resembled a battleship and a surfaced submarine parked in the current. Structures had been built on the islands during the World Wars to deceive the periscopes of German U-boats, and from the Kinghorn tee boxes, they still did the trick. He pointed out the nearby peak that locals called Crying Hill, as it was the vantage for a final view of loved ones leaving Scotland by choice or by force, and he made note of the town graveyard below number eighteen where witches were once strangled and burned on Witches' Hill. I assumed these slaughters were the reason the eighteenth tee was cursed with a twenty-degree upward tilt and a blind skyward drive that felt like hitting from the depths of the netherworld. He showed me the Kinghorn beach, where Scottish King Alexander III died in 1286 when his horse fell off a cliff, and he translated my favorite hole name in all of Scotland for me as he took a picture of me standing by a tee box sign on fourteen that read *Lang Whang* (long path, or long hit, in the local dialect).

John's pride in Kinghorn was matched only by the pride he showed in his gear. I was a longtime Mizuno devotee and couldn't help but notice he was playing Mizuno everything (including Mizuno balls, which I had never seen Stateside), with bag and glove and jacket to match. I remarked about our shared brand loyalty, and he promptly put my dedication to shame by rolling up his sleeve and showing me the Mizuno logo tattooed on his forearm. Because his tattoo made perfect sense to me, I knew I had found a kindred spirit, and it was comforting to spend some time in the company of one of my golf-afflicted brethren.

I had been collecting logo balls and ball markers during my visit and was disappointed that I wouldn't be able to add Kinghorn to my gallery at trip's end. There was no pro shop or club paraphernalia to speak of, but John, being golf mad and knowing what a golf souvenir meant to our lot, offered to find one of his Kinghorn ball markers at home and deliver it to me that week in St. Andrews, a good forty-five minutes' drive up the coast. I described our location to him but didn't expect him to actually go through so much trouble. And then I arrived home from golf a few days later to find a Kinghorn ball marker waiting for me on South Street, a kind note from John attached. His wife had stopped in and met my entire family that afternoon, charming them in full and leaving my souvenir. She told them she wished me health on my journey and a quick return.

I don't play tennis or racquetball or pickup basketball, but I don't think you meet these kinds of people when you do. Maybe I'm wrong. But I doubt it.

•   •   •

Perhaps it was collective guilt in this southeast corner of Fife about all the witch-broiling (the area had been an epicenter of Scottish witch-purging) that made the inhabitants so affable today, but that afternoon, after being offered a bacon roll in the clubhouse, I found a playing partner as joyful as John in Kinghorn's neighboring town of Burntisland. Golf at Burntisland dated to 1688, and the club called itself the tenth oldest in the world. The parkland/links blend was carved into cliffs overlooking the firth and had Morris and Braid and Willie Park Jr.'s fingerprints on it, but I found its architectural vintage was upstaged by the company of Edward, a host who was a few years my senior, with a thin build and a bespectacled-schoolteacher vibe. I thought I had joined up with a reserved historian for my tour of Burntisland, but I soon discovered I'd been partnered with one of the resident characters who provided not only an education in playing Burntisland but also instruction in how to enjoy it, a golfer who could both laugh and lament in the same breath.

Edward pointed out the former mining villages that had once thrived in the hills around the course, the remains of formerly bustling towns grown over with forest. History was always close along the coast of Scotland; I had expected plenty of golf lore, but it was the remains of World Wars and ancient clans that reminded me that golf was relatively new to this landscape where legends had been born and embellished before my country had even been discovered. Burntisland took its name from either the Romans' attempts to burn the village to the ground, fishermen's charring their huts on its coastline, or the appearance of a nearby island of dark, sooty rocks. Romans were more exciting than rocks, so Edward gave naming credit to their legions.

As a course guide, Edward was handy at pointing out sight lines for my drives on the tight and tumultuous track—"That red van in the distance is a good line . . . well, if it would stop moving"—while he described to me his role as one of the caretakers of the links. The course was dotted with a few tiny ponds that he explained were old quarry pits, each precariously deep. In one of the pools, dead fish had recently been spotted floating on the surface.

"One of the lady members was on to me about it," he said. "She wrote an email: 'Something must be done about it!' So I thought, *Yes, I will do something*. I hit delete."

His teasing the lady members was mild play compared to Edward's welcome routine for newcomers to Burntisland (which for some reason I was spared). Like most Scottish courses I'd played, the grounds were shared with rabbits and occasional piles of their pebbly scat. Edward would put a few coffee beans in his mouth before heading out onto the links with first-timers, and later on would inconspicuously drop the beans around his ball on the fairway. He would call the guests over to explain a local rule stating that you were allowed relief from hare droppings.

"Like this here; I'm entitled to a drop," he would explain, pointing to his ball sitting atop a pile of wet brown beans, "as long as you're sure it's rabbit shit. I'll check." His partners' eyes would go wide as he picked up one of the beans and popped it into his mouth.

"Yup," he would say, swishing the bean around his teeth. "Rabbit shite for sure."

The crisscrossing quarry course was unlike any I had played in the UK, all serpentine holes wrapped up in wild knots, with cliffs and bumps and stone embankments that had me unable to find a boring bit, and its blind par 3 seventeenth was as much joy as a golfer can find in 150 yards. I scraped together a decent 74 on a course you would want to play a dozen times before claiming to know all its angles. Edward had struggled and lipped out a half dozen putts during our round, and after burning yet another edge on seventeen, the mild-mannered club historian noted, "I've shaved more holes today than a maternity ward."

I thought I'd heard every clichéd golfing depiction ever concocted, but at Burntisland, my putting lexicon expanded with unwholesome glory.

In my search for golfing miracles, I found a pocketful at St. Andrews. They aren't difficult to locate around the Old Course, where even the divots hold a puff of magic. Divots on the Old explode in the wind, a sandy burst instead of a scalp of turf being the mark of a genuine links. Unless, of course, those puffs were breezes full of grandpa; a caddie informed me that visitors' sprinkling Dad's ashes on the Old was a weekly occurrence—a cloud of smoke, and *There goes another one! Rest in peace!*

It was a course that did not require a case to be made on its behalf. It actively hosted more majors than any venue save Augusta National; it was highly accessible and had been experienced by traveling golfers the world over; and its history, from Robertson to the Morris men, from the origins of the eighteen-hole round (golf as an eighteen-hole affair was born on the Old Course) to the seven double greens with two pins in each to the Road Hole and the Swilcan Bridge and the Hell Bunker to the fact that you could actually play the course clockwise or counterclockwise, made the place more catalogued and chronicled than any property in golf. But the Old never gets old, not when you're standing on the first tee and you understand that this patch of tight grass is the only space on earth that has been shared by everyone who ever meant anything to the game of golf (save Ben Hogan, who never did cross the Swilcan) and that they all did precisely what you're about to do—albeit in a straighter and farther fashion.

Playing a few months before the 2015 Open, with grandstands already erected around the course, was an unplanned thrill, but doing so with my eighty-one-year-old father whose ocean-crossing golf trips had seemed a thing of the past was true grace, a blessing I could not earn nor repay. I suspected I was the luckiest golfer on the planet. And then I *knew* I was the luckiest golfer on the planet when I returned home that afternoon from the Old Course with my marriage still intact and my vows still wrapped firmly around my finger.

A mutual friend had made an introduction for me to John Boyne, a top looper at St. Andrews who looked like a fitter version of Darren Clarke. John took my bag and enlisted his friend Denny Coyne to carry for my father. I couldn't recall the last time my dad had walked a golf course; it was likely eight years before in Ireland, where at Tralee he had purchased the wool cap that was now pulled snugly down around his ears. For months, I had compiled a list of hopes for my round on the Old with Dad: shoot a low score on a course where Rory and his ilk would be teeing it up that summer; own the Road Hole/take on the hotel without fear; pose for an album's worth of shots with my father on the Swilcan Bridge, one foot propped up on the wall in my best Nicklaus impression; win applause from at least one tourist watching golfers finish on eighteen. Some of these hopes would be realized, but they would all be supplanted by a new dream for that afternoon: that Dad and I both remain upright for most—perhaps all—of our five-hour round on a frigid day that would have sent meeker souls to church instead of the golf course. It was an end-times wind.

Denny Coyne kept the mood bright by educating us on the history of the Coyne clan, and even presented my dad with a copy of our family coat of arms. They got along like the cousins they might have been, and on the third hole, Denny inquired about the course Dad played back home.

"Oh, it's a course outside Philadelphia. You wouldn't know it. LuLu Country Club."

"LuLu?" Denny said. "In Glenside?"

My dad's eyes widened. *My caddie at St. Andrews knows LuLu?* He stammered at the inconceivable coincidence, explaining that yes, that was the very course.

"Is Jonny Rusk still there?" Denny asked, invoking the head golf pro.

Dad was astonished to near speechlessness. He laughed and shook his head, then said that Jon was there and was doing a great job. Dad talked of LuLu and his head pro until they reached the fourth, when he stopped and asked Denny, "So how do you know Jon and LuLu?"

Denny shouldered his bag and walked ahead. "Don't have a clue about either," he said. "But I can read your bag tag."

On the wind-ruined sixth hole, as we watched our balls play Ouija on the green, sliding around in circles with no help from us, John confided that they would have suspended play if this were the Open. I decided bogeys were fair scores and went about making plenty of them. On the twelfth tee, we watched players to our right go sprinting after windblown trolleys, their golf clubs blasting across the fairway at a good twenty knots. When one trolley launched off the edge of a pot bunker, the wind lifted it up into the air for a moment—a poignant breath, poetic almost—and then slam-dunked it into the pit, bag somersaulting and clubs exploding like gear off a wrecked skier. We chuckled without moving our mouths, lips frozen into thin grins and lines of dried tears traced along our temples.

I'd had too many such moments so far in the UK, where the elements seemed so set against my endeavor that I felt I was practicing endurance instead of golf, and where I wondered how there was anything fun about this game that was FLOG spelled backward. The frozen fingers and the pin-snapping wind did more than push our balls around—it blew away the artifice and whipped back a curtain, revealing golf to be a silly, sinister endeavor of placing tiny balls into tiny holes using glorified garden hoes. It made you forget what you loved about this expensive and demanding and delinquent spouse and wonder why you were with her in the first place.

Scores quickly became irrelevant, and the dream round's dream was again streamlined: get Dad to dinner in good-enough shape that Mom wouldn't have to spoon his soup into his mouth.

A retired stockbroker from an era of smoky trading pits and deals done via handshakes, Dad had been through a lot; he beat cancer and buried a brother, survived his kids' calamities and scraped through grim markets. Age had worn some curve into his stature over recent years, and the unsteadiness of eighty-one was more noticeable now in his hands and steps, but his mind was clear, and at St. Andrews he once again proved himself a tougher man than me. While in my head I was whining like an infant spoiled by too much golf, an insufferable brat who got everything he wanted and found it lacking, Dad played on without complaint. He even smiled, and he showed me what it was to love a day—a single day—as he savored good shots and bad. He popped his ball out of Hell Bunker in one shot and made a solid six on the Road Hole. His quick smile on the Swilcan Bridge (we didn't pose for long) was entirely real. And so was mine, because I had just narrowly avoided one of the most tragic rounds in the history of husband golf. The Old Course had thrown her best shot at us, and for our resilience had rewarded us with a fantasy outcome of Tolkienesque proportions.

Allyson had given much to the golf courses of Ireland and Scotland, losing her husband to the links for months at a time. But when I looked at my fingers on the thirteenth to check that they were still there, I noticed that the blue and bony icicles looked wrong. Curious; was something missing? My left hand was too light, too bare—and a shot of instant guilt ran from my throat to the bottom of my ass. Now the links had taken the ring Allyson had given me, too. I'd never thought it unwise that I played golf wearing my wedding ring, or that I took my glove off after almost every shot. It turned out that it was.

Lost pounds had made the ring loose without my noticing, and that afternoon's freeze shrunk my fingers two more sizes. I looked out over the links that now seemed to expand into a vast continent of shoulder-height shrubs and wondered where that golden hoop might be hiding. So many shots, so many steps, so many trips into the high stuff. I imagined two hobbits hiking the dunes and pits, but their ring hunt was duck soup compared to the impossibility facing me. A cliché came to life in my imagination—a needle in a haystack had nothing on a wedding ring on a golf course.

I was technically still golfing, but in my mind, I was forecasting a conversation: *Do you remember that time you lost my sunglasses and how I didn't get upset? Even though they were prescription?* I hadn't wept since high school and worried about my ability to conjure tears at the appropriate time. The girls would be waiting at eighteen, so maybe if I burst into sobs after picking my ball out of the hole—*My day at St. Andrews! Ruined!*—I could turn resentment into sympathy. Perhaps I could talk John into staging a greenside mugging. Worst case, I was sure there were jewelers in St. Andrews. *Dear, what better way to commemorate our time in St. Andrews than with new wedding bands?* I didn't notice the caddie running toward us as we waited on the sixteenth tee, and if I had, I would have probably hidden out of shame.

He was out of breath when he reached us, but what a beautiful breath it was that he had left in him: "Did anyone lose a wedding ring?"

I've had only one hole-in-one in my golfing life—a weak sum, really, considering the amount of golf I've played. But all the near aces were redeemed, and no albatross or triple-eagle could have felt more inexplicable. The ring looked brighter this afternoon than it did on my wedding day; on that morning, it had arrived as no surprise. But at St. Andrews, life proffered a miracle. Luck, coincidence, providence—I rarely noticed them when I wasn't on a golf course. Maybe that's what kept all of us sadists coming back.

The small stone hump of the Swilcan Bridge on eighteen gets all the photos, and there are some corners of Augusta that must feel pretty special, but for me, the shared expanse of the first tee and the eighteenth green on the Old at St. Andrews is the altar of golf. My favorite golf shot out of many thousands was played to the center of it, where I saw two redheads in pink St. Andrews ski caps bouncing around behind the green, waiting for their dad to come take them to dinner.

I putted out for par and Dad saved a scrappy five, and Maggie and Caroline ran down onto the green to hug me and their grandfather, entirely unaware of the hallowed ground upon which they were standing. That was what was so unique and so transcendent about St. Andrews: it wore its lore effortlessly, and it gave me my moment on eighteen at the Old. No matter who lifted the Jug there in July, I would know a small piece of what they were feeling as they stepped to the green and understood perfect in a whole new way.

As divine as an afternoon that ended on golf's altar was, the following evening I learned that there was an even more celestial experience nearby, back behind the altar in the sacristy known as the clubhouse of the Royal & Ancient Golf Club.

I allowed myself certain prejudices in life and in golf. Scientologists, golfers who buttoned their top button, and links built in the last fifty years were all a priori suspicious in my estimation, so I took some baggage with me to Kingsbarns, the raved-about new links down the road from St. Andrews. In fairness, golf had been played in the area by the Kingsbarns Golfing Society since 1793, but their course had long since been plowed under, and its latest installment was opened in 2000 and designed by Mark Parsinen and Kyle Phillips, the latter of international design fame for recent courses in Korea, America, and the UAE. I was prepared to dismiss this course as overpriced and tailored to foreign visitors (a round plus caddie will run you north of $400), convinced through much research that the greatest links were discovered, not shaped, and therefore courses built after the advent of bulldozers should be discounted as man-made imitations instead of true, organic gems. I felt confident in my closed-mindedness and satisfied with my antidesign proclivities, and I was almost sad to see my philosophy discarded at Kingsbarns. I had been invited to come play the course in a Scottish tourism outing, where I quickly learned that I had been dumb to judge the new guy for being new. He had plenty to offer, it turned out, as Kingsbarns earned its place on a short list of courses for which I would sign a credit card receipt without looking.

From the pro shop welcome to the practice grounds to the perfectly diminutive clubhouse—a small stone castle where I enjoyed a bacon roll and views of a mountain range of golf holes set against blue-black seas—Kingsbarns seemed to have nailed a kick-ass golf day before I even stepped foot on the course. And when I did, I found a links where the ocean seemed to watch every shot on a property that had not compromised the landscape for any sort of phony drama. With each new tee box came a fresh smile and another highlight; I was having too much fun to mind losing Open tickets for closest to the pin on number eight, where my invincible fourteen inches was bested by a hole-in-one. *Did that roar come from eight? You're joking.*

"Hard lines," my Scottish playing partner told me, a native lament I had come to learn meant tough luck.

Hard lines indeed. I had plans for getting my own Open tickets, anyway.

It would have been a great day of golf if it had ended on eighteen, but this was the first time on the trip when I was more excited for dinner than I was for the round. The tourist board had special plans for us back in St. Andrews, so I showered and dressed in jacket and tie and left the family with meat pies from the butcher across the street (let us all pray that someday meat pies will come to American ovens) while I walked alone through town to my dinner reservation.

Set at the end of the Old Course, the tall gray stone of the R&A wasn't surrounded by any fence or barriers—just another old building in an old town—but in my mind, it was enshrined inside a force field of history and legend. The idea that I was going to enter it, to walk through its doors without an alarm sounding—I didn't quite believe it, especially when I went to the wrong door and stood there knocking, nervous and ready to cry. A butler showed me into a drawing room where golfers from our outing were cocktailing amid trophy cases and bookshelves crowded with golf tomes. There was an excitement among us as we talked about matters of no consequence, a collective energy about where we were standing that made chitchat feel joyful and rare. And then suddenly my shoulders jumped at what sounded like gunshots, and we all turned to find a butler banging a gavel against an old, certainly historic board that he had set against the sash of the doorway.

"Dinner is served!" he informed us with an almost angry formality that felt pitch-perfect in context. I lagged behind the group as we were shown upstairs, searching the shelves of books for any that might resemble my own—it was the longest of shots, but so was my having dinner in the R&A. No such luck, and with a fresh dollop of humility in my pocket, I scrambled to catch up and find a seat at one of two long tables where a description of the coming meal was waiting at my place—*Beef Wellington, yes, that will do nicely*—with R&A stamped in the corner, a menu that somehow found its way into my jacket that evening and ended up on my office wall. (I don't always eat beef Wellington with the Claret Jug set at the head of my table, but when I do, I steal the menu.)

We worked our way through a parade of dishes as I soaked up stories from my neighboring golf journalists and power players, gents who spoke of pints with Ernie Els and weekends in Spain with Rory. We finished our custards and were escorted back down to the first floor and into what looked like a small ballroom for after-dinner drinks. I could tell by the angled windows that we were in the room I had always wondered about from outside, where the walls of the R&A bowed outward toward the course and, from afar, looked like the greatest seat in golf. There were a handful of sharply dressed men drinking from glass tankards in the light of those famed windows as the sun set over the course. We presumed them to be members, and the rest of us kept a safe distance on the other side of the gallery with our cookies and tea.

A giant portrait of Queen Elizabeth guarded a fireplace wide enough to sleep in, and paintings of men in red jackets adorned the high walls. The lower portions of the walls were covered with old oak panels with names etched into the wood. I wondered to one of my compatriots about the names—were they past captains? Golf Hall of Famers? Knights Templar? He told me that the panels were actually doors. He pointed to small keyholes and explained that what I was essentially standing in was the grandest locker room in the world. There were golf shoes and dirty socks and golf bags behind those doors; this room that seemed appropriate for royal nuptials was a place for members to change their shoes. The longer you were a member, the better your locker position, so this was a room of R&A old-timers who might rarely play, while the newer members had to put on their trousers down in the basement, which I was sure was the greatest basement in golf. There was cool in golf, and then there was changing-your-pants-in-this-room cool. All these names of old men—do they appreciate their forgotten lockers, or how much we would have given to drop our wet socks into one? *Privilege*, I thought; *it's so wasted on the privileged.*

On my way out that evening, I stopped by the glass case in the lobby for a picture. Inside was the genuine Claret Jug (not the winner's replica that we had dined with), which I would learn was named not for some golfing Earl of Claret but for the Claret wine Brits enjoyed from jugs of a similar style. Next to the Jug was the Challenge Belt. I'd always thought of the Claret Jug as the oldest trophy in sports (though if you count yachting as a sport, the nod actually goes to the Americas Cup), but the Jug is predated by the maroon leather and silver buckle of the Challenge Belt that was originally awarded to the Open champ. The rules stipulated that any three-time winner got to retain the belt, which Tom Morris Jr. accomplished in 1870, so with no trophy to play for, the Open wasn't held in 1871. The golfers came back when Prestwick, St. Andrews, and Musselburgh chipped in for the Jug, but it wasn't ready in time for the 1872 tournament, so that year's winner got a gold medal, and Open winners still do—today's victors are announced as "champion golfer and winner of the gold medal." Jug, belt, and medal—it was the only championship I knew that celebrated its winner with a trinity of trophies, as if everything an Open win embodied could not be contained in one vessel, no matter how fine the silver. I left the R&A more convinced than ever that the Open held no rival as a golf tournament. Perhaps it was the beef Wellington talking, but from my view in St. Andrews, green jackets were nice, but you couldn't leave the house without a belt.

When Caroline woke up with a scary fever the following morning, I was shaken from my golf myopia and reminded that I was a father with responsibilities larger than a tournament in June. My morning tee time at the Panmure links, a renowned Open qualifier, would have to wait for the next trip to Fife. It felt strange to pause the obsession for a moment and put something—or someone—ahead of golf, but I needed a rest as much as my daughter did. I found a doctor in case we needed her, and that afternoon I took Caroline's sister, Maggie, out for a walk on the beach and a visit to the aquarium down by the water, just behind the R&A. We climbed down onto the strand, and she clambered over the beach rocks and found tidal pools with shells and strange seaweeds that she wanted to bring home to show her sister.

The sun was bright, and we were warm in our thin jackets, and on an unhurried day, it became clear to me that I was not a jug hoister or a belt wearer. When it came to my golf, I wasn't destined for so much as a plastic spoon, and that was fine. As I watched Maggie run circles in the sand, I was a dad. A pretty good one, I hoped. I wanted to qualify—more than anything, I wanted to play on—but in the sun in St. Andrews, I felt my need to prove something slipping away. Standing here in front of me was proof, four feet tall in yellow boots, that life was stuffed with the extraordinary. I thought I had to keep fighting and grinding to grab it, but it turned out that I just needed to notice. And because I did notice now, I could give this shot my honest everything without worrying about its results, hoping that it would help Maggie do the same someday—to see her dreams and be unreasonable in her pursuit of them.

• • •

On my list of many courses, there was only one whose name conjured actual fear. Perhaps the panic came from the 1999 bloodbath of an Open Championship, when the links famously left a poor Frenchman barefoot in a burn, and where the winner's score of six over was a throwback to the days of hickory-shafted champions. But if you gave most golfers a free-association test and threw them the word "Carnoustie," the flinch responses would be "Hard," or "Really hard," or perhaps, as the locals called it, "Car-Nasty."

When I told Dad that the last round of his week in Scotland would be at the site of Jean van de Velde's unwatchable collapse, I could see the apprehension in his eyes as he gazed off into the distance and nodded, whispering "Carnoustie" with the look of a willing but outnumbered soldier.

In case you missed it—and you're lucky if you did—in 1999, the French pro brought a three-stroke lead to the final hole, prompting the Claret Jug engraver to begin etching his name into the trophy. He would soon go hunting for sandpaper as van de Velde knocked his ball around the grandstands, taking off his shoes and standing in a stream to contemplate a water blast, and eventually getting up and down out of the sand for a triple bogey that led to a playoff he would lose to Scotsman Paul Lawrie. Sadly for Lawrie, few remember that his record-setting *ten-shot* comeback on the final day was one of the greatest feats in golf; it would forever be overshadowed by one of the most tragic.

Some might remember Carnoustie for the Irish pride of Pádraig Harrington's breakthrough win in 2007, or the birth of Tom Watson's links love affair in 1975, or Ben Hogan's victory during his only trip to the UK, where his gutsy play on number six between death bunkers and out-of-bounds led to the hole being named "Hogan's Alley." But most of us recall watching golf on a Sunday morning back in the 1990s and feeling that sick excitement the Romans must have felt in the Colosseum as lions had their lunch. For all the pain and empathy, I remember feeling a tinge of relief as well—golf was hard for everyone, it turned out, and it could embarrass us all.

I expected to find black clouds swirling above a haunted clubhouse, with a soundtrack of grim organ music and a staff dressed in funeral colors. But there were no hearses queued up in the parking lot at Carnoustie; rather, it was a bright and cheery place with a modern clubhouse and a laughing starter eager for us to have a great day. Like St. Andrews, the course was a true municipal track shared by six golf clubs, and the spirit of welcome was palpable, most notably in our sage caddie, Steve, who came along to carry for my father.

In his early thirties, Steve was wrapped up in wind gear and tattered hiking boots with a cigarette held in his teeth, but I could tell before shaking his hand that he was a player moonlighting as a looper. I had learned to spot the sticks over the years; it was their comfort on the course, combined with the sinewy frame of someone who spent more on tournament entries than on meals. Steve had that lean, unshaven, unimpressed look of a person who golfed with his rent check and for whom an Open venue was his natural setting. For Steve, it actually was—he had grown up on the Carnoustie links and played on professional tours around the world. He was a journeyman on hiatus, making a few pounds and visiting his family before plotting his next season on the minitours. Maybe it was the way he skillfully lit his cigarette in a thirty-mile-per-hour wind or how he didn't flinch at Dad's mishits, but his was the look of a golfing creature, and this was his living room, while I too often felt like I was crashing in somebody else's. I wanted that look and that feeling. I wasn't going to leave Carnoustie without asking him how he'd gotten it.

Dad played steady golf around Car-Nasty, knocking low and short shots along the fairway but keeping his ball in play and out of the bunkers. Steve coached him around with enthusiasm and good humor, handing my dad the 4-wood without his having to ask for it and reading the requisite two inches of wind into Dad's putts. On the sixth green, Steve knelt down behind Dad's ball and confidently declared, "Two cups outside left." When Dad missed left by a good four feet, Steve explained, "I didn't say two Stanley Cups."

Perhaps it was my pent-up Carnoustie anxiety, but I played my nines by a flip-flopped script. The back nine and the final five holes were supposed to be the card-wreckers, but I played them in one over par, making the four on the final hole that van de Velde had so needed, and I parred the 446-yard tenth that had the best name on the card. It was called South America, and Steve explained that its curious moniker came from a clubhouse party many years before. A local lad was shipping off to seek his fortunes in South America, so they celebrated him with a proper sendoff, at which most of the Scotch in Scotland was consumed. The merriment inspired him to set out on his trek to South America that very evening, and when he was found asleep near the tenth hole the next morning, the name of his destination stuck.

I flailed my way through the front nine, where I attempted to play down Hogan's Alley on six but instead blazed a new path down Coyne's Crumbling Sidewalk, sampling a medley of bunkers on my way to double bogey. I feared I wasn't going to be able to summon the courage to ask Steve about the secrets to his game, not after a front-side 44; surely he would dismiss me with a charitable "Keep your head down, and keep swinging." But after navigating my ball safely over the famed Spectacles on fourteen in two shots (the two side-by-side bunkers that gobbled approaches on the par 5 resembled spectacles if you missed them but looked more like giant sheep balls if you didn't), my confidence was buoyed. I managed a par on the 245-yard sixteenth, a hole Watson called the hardest par 3 in golf, and I somehow kept my ball out of the snaking Barry Burn on seventeen and eighteen, both played into a wind that doubled their already punishing length. The looping burn plagued the closing holes and seemed to defy the rules of nature—water was not meant to flow in nine directions at once, and Bernard Darwin had aptly described the stream as "the ubiquitous circumbendibus." As we approached the finish I closed with a string of hard-fought pars, so I sidled up to Steve and asked him what was going through his mind when he was playing his best.

"I don't know. I'm not thinking about much, really. I'm just thinking about going low. If I'm swinging well, that's it—just go low."

Just go low. Easy enough. I should have expected an unsatisfying answer to such an obvious question. I already knew that when you were playing well, your head was mostly empty. But Steve did elaborate after a drag.

"In a tournament, I'm just thinking about fundamentals. I'm thinking about using what's working on that day. Every day, your makeup is different.

Your nerves, your muscles, your head—it's always different. You can't change it. So you go with what you have on the day. Stay on your fundamentals, use the shot you have with you, and make birdies."

I was interested to hear him hint at acceptance and not forcing a game you didn't bring with you. His keys might have seemed overly plain, but as with all grand mysteries, the answers were wrapped in simplicity. The player's mind-set was not one of *Go pretty good* or *Go to not shame yourself* or *Go look good* or *Go make the right swing* or *Go find that backswing position you've been working on with your coach for a year but can't quite find this morning* or *Go make them think you can play* or *Go so they'll say generous things*; rather, it was go to one place, and fuck everywhere else: *Go low.*

Steve also shared that he would not have played golf today. He was glad he was caddying, because playing in wind like this had wrecked his swing in the past.

"My coach tells me to take two days off if I play in bad wind. You start making swings in this stuff that you need to forget about. You can learn a bad way."

I understood what he was telling me, and it hit a vulnerable spot. I didn't have the luxury of two days, let alone two hours to put down the clubs, and I could feel how this week's tempest had left my swing feeling like I was throwing wild haymakers at my golf ball. With a little more than a month to go, I'd expected my links moves to be thoroughly grooved by now, but there was nothing groovy about punchy stabs at a wobbly golf ball.

Acceptance, he said. Well, the wind would have to change, because my itinerary wouldn't. I was sticking with the plan that brought me here, and I was trusting the powers that had me completing Carnoustie with my eighty-one-year-old father, who had just finished the toughest closing stretch in golf in a wind that would have kept a Tour player indoors, and neither one of us took off our shoes even once. Who knew—maybe the wind would be blowing fifty miles per hour at Bruntsfield. If it was, I would have to find a bookmaker and double all bets.

• • •

As we loaded my family's car seats and suitcases into the back of a taxi van, I was reminded of the rationale behind my irrational itinerary. I recalled thinking as I filled my spreadsheet with two or three rounds per day, loading up blank dates once reserved for rest, that not only did I want to cover every corner but I didn't want to leave any gaps to mull or meander. My mind was safest when occupied, and on departure day, I was grateful for the diversion of the busy week ahead as I kissed my girls and buckled them into the cab. I'd left myself no choice but to get on the road and race for the next tee time at Montrose before my afternoon round at Stonehaven. And thank goodness, because if I didn't have the obsession to distract me, I would have pondered the upcoming month away from Allyson and the kids, imagining my new trajectory up into the Highlands where the golf grew sparer and had me hopping ferries and planes to far-flung islands, and I might have climbed into the taxi with them.

As I plugged Montrose into my car's GPS, I took consolation in the knowledge that we would someday revisit St. Andrews, and that my kids would again play in the garden behind Cowper's Close. Allyson wouldn't leave without insisting we come back to this new home away from home. Now it was up to her husband and his sack of clubs to find out how soon that return would be.

Honor

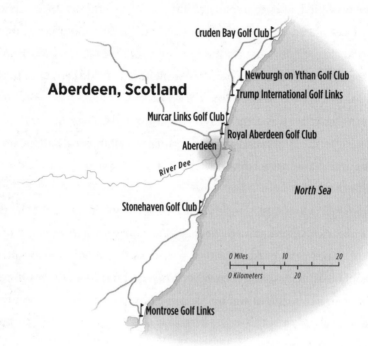

Cruden Bay Golf Club

Newburgh on Ythan Golf Club
Trump International Golf Links

Aberdeen, Scotland

Murcar Links Golf Club
Royal Aberdeen Golf Club

Aberdeen

River Dee

North Sea

Stonehaven Golf Club

0 Miles   10   20
0 Kilometers   20

Montrose Golf Links

I feared that I had set off Scotland's fireworks in the third inning. I'd surely read its finest and final chapter too early at St. Andrews, and by going counterclockwise, I might have gotten Scotland all out of order. But as I blazed my path up toward Aberdeen and Inverness, I discovered that St. Andrews, though it would remain unrivaled as the universe's ideal municipality, was just a golfing amuse-bouche for the links bacchanalia ahead of me, to the point that in a week's time I would be playing the course I would come to call the finest in the entire home of golf.

My Irish travels had taught me that once you'd played all the links, you would consistently be asked to confess your favorite. Carne in brilliant

Belmullet was my go-to Irish medalist, but I needed to identify its Scottish counterpart, so my eyes and feet were on high alert for a darling. Just as I had at Carne, I would know it before I knew it, an epiphany of spirit and body born of a cosmic confluence of circumstances that fired my every neuron, leaving me weightless and overwhelmingly aware. It was Faraday in the laboratory, Newton under the apple tree, my kids at Chuck E. Cheese's: a click of discovery and relief wherein all was revealed, right before you bought every last shirt in the pro shop. I trusted that it would happen for me in Scotland, not knowing that it was going to happen twice, and that the first such revelation lay just up the road in the shadow of Dracula's castle.

My search for golf's secrets was designed to include the first, the finest, and the farthest courses of the UK—the westernmost, northernmost, and southernmost links, the longest courses and the shortest—but I couldn't have expected that I would visit the most holey of all golf courses, until I showed up for my round at the Montrose Links with a Scot named John Adams. Given the history of the place, his name sounded about right.

John explained how golf had been recorded on these links as far back as 1562, making it the fifth-oldest recorded links in the world and, at one time, a golfing loop that held more holes than any course in the world. Montrose formerly boasted a layout of twenty-five holes, and in 1866 it hosted the first and only twenty-five-hole pro golf championship, at which Willie Park and Old Tom competed for a purse larger than they were offering in the Open, where you just got a belt.

Scotland's original links varied in their tally of golf holes; most held closer to five or six and were meant to be played two or three times, until St. Andrews's twenty-two-hole rounds (in which ten of the holes on the twelve-hole layout were played twice) were shortened to eighteen-hole outings by way of combining fairways and enlarging the putting greens. It was Allan Robertson who stretched the carpets and gave birth to St. Andrews's famed double greens, where two pins share the same putting surface; one pin to be played to on your way out, the other on your way in, allowing for an ingenious method of course preservation whereby the Old was alternately played in clockwise and counterclockwise directions to manage wear. The R&A's

rules of 1842 decided that eighteen holes consecrated a match, and its members' broad sway eventually saw other courses following St. Andrews's lead.

It took a while for that number to become the standard, but the move toward the eighteen-hole round signaled a shift in golf's power structure. Golf's original standardized Leith rules had the Honourable Company of Edinburgh Golfers taking the lead as golf's trendsetters, but in the centuries-long pissing match among the gentlemen of Musselburgh, Muirfield, Prestwick, Bruntsfield, and the like, the acceptance of the eighteen-hole round perhaps marked the moment when the R&A's influence outdistanced that of its club peers. Golf, once a tribal miscellany of rival clubs playing a variable sport in their own showcase invitational tournaments, began to coalesce into an identifiable form under the leadership of the Royal & Ancient, a post the R&A still occupies. For a game so tightly governed today, it's strange to think of golf as an untamed and blithe pastime unencumbered by convention. Six holes or twenty-five, played clockwise or not, with a list of rules you could fit on a business card—there was once a little rebel spirit in golf, with innovations and nuances in one club's version that might not be found in another's, and as we search for ways to make the game quicker, cheaper, and easier (twelve holes, anyone?), we might do well to remember that golf's traditions were often born of accident and not of tablets on a mount.

The Montrose Links were the first to follow St. Andrews's lead and make the move to eighteen holes, before deciding that if eighteen was good, twenty-five must be great. They eventually rounded back to eighteen holes by 1888, and what an eighteen holes it was: shaped by an all-star cast of Old Tom, Willie Park Jr., and Harry Colt, Montrose was a natural links with a front nine stretched along the strand and a back nine cradled by lumpy dune land thick with blooming gorse. John Adams proved as knowledgeable as his namesake on matters beyond golf, as he taught me the difference between gorse and broom, and how the stems of the latter were traditionally used in the making of—you guessed it—brooms. He was fiercely proud of his club's ancient legacy and thought too many skipped it when coming to play Carnoustie. I agreed. Unlike at its Open neighbor down the coast, where the sea is largely out of view, at Montrose you felt and saw the water on most of the holes, and as a breezy walk on a pure links, I would take it over Carnoustie for the fun.

Playing with John made for a good part of that fun; it never got old for this American to hear him exclaim, "John Adams!" when he botched a shot. He explained that while the links didn't bear the duke-decreed Royal designation, one of its golf clubs did—the Royal Montrose Golf Club was one of the three clubs associated with the Montrose links, alongside the Caledonia and Mercantile clubs, and it was one of the sixty-something clubs around the world with the Royal designation. The moniker is a label of somewhat unspecific prestige: There are no set criteria for a Royal club, outside of it residing (or once residing—see Royal Dublin) in the British Commonwealth. A member of the royal family simply had to grant the title, often by way of a yellowed letter that one could find hanging in the clubhouse. It meant your club was well connected, I suppose, and it granted you reciprocal playing privileges among the other Royals. John was keen to point out that the oldest Royal club was not the Royal & Ancient but rather a golf club in Perth. I was stunned to hear that they were golfing in Australia before they were at St. Andrews, until I realized I would need John to further educate me in Scottish geography—he was referring not to the Perth Down Under but to a very old city in the heart of Scotland, home to the R&A's rival for royal longevity.

As the Montrose links expanded and contracted over the years, John explained how its metamorphosis was ongoing. Two of Montrose's best holes were threatened by coastal erosion, and the course would have to be replotted in upcoming years in order to maintain an eighteen-hole layout. It was not a unique story in links land. As tides swelled and winter storms grew more severe, courses were suffering around the British Isles—one of my Irish favorites, Mulranny in County Mayo, had already conceded nine holes to the sea, and its remaining nine were nearly washed away entirely in a storm in 2014. But Montrose was the first course I encountered that was already preplanning a redesign ahead of an inevitable defeat. Receding tides conceived these dune courses, and encroaching ones were coming to take them back. It gave me pause to consider how many other courses were vulnerable, and how many of my favorite tracks might not outlive me. I was lucky to be playing them now, and would encourage any links lovers to do the same.

One of the on-course features at Montrose, however, was built to outlast the floods. I thought I'd played out of every conceivable style bunker until I found the concrete World War II pillboxes cradled in the dunes. It seemed a humbling reminder of the soldiers who once stood here, looking out for U-boats and bracing for German boots on this very beach. The irony that golf-loving Germans now played their way around these fortifications less than a lifetime later felt both strange and hopeful. Such remnants were not a unique discovery—I had found beach paths built for brigades all along the UK's coast, and regularly came across gray blocks tossed into the dunes, anti-tank blockades around which I chased a golf ball. On the radio just that morning, I'd heard of a football match at Wembley being delayed because nearby construction had discovered an unexploded German bomb from the Blitz. It all reminded you of the guts of the place. The sense of honor that the Scots wore and had imbued the game with—the stone boxes reminded me where it came from, and what it had endured.

A score of four over par felt reasonable for the family getaway day, as John Adams kept me distracted from visions of my wife chasing a toddler around the Edinburgh airport, having to beg help from strangers to carry the car seat. Surely some traveler would take pity on her, forced to raise two little ones on her own. Parental guilt set in for a moment on the drive to Stonehaven, but it didn't last. Upon eyeing the course from the parking lot, my imagination fired, and in my mind Allyson's seven-hour flight transformed into an opportunity for some quality bonding with the kids, real memory-making time. What a generous partner I was, I thought as I skipped my way down to the Stonehaven clubhouse for a bacon roll and a crack at a golf course that seemed to be sliding off a clifftop and into white breakers below.

If Montrose was a breezy walk on a happy course, Stonehaven—one of Gene and Gramma Billy's picks—was a spelunking expedition packed with deep belly laughs. It was a good course to play alone, my confusion at the preposterous layout just another part of the adventure. Better to not have a member try to explain the overlapping fairways or the glacial gulley that required a ten-minute walk—twice—beneath a mammoth stone railroad bridge splicing the course or the seventeenth fairway that was literally impossible to hit (it was wide enough, but at a sixty-degree sideways slope, you couldn't hold it unless the greenskeeper forgot to mow). It would have been useful, though, to have a local there to tell me that the pit between one and two had a designer of international reputation. Forget Morris and Braid—Stonehaven had "Hitler's Bunker," put there by a German bombardier returning from a raid.

As a whole, Stonehaven was a head-scratching course on the edge of the earth, the cliffs of Aberdeenshire's coast haunting nearly every swing, with the best collection of par 3 tee shots I had ever seen on one property. Gully Cup, number fifteen, had me teeing off next to a crumbling chimney—the only remains of the original clubhouse—across an unreasonable gulley that shined yellow with gorse to a lofted green that looked more like it was 161 acres away than 161 yards.

I went around the short course in 70 swings, but I wasn't considering my score as I finished eighteen on a green the size of a kiddie pool set next to the ruins of a cliffside church. I was too busy studying the tombstones and considering the lives of the people who called this jagged landscape home. Though it was a bit shaggy with fuzzy greens, the place had shades of Old Head drama, with gnarly black shipwrecking rocks holding up the golf course. I felt waves of vertigo on at least three tee boxes, and at 5,103 yards on the card, it was a walk to make you feel old as you took twice as many steps to cover the place. Still, it was worth the fatigue. The view from the modest clubhouse of a golfing battlefield on the brink of Britain was a tonic to revive one's feet. Stonehaven was one of the few courses where I needed to stop in the nineteenth to catch my breath, and as I watched the lads play snooker while I quaffed a life-restoring ginger beer and devoured a bag of peanuts (if there was any doubt as to whether a human being could subsist for two months on bacon rolls and peanuts, I was blowing it away), I was again thankful for Gramma Billy, the former stranger turned golfing spirit guide who cracked open another one of golf's secrets at Stonehaven: to the open mind go the happy surprises. What I expected to be my heaviest days had become my lightest, and as I sat alone in the Stonehaven clubhouse, I thought of my friend and wondered what she must have felt like after that trek. She probably felt the same as I did—absolutely wonderful.

I was in need of a game, and I found one at Peterhead. Solo 74s were hardly worth the cardstock on which they were scribbled; I required a test replete with signed cards and entry fees and first-tee reflux. Lucky for me, the Scots were an intensely competitive golfing lot, and on most Saturdays, I could find a taste of tournament golf, as I did the following morning at Peterhead.

I had attempted to book separate Saturday rounds at the Peterhead Golf Club and the Craigewan Links, only to find that they were both busy hosting tournaments, but that I could enter if interested. I was, especially when I learned that Peterhead and Craigewan were the same course, thereby trimming my day's agenda in half. Still, I was nervous as I crossed the bridge separating the Peterhead parking lot from the clubhouse—and I told myself that was good. A golf club felt differently when wrapped in that thin film of nerves, and I had better get accustomed to it again. I paid my modest entry fee and was shown into the breakfast room to meet my playing partners. The Americans were easy to spot in baseball caps and layers of new rain gear; we stand out for our bulk, and for the money we spend on negating the elements. I interrupted their bacon rolls to introduce myself, and one large Californian (we also stand out for our height) greeted my greeting with, "You don't sound Scottish!"

"No. Sorry, I'm from Philadelphia." I'm not sure why I apologized, but I did.

"You're playing with us?"

"I am."

A collective hush of disappointment settled over their table of six. The revelation that one of their threesomes had been filled out by an American sent their nearby tour operator into a bit of a flurry—he must have promised them local wisdom, or a genuine Scottish experience.

"Don't worry, lads, I'll sort you a forecaddie," he explained, hurrying off to the starter. They were concerned that they wouldn't know where they were going out there without a local, and when I told them such naiveté was often part of the fun on these courses, they eyed me with pity, some hack who must have taken up the game that morning. They were here to compete, to best their buddy from San Francisco who'd nipped them by two shots at Royal Aberdeen yesterday. I sympathized with their wanting to score well, but I also recognized the traveling golfers' flaw that I had lamented on many a trip: folks roamed so far only to weep at their scores and bury their heads in their cards without seeing where they were. Hell hath no fury like an accountant from Minnesota who paid $6,000 to golf Scotland and just shot 104. I often advised people to forget about their scores, or to play Stableford; don't let not playing to your handicap ruin your one trip around god's courses.

When no forecaddies could be found, the threesomes were juggled so that we would all have a Scot in our group. Being that guy nobody wanted to play with was a bit of karmic payback for me. How many times had I tried to rig a tee sheet so that I wouldn't be stuck with a slow or whiny player? Any residual nerves quickly melted into quiet resolve. Bring on those boards in the bar where our scores would be posted next to our names and hometowns: Philadelphia was going to kick California's ass.

The Peterhead Golf Club dated its origin to 1841 when, at its first membership meeting, it was decided that the club uniform would consist of a green jacket with distinctive buttons, in contrast to the red coats of the R&A and the Honourable Company. The introduction in the yardage book boldly suggested that Augusta members perhaps had a peek at these Peterhead coats at some point, a bit of fake golf trivia that I appreciated for its cheekiness. In fact, the Augusta green jacket came about as a way for members to stand out at the Masters so they could assist visitors; golf's most coveted garb originally identified the guy to ask where the bathroom was. Sunk deep into hulking dunes, Peterhead's Craigewan course did not feel much like Augusta, but was just as good a test in the rib-rattling wind. The Californians would be glad for their layers.

After a sloppy bogey on the short opener and three birdies missed from within ten feet, I felt some confidence at the turn. Anything around par in these gales would surely have me in the running for some silver for the fireplace. But as the front nine turned homeward and steered us straight into the gusts, my chances whooshed away like seeds off a dead dandelion. I had been a few shots up on my Scottish playing partner, Gordon, whose card I was keeping, but on the back nine, I could reliably take his score and add two to make my own. He had a homegrown swing that I would have bet against, but he knew his way around the course and through the wind. Eleven through fifteen felt like a mountainous death march of unreachable par 4s, and as my ballooning drives and rejected hybrids got slapped down and knocked sideways into the badness, Gordon suggested I try to hit "a little hooky something," because regular upward spin into this air was an idiot's errand. It was the first time in all my golfing life that it occurred to me that a straight ball was the absolute worst shot, and this realization was proven as I penciled in doubles for myself while Gordon hit sneaky low hooky somethings along the fairway, creeping up on the holes and snatching unlikely par after unlikely par.

For the buffet of humble pie that I consumed after having to sign for a 45 on the back and post a total of 81, it was worth the ego reduction to watch a Scotsman manage an untamed wind. I had bested the Californians, but it was bland consolation—my score was a worrisome tally. One month to the qualifier and I was posting laughable competition scores, and our Carnoustie caddie's prophecy about too much golf in the wind was weighing on my mind. Was I getting worse? Had my game peaked back in East Lothian? Did I have the slightest clue how to hit a low hooky something?

I took a long drive back down to Aberdeen to consider it. My eagerness to visit the Peterhead tournament had me playing the Aberdeenshire courses out of sequence, so as I worked my way back south along the coast toward Scotland's oil city, it occurred to me that my ball-striking wasn't the thing holding me back. I'd proven I could hit low shots, and tee to green, my game was tidy enough to the point where a few putts should have me around or under par on most days. My back nine at Peterhead wasn't about the wind; I'd been here too long to claim breeze as an alibi any longer. I had simply stopped caring once I figured myself out of contention, violating another one of the commandments of good golf that I'd learned long before this trip: Thou shalt grind. I had played with a lot of elite golfers over the years, and they all had their own way of arriving at 67; bombers, scramblers, technicians, one-putters—the styles varied, but there was one trait that every great player I had ever watched possessed: they never frittered away a single stroke. Even if they were putting for triple bogey, they studied and processed that putt as if it were for eagle.

They all mattered. How had such simple math remained a mystery to me? Birdie putts mattered more to me, and early strokes were of more importance than the later, thoughtless ones. Yet my scorecards never shared my perspective. A shot was a shot, and I was too much of a genius to understand it.

I resolved to respect every stroke for what it was—a stroke. And the more scores I tallied in Scotland, the more I believed another law of the golfing universe: The putter is three times more important than any other club in the bag. Missed birdies infected my next drive, which polluted my approach and poisoned my bunker shot. So small there in the bag against its taller neighbors, my flat stick was a sneaky little Napoleon that was running the whole show.

I felt I had figured something out on my drive down to Aberdeen. If nothing else, Peterhead had identified a specific shortcoming in my game. As I drove, I told myself, *I am a great putter, I am a great putter*, a mantra my former golf shrink insisted I believe before teeing it up in a tournament. What I couldn't figure out was why that police car in the rearview mirror had been following me for so long. If it was going to pull me over, wouldn't it have put its lights on already? And then it did. After many days spent trying to acquire the experience and insights of a Scotsman and blend in among the locals, I pulled over and quickly changed suits, donning my best dumb American.

"Do you know why we pulled you over?"

You pulled me over? Is that what's happening here? "I'm sorry, I don't."

The officer was a kind-looking woman in the unintimidating neon yellow coat of the British police, with a sort of Mary Poppins–ish police hat that suggested to me if I just continued to play stupid, I might appeal to her hospitable spirit.

"You were driving at thirty miles per hour over the posted limit."

Or maybe not.

"I'm sorry, I'm not from here. I'm traveling, and this is a rental car—I'm over here golfing, I'm not from here, and I'm in a rental car and I didn't see any signs . . ." *Did I tell her I'm not from here yet?*

"Yes, we know this is a rental car."

"I thought the speed limit was sixty, I'm sorry . . ."

Turned out that the speed limit was sixty for some of the coastal drive in Scotland, but thirty when passing through "built-up" areas. I honestly hadn't taken note of the switch—not that it would have altered my pace much. This little Beemer cooked.

The officer conceded that the speed limit did change over the course of the road I was traveling, and her eagerness to ticket seemed to subside.

"Are you known to British police?" she asked.

Am I *known* to them? I resisted the chance to say, *I might be if they love golf books!* and told her that my British rap sheet was squeaky clean.

"You're on a golfing tour? Are you playing Cruden Bay?"

"I am!" I exclaimed, overjoyed that the conversation had turned from speeding tickets to golf.

"We're just going to give you a warning today. Please mind the posted limits. Enjoy the rest of your stay," she said. "Happy golfing."

Happy golfing indeed. I just had no idea how happy it was about to get.

I knew very little about most of the courses on my list, but when it came to Murcar, I knew less; I didn't even know how to pronounce its name—not Mur-*car* but *Mer*-ker. All I knew was that I was hoping my ticket-dodging luck would extend to a less windy afternoon, but I soon found that I had expended that day's good juju on the carriageway: the pins on the practice range bent over like they'd been gut-shot. Pellets of rain bounced off my windshield as I sat in my car in the parking lot, wondering if this Murcar was worth four hours of *Fuck this*. But I had a poster to gift and a course to cross off its map. And thank god I did, because Murcar turned out to be more than a golf course. For this weary golfer, it was a renaissance.

Originally laid out in 1909 by Archie Simpson, the pro over at Royal Aberdeen, and then updated by James Braid in the 1930s, Murcar was a jewel of a track that I thought out-joyed its royal neighbor. The two links literally overlap one another; in later years, it was discovered that each course had a tee box on the other course's property, but as the members get along well enough (they play a yearly tournament across a routing that combines the ocean holes of both links), the encroachment was overlooked. Murcar was often missed by visitors on their way to the new behemoth links up the coast, built by an American whom the Scots loved to hate, and that was a shame. Bigly. Because Murcar was the rare course—perhaps the only one of its kind I played in Scotland—where I didn't feel the rain, not even as it cleared the course of golfers save me and my playing partners, an Irish pro named Cullan and a quiet Swede named Clem, whom I got to know about as well as a highway toll-taker.

Cullan was in his early twenties and from the town of Doonbeg in County Clare (I assured him that he didn't need to explain where that was) and had played on scholarship at a college in the States. I learned early in our round that he would also be teeing it up next month at Bruntsfield in the qualifier, so our friendly tour quickly became an unspoken competition whereby I might gauge my game against the fresh-from-college pros who attacked golf so fearlessly, and who would make up the majority of the field down in Edinburgh.

"How are your legs holding up?" Cullan asked me as we made our way down the first fairway. "Two rounds a day. You must be knackered."

"They're holding up," I told him. "I was pretty sore at the start. I've lost some weight. That's helped." And I had; I was down at least twenty pounds and a notch and a half on my belt. In the first fairway, I pulled a 9-iron from my bag, ready to impress Cullan with my new Scottish shot-making. I'd been working on taking two extra clubs and playing low and punchy approaches. It took some humility to hit a 9-iron from a hundred yards, but it was fun to make the wrong club go right; there was wisdom in the low ripper I was about to make hop, check, and release to the hole. Cullan would witness the stylings of a genuine player and wonder where an American had learned to golf that kind of ball.

I set the ball back in my stance and delivered a hard upper-body blow at the turf. Cullan was indeed wondering where this American had learned to golf his ball that way as it shot sideways off my clubface like a frightened grouse.

"You were asking if I was tired?" I said, still posing in my low-hands follow-through, as if I were waiting for the ball to decide it was just kidding, hop out of the tangles, and trickle down to the cup. On the shank scale (1 being a gentle forward-moving brush of the hosel, 10 being the rightward rocket of a pitcher trying to pick someone off third) it was a 4 from which I would scramble my way to a putt for par, but that quiet neck-click held enough gunpowder to destroy the next eighty-four strokes and blow this round to pieces. There was no sight in golf as emasculating as watching your golf ball travel on a path completely at odds with the physics of your swing; worse than a whiff, a shank was bad in an almost magical way. So it would have been easy to spend the next seventeen holes paralyzed by the fear of the next one, playing simply to prove I had played golf before, apologetically limping my way across the Murcar dunes.

It was my default golf setting: self-doubt and self-critique, reinforced through long strings of heavy numbers. But as I holed out my par, it was clear that my default had shifted. I didn't have the energy to be embarrassed. I had come too far and played too much to doubt anymore. I knew this game. It was an attitude I had formerly tried to fake, a mode of thinking I'd pursued through meditation and psychologists, through books and tapes and visualization, but my new conviction that I had to go out and play my way into the player's mind-set was bearing fruit.

I couldn't think my way into better play; I had to play my way into better thinking, and that thinking was: I shanked it. So what. Fifty-two rounds in thirty-one days on the landscapes where this game was born: I wasn't just playing at golf anymore. I *was* golf. The golf bullies in my mind had turned to wispy specters. It might still beat me on the scorecard, but there was nothing golf could do anymore to scare me.

Finally.

Cullan and I both hit one or two weird ones that cost us a ball and a double bogey, but our games were well matched that afternoon. I didn't keep his score, but I held the honor on half the holes, and my 76 would have been a shot or two within his. On such a nasty day, and for first peek at this track, I had to take encouragement from a three-birdie round on a course full of holes that gave you no peace. Holes called Ice House and Pool were tests that snaked through the dunes. Even snakier was the killer seventh, Serpentine, which saw us slicing our way around a mountain of golden thorns with the ocean blasting us from the opposite side. The biggest difference in our golf was when Cullan's ball arrived on the fringe and he reached for his lob wedge. From even an inch off the green, Cullan hooded his wedge and firmly chipped his ball, and he never missed the hole by more than a grip's length. It was reinforcement of the old golf adage that they don't ask how, but how many. It took some guts to chip that way—I felt like I was watching a basketball center shoot foul shots underhand but swish every one—and it was a reminder that what anyone else might think about what or how I was playing was none of my damn business. Just get the ball underground.

More unanticipated than the quality of this mystery links were the views from the tee boxes. From our vantage point, the sea vista looked more like Kuwait than Scotland. I counted eighteen oil tankers parked on the horizon, a literal traffic jam of vessels waiting to dock in Aberdeen. Cullan explained that they were charged thousands of pounds a day when docked in port, so they queued at sea until their slot opened up. The ships beyond the dunes were a juxtaposition of nature and industry, leviathan watercraft lurking offshore as if awaiting the signal to invade. Yet it didn't feel unsightly; it looked like new brushing past old, today nodding at yesterday in a place far from home. You didn't see that at the Jersey shore.

I didn't exchange many words with Clem, who was quiet from what I assumed was a language barrier, but I appreciated his guts for sticking it out through stinging rain in a Windbreaker that, by the third hole, was hugging his large frame like soggy Saran wrap. Water dripped from his nose as he carried on, lugging his rental clubs with the resolve of a man who had come to Aberdeen for the weekend with his wife and was set on playing golf while she got nine hours' worth of spa treatments at the hotel. He was going to have fun, goddammit, as he fired a half dozen meatballs into the Murcar vegetation. He played quickly and never complained (or maybe he did—I don't know how you say *son of a bitch* in Swedish), and Cullan and I cheered him along, exclaiming *Good shot!* when he hit one, confident that our English was easier to translate at higher volume. It was around the fifteenth hole when Clem hit one so far off the map that the oil tankers were suddenly in play, and I found myself unable to summon any hopeful commentary. *Hit a turtle? I love Ikea?* But Cullan knew what to say as we watched the ball move sideways on the wind on its way off of Scotland:

"That one's in the lap of the gods."

I scribbled it down on my scorecard: *In the lap of the gods.* I suspected that he meant the ball's fate was unknowable and left to fortune, or perhaps that Clem's ball had left this earth and now rested in a happier place. Either way, I liked the idea. I liked the sound of that place.

"You see those dunes out there?" my friend Neil said, pointing at gray mountains in the distance. From our view atop the Newburgh on Ythan links, I could see where it looked like a storm had tossed the coastline upward into a wavy pile of peaks and valleys, an angry dunescape at odds with its more serene surroundings. It looked a little frightening, and a bit unreal. "That's Trump," Neil said. "That's you tomorrow."

Miles from its first tee, the developer's course already loomed large, not just in its size but in the lore surrounding its origin. I didn't want anything to interrupt my day at Newburgh, where I was relishing the company of my two playing partners, Neil and Graeme, as well as I had enjoyed any of my new Scottish friends, but it was impossible to play golf in or around Aberdeen and not think about the course my countryman claimed was the greatest ever built. You were either playing it, asked if you were playing it, or asked why you weren't playing it—put the words *golf* and *Aberdeen* together and suddenly you were confronting a reality-TV world of trumped-up heraldry and hairspray.

I could dismiss the hyperbole easily enough—*Greatest course in the world?*—exaggeration was his brand. But I'd wavered on whether I was going to play his course on this trip. Too new, too controversial, too Trump-tastic, I reasoned. I was determined to play courses that could teach me something or reveal a glimpse of this game's soul, and there was nothing soulful about self-branded glamour-turned-golf-course. But primary among all my strategies for this course called Scotland was to keep an open mind, so I said thank you when offered a tee time at his International Golf Links Scotland and prepared to learn what all the fuss was about. Besides, who knew if the high-ticket course was going to make it, or if its developer would be around much longer before another bankruptcy exiled him to irrelevance? Better see it while I can.

I didn't dislike the developer, at least not as much as some people I met in Scotland did (I also met others who loved his golf course and applauded his ventures in their country). His politics and persona aside, I appreciated that he invested in the game I loved. No matter that he scooped up financially distressed courses and paid a fraction of their former worth (à la Doonbeg, Turnberry, and Pine Hill); he put money where others wouldn't, at a time when courses were failing daily and golf was in a dangerous decline. One could have resented his golf takeovers and his plan to buy his brand a major championship, but I honestly couldn't. If I had millions to shed, I would buy myself some golf courses, too. As long as his Aberdeen course honored the game, the landscape, and the community, I could overlook my aversion to his bluster and appreciate the site as a contribution.

I really tried. I wanted to love the International Golf Links Scotland as much as the gregarious pro shop staff told me I would, to care about it as deeply as the convivial starter did, but in the end, I couldn't look past so many of the developer's sins against the game. The most mortal among them was evident before I even set foot on the property—before golf, before course, before Aberdeen, on the sign there was *TRUMP*. I believe real golfers understand that the game we play is bigger than us; its beguiling beauty is in the way it demands our respect and humility. You cannot truly honor the game if you're using it as a platform for self-aggrandizement. Slapping his name on courses, turning Doonbeg into Trump International Links Ireland, Doral into Trump Doral, and Turnberry—*Turnberry!*—into Trump Turnberry was an iniquity beyond forgiveness. They didn't call it Bobby Jones's Augusta National or Tom Morris's Prestwick. A great golf course should not be a personal billboard, as it turns a round played there into an awkward homage to its owner. And in the case of this particular developer, it blended golf with politics, a recipe for which I have no appetite.

I endeavored to try to overlook such hubris, hopeful that his course honored the land or the community in Balmedie, near Aberdeen. It was an effort that I would be spared. In the construction of his Aberdeen links, the developer didn't play well with his neighbors. Anthony Baxter's award-winning documentary *You've Been Trumped* (which the developer's lawyers tried to block from airing on the BBC after Baxter was arrested for filming on the Aberdeen worksite—so much for the Scottish Right to Roam) shows the American bullying his course into existence. He accused one longtime resident whose farm was perceived as an eyesore against a future luxury hotel of living "like a pig" in "disgusting" and "slum-like" conditions. The farmer was later voted "Scotsman of the Year" at the Spirit of Scotland Awards by his countrymen for holding out. Eminent domain threatened the homes of long-standing Balmedie denizens, and the 6,000 promised jobs for locals came in closer to 150. A ninety-year-old woman who lived next to the site had her clean water supply cut off, not for days but for *years*. Such large-scale construction was an untidy business. Might the ends justify the means if what had been created lived up to its billing as the greatest golf course in the world?

If only it were the greatest golf course in Aberdeen. His International Links was good—very good: an extraordinarily dramatic layout, a course of eighteen signature holes. It played like a meal of exclusively mains, no starters or salad, just T-bone after T-bone, all overcooked with a slathering of ketchup. It felt forced. Manufactured. Whether it was the six sets of tees, the ten-foot-wide cart paths cut into the dunes (I was told the developer insisted on paths wide enough for golf carts to pass one another), the forced walks to another sky-scraping tee box, the ubiquitous signage directing golfers to so many different tees—there were fewer arrows at an airport—the placards and markers smothered with his heraldry (is there anything less regal than an American's faux royal crest?), or just the knowledge of how much earth had been moved in its construction, the place seemed so relentlessly over-the-top that I couldn't help but feel the human handprints all over it. Though Martin Hawtree had succeeded in designing a procession of postcard holes for his client, I couldn't shake the notion that I was playing a man-made imitation. Perhaps all the coverage of its creation gave me too much insight into how this particular sausage was made.

As for my morning round at Trump International Golf Links Scotland: It was nice. It was hard. I shot 77. But I had more fun at nearby Newburgh on Ythan.

Newburgh had been stretched to eighteen holes only in recent decades, so the course played like two distinct tracks: a front nine up and down pastoral hillsides, and a links-ier back nine along the river Ythan. I was well shepherded around both halves by two locals, Graeme and Neil. Graeme met me outside the clubhouse, his summer sweater seeming to mock my three layers and wooly cap. He was tall and thin, with gray hair and a careful smile that hinted at a dry wit, while Neil was a stocky bomber around my age who we found looking for a game in the pro shop. Between the two of them, they knew every ounce of Newburgh history, reminding me that if you played with a local, every course in Scotland held enough legends to rival St. Andrews.

The fourth hole, Drovers, made it directly onto my list of the top holes in Scotland as I eyed the short stone wall in the heart of the fairway, remains of a former drover's (shepherd's) sheep pen. I thought Graeme was kidding when he told me to aim for the doorway, but it turned out to be a joyful touch of minigolf, my drive miraculously rolling through the slim opening and gifting me one of my five birdies that afternoon, modestly balanced by six bogeys for a 73. I so wanted to birdie the final par 5 for a round of one under but turned a good drive into a bogey when my approach found a curious rectangle of low, marshy ground. Neil and Graeme had different stories on the origins of this patch—one said it was an old curling rink, while the other claimed it had been used to lay out and dry salmon. They both agreed that sticky toffee pudding had been invented in the kitchen behind the thirteenth tee, the most exciting history I had heard since visiting Archie at Gullane—sticky toffee was a spongy fig cake (not pudding as we Yanks know it) covered in caramel syrup that I had yet to pass up when it appeared on a menu. As to the origins of the name of the hollow on the fifteenth hole, Neil deferred to his elder playing partner. Old members disputed whether it was a World War II bomb crater, but Graeme explained that it was better known as Rosie's Hole, named for the local lass who enjoyed canoodling in it with the lads, thus sharing with me the least likely hole name to ever make it onto a scorecard (Newburgh's card more modestly dubbed number fifteen Boathouse).

As we made the turn down to the lower, waterside back nine, Graeme pointed my eyes to a beach across the Ythan where seal watchers flocked, and said that the hillside overlooking the lower course was called Gallows Hill. I assumed witches were hanged there, from my education in Kinghorn, but Graeme explained that it was for golfers who didn't pay their greens fees. "Or unkind golf writers," he added with a nod.

Toffee pudding, Rosie, seals, gallows—local knowledge flavored our every shot. We got to talking about place names, and Neil explained that *Inver* and *Aber* both denoted the mouth of a body of water, as in Inverness at the head of the River Ness and Aberdeen at the start of the River Dee. I was still unsure of the meaning of *Inch*, a word I had seen on road signs around Scotland, so I asked him for a translation.

"Ah, Inch," Neil said. "That would be one-twelfth of a foot."

"Actually," Graeme corrected him, "I think an inch is a piece of land protruding out into the water."

"Really?" I said.

"Yes," he said, and smiled. "As in, Pen-inch-ula."

The origins of *Inch* remained unknown, but I did learn of a British

Olympic track hero named Sally Gunnell. The back nine held a few drivable par 4s guarded by thick, marshy brush, and Neil encouraged me to try to drive the fifteenth, "if you have enough balls." I stopped; *They say that over here?* "Balls in your bag," he added.

I grabbed the bait and ripped my driver, catching the bottom of the club-face in an almost perfect miss that skipped, ran, and hopped its way up to the mouth of the green. As I groaned at my meager contact, Neil exclaimed, "Sally Gunnell!"

"Sally Gunnell?"

Neil nodded. "Not pretty, but she runs a mile."

We discussed the courses coming up on my list. They told me I was in for some special days, especially at Cruden Bay, and they would have known; aside from Trump, they'd played all the links around Aberdeen and Inverness. The price at Trump was hard to justify, they explained, at 165 quid ($235), when golf everywhere else in Scotland was so inexpensive. Graeme had just joined the local seniors' golf society, where, for thirty-six pounds, he was entitled to twelve rounds of golf at area courses.

"I couldn't afford not to join," he said. "It's an incredible deal. Golf in Scotland, you may have noticed, is very reasonable."

I said that I had noticed, and asked how he'd gotten into such a group. There had to be a waiting list at that price.

"Well, you see, as they're seniors," Graeme explained, "they tend to die. So it works itself out."

It was always better to play with partners matched in sense of humor than in playing ability, and in Graeme and Neil I had found two friends with whom I knew I would be teeing it up again. I left Newburgh on Ythan with the energy of my first day in Scotland, not yet aware that this would become one of the days in my golfing life for which I would trade so many others.

The Kilmarnock Arms Hotel seemed like the only place to stay in Cruden Bay, and while previous travels around the British Isles had proven that any accommodation with *Arms* in the name was actually the prescribed length one should keep from its front door, my limited options in the area resulted in a happy accident. The three-star hotel with a cozy pub had clean, spacious rooms in a new addition toward the back. Upon checking in and studying the small lobby, I soon learned this was the hotel where Bram Stoker, Irish author of *Dracula*, had spent his holidays, his novel inspired by the nearby ruins of New Slains Castle overlooking Cruden Bay from a perch atop the cliffs. I set off to the golf course, where Dracula's castle would be in view from nearly every hole, its walls golden in the late-afternoon sunlight. A rainbow was touching down on the ruins as I arrived at the Cruden Bay pro shop, and if you hadn't already known it, you would have guessed that the place had inspired a masterpiece.

It was appropriate that I had an Irish author on my mind as I was about to meet another one for my round at Cruden Bay; Kevin Markham was a less gothic author than Stoker, but he was still a bit mad. In his wonderful book *Driving the Green*, Kevin and his camper van embarked on a seven-thousand-mile journey around Ireland (I didn't know there were that many miles *in* Ireland) to play every eighteen-holer in the country, some 351 in total. He was the rare golfer who could look at my itinerary and think, *Well, that's a bit tame.* We'd never met before but had exchanged emails over the years as the two wandering chroniclers of Irish golf, one by car and the other by foot, and the quality of his driving narrative gave me license to drive this one—not that I was ever really tempted to hike the Highlands.

I expected to find a long-bearded and zombie-eyed waif falling out of a van in the parking lot, thick Irish fingers trembling for another golf hole or dram of whisky; I knew the lonesome obsession behind adventures like his, but mine had been only a quarter the length of his quest. Surely he would be unwell. I prepared myself to meet a golfing gypsy who might beg a sandwich off me or lift a putter in the pro shop, but Kevin turned out to be a very reasonable Irishman of good humor and genuine class. He was bearded but neatly so, and was already snapping pictures of the golf course from where the hillside clubhouse overlooked the first hole. We greeted one another like old friends, an instant comfort shared between two men who knew the trials of the golfing road. It was an unspoken bond—we both understood the small joys of smiles in the pro shop, of empty club parking lots, of pubs that were still serving food at 9:00 p.m. And we knew the sting of hostile starters and the despair of tour busses in the car park, and the pain of playing through arctic monsoons because the calendar said we must. The fact that we met for the first time at Cruden Bay turned out to be no accident. It was as if the golf gods were jointly rewarding us for the blisters and the credit-card debt with a visit to a course I quickly knew was my Scottish beloved.

I worked to resist comparing Irish links to Scottish ones during my trip, but it felt as if this was a day when I was supposed to stop trying—from Stoker's castle to my Irish playing partner, I couldn't help but think of the dunes of Enniscrone and Carne and the blind shots of Lahinch and the drama of Tralee's closing nine and the welcome playability of Waterville as I experienced Cruden Bay. Designed by Old Tom Morris, like so many courses in Ireland and the UK, it was a railway course, commissioned as the railroads spread around the British Isles in the late nineteenth century for all the new-money travelers. With British industry came wealth, leisure time, travel by rail, and golf on the coasts of their islands. Golf might have remained a pastime for a few pockets of Britain had steam engines not come along and spread holes far and wide.

Kevin was a thoughtful playing partner, far more interested in photographs than his score—he took three times as many pictures as swings—and our conversation naturally turned to our impression of Scottish links versus Irish. We both agreed that there was something more subtle about the Scottish layouts, courses with hints of restraint that needed to be studied in order to understand their quiet quality, whereas Irish links were often as subtle as a slap, knocking you across the eyes with their drama and peculiarities. Cruden Bay was far more the latter, with towering dunes and views that had smoke pouring from Kevin's camera. The tee box perches at the ninth and tenth made us both giddy about the par 4s awaiting us below, and the fifteenth, a 195-yard doglegging blind par 3, was my best par in the UK. Everything about Cruden Bay felt as organic as a Morris course should—the honest drama of an old landscape, not a manufactured note to be found— though my favorite feature on the fifteenth was man-made. A buried pipe allowed one to pull a rope beside the green, flipping a lever by the tee to signal to players that you had cleared.

Golf pundits and course-raters talk of "shot values," "design variety," and "resistance to scoring" when assessing a course's greatness. I know what some of those terms mean, and I appreciate that a rubric needs to exist if our cherished annual course ratings are going to have any proper measures of assessment. In a recent *Golf Digest* ranking of the world's top one hundred, Cruden Bay ranked seventeenth in the world, somehow fourteen spots behind the International Golf Links down the coast. You could probably throw most of the top one hundred in a bag, pull one out, and make an argument for why it belonged in the top slot. And my argument for Cruden Bay would have nothing to do with shot values or design data; it would be the utterly subjective flight metric by which I would find myself sprinting from Aberdeen or Edinburgh if you told me I had a tee time at Cruden Bay tomorrow. Hopefully Kevin would pick me up in his camper van along the way.

I'm sure our weather had something to do with my fervor, the sunshine only briefly interrupted by a few passing rainbows, and Kevin's company no doubt hoisted my Cruden Bay impressions. Or maybe it was that I made the best swing of the trip on my approach to fourteen and Kevin caught it on camera, a zippy wedge fired up to a deep green that was cradled by swollen mounds of sand. Maybe it was that I closed with a birdie to make the post-round ginger beer so much sweeter, or perhaps my affinity had to do with the fact that at Cruden Bay I saw something more beautiful than rainbows and eagle putts. On sixteen I stopped Kevin and said, "Look at that. That is a sight I haven't seen in six weeks."

And there it was, more elusive than Nessie herself: a flag sitting still atop a Scottish flagstick, hanging dead as a wet rag. I had to rub my eyes at this miraculous vision. I would have been no more gobsmacked if the Virgin herself appeared and told me to keep my shoulders square.

I wanted to think that the heavens had something to do with why Cruden Bay struck me deep in my golfing soul. I wanted to believe that they had something to do with many things, and I had been trying to get there in recent years. Every morning on this trip, I woke up and said, *Whoever you are, whatever you have in store for me today, with some help, I'm up for it.* It was as much of what one might call faith that I could summon, and so far, so good. And the golf course seemed to agree.

On seventeen at Cruden Bay, a small wooden well sat tucked at the edge of the fairway. An old sign above it read: *St. Olaf's Well low down by the sea, Where pest nor plague shall ever be.*

A thousand years before, a battle between Scots and Vikings had bloodied these dunes, and to commemorate the lost lives, a chapel was erected in Cruden Bay to St. Olaf, king of Norway and an early defender of Christianity. Built in 1012, his chapel marked the start of Christian services in this part of Scotland.

Out of Cruden Bay grew a millennium of faith, and that was plenty good enough for me. All I was asking for was a day.

Contact

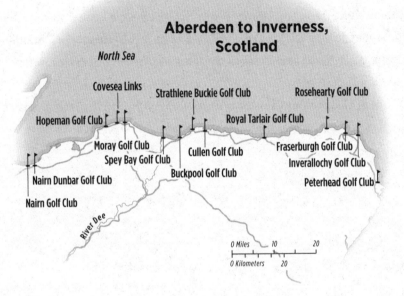

Aberdeen to Inverness, Scotland

North Sea

Covesea Links
Strathlene Buckie Golf Club
Rosehearty Golf Club

Hopeman Golf Club
Royal Tarlair Golf Club

Moray Golf Club
Cullen Golf Club
Fraserburgh Golf Club

Spey Bay Golf Club
Inverallochy Golf Club

Buckpool Golf Club
Peterhead Golf Club

Nairn Dunbar Golf Club

Nairn Golf Club

River Dee

0 Miles 10 20
0 Kilometers 20

My name in Scottish Gaelic is Tòmas or Tam, and it means twin. I don't have a twin, nor did I hear much Gaelic at all in Scotland (supposedly it was still spoken in the Outer Hebrides, where I was headed at trip's end, but the Scots' erstwhile language was known by only 1 percent of the population). Plenty of Toms had left their mark on golf—few golfers are more popular in the British Isles than Tom Watson, and the Morrises elevate the Tom brand for sure. It was a fair golf name as far as forenames went, but there were some first names that just sounded like six under.

You can't be called Bubba and hack. Bob, Joe, Frank—they might all cheer for net bogeys, but I never met a Chandler who couldn't play (I've met only one, but he can). Bradley—he probably stripes it, and Alan is a stick; he takes money off Al every time out. Jimbo and Jimmy mash it, while Jim plays in cargo shorts. And then there was Garth. Garth golfed his ball. Garth was a country-club rat who played on scholarship at a Christian college down South and had a cushy sales gig at his dad's insurance outfit waiting for him, where his job would be to dazzle clients on the golf course and sip transfusions full-time.

I had never actually met a Garth, not until the winter before I left for Scotland and learned that, just as I couldn't judge the Scots' playing abilities by swings that sometimes looked like an angry janitor mopping the cafeteria, I shouldn't judge a player by their moniker. This Garth was not a born linksman. He had the name, the carefully parted hair of a corporate hustler, the starched Brooks Brothers shirts, and the Ivy League education. But he was also raised in Altoona, Pennsylvania, in that red center of my home state where schools closed for the opening of deer season and a trip to Sheetz was reason enough to iron the Dale Earnhardt T-shirt. He was thirty-four but had taken up golf only the previous year after marrying into a golf-mad, mainline Philadelphia family, and was now scrambling to catch up to their handicaps and win himself a spot in the Thanksgiving foursome.

When I threw out a Facebook invitation to friends to join me for a few rounds in Scotland, I was shocked when Garth came back as one of the instant commits. His local handicap was 38.4, and he had just recently achieved his goal of making his posted scores actually count, shaving a few strokes off the default max of 40. We met over coffee to discuss the trip at hand. I needed to make sure Garth knew what he was signing up for in links golf, in wooly-hat golf, in buying-more-balls-at-the-turn golf. And he was in, without a breath of hesitation. He had a line on a gross of golf balls through DrMulligans.com and was eager for the test, as long as, he explained, I didn't mind playing with a beginner. He knew my golf had earnest ambitions and didn't want his learning curve to interfere.

Any golfer who busted his ass to shrink his handicap from 40 to 38.6, who counted *every single stroke* with an almost agonizing veracity, who was ready to take a winter's worth of lessons and wanted so badly to be a golfer without cutting a single corner or taking a single putt, was as worthy a partner as I could find. I assured him he would be doing me a great favor in making the trip to come find me up in Aberdeen, but I didn't tell him that it would be a treat to see a links course through the eyes of someone who had never imagined one, and to again see the game from the perspective of someone who was still courting it.

A round of golf is full of silent rhythms and nuances that players take for granted: Where do you position your bag, stand on the green, drop the pin, take a leak? Contact is hard enough, but the etiquette and flow of a game takes years to master, and I wonder how many beginners give up for feeling like outsiders, unwelcome because they don't know all the secret handshakes. I once heard a Tour pro say that he didn't golf with members at his club because he didn't want to play "with a bunch of chops." But the chops are the future. They're the most important players on the course, and they need our stewardship. So hug a chop, because we are all chops at least a few times every round.

I wasn't a benevolent guru inviting a beginner along to marvel at my drives; rather, I was fortunate for a playing partner who loved golf more than I did. He must have, because I wouldn't have spent the money on a ticket to Scotland for the chance to add up to 124. I was born in the church of golf and had watched my faith lapse, while Garth was freshly converted and chased the game with the fervor of the born-again. He wouldn't teach me anything about the golf swing, but that was fine, because I suspected he would show me something about golf guts.

And he did, straight off the plane. We might have oriented him on a wee parkland nine-holer or warmed up on a practice range, but the schedule demanded Garth belly flop into the deep end, teeing up his first Scottish ball on a course that had hosted the Scottish Open and the Walker Cup, the sixth-oldest club in the world, where King Edward VII himself added the royal to Royal Aberdeen.

After a kind welcome and a tour of the aged clubhouse that showcased trophies older than Texas and an encased sample of the members' red coats, I felt the nerves myself. I hoped Garth didn't know enough about the game's history to be daunted by his surroundings. His goal on this trip was to break 100 in Scotland, and I hoped this course wouldn't prove that goal a pipe dream on day one. On the opening tee box, Garth turned to me. I expected him to make some excuse about jet lag or his new golf shoes, but instead he smiled and said, "Guess what, Tom? We get to golf today."

Unafraid, he stepped up and knocked his ball down the first fairway in a mostly forward and airborne fashion. And suddenly, the trip had changed: I was no longer the lone seeker, and as I walked the opening hole, a par 4 that rolled downward toward an ocean horizon, I felt a lightness in my steps. What a relief to take a break from worrying about myself and my scorecards and cheer for someone else for a while.

It turned out that my cheers weren't going to be enough—not on this afternoon. Royal Aberdeen flogged Garth with contempt and abandon, but his spirit never wavered, even as his carefully calculated ball budget took a hit that threatened his Dr. Mulligans stash. I didn't have to explain that the five-minute rule for ball searches was invented at this very club (if you don't play the gorse as a lateral hazard in Scotland, dropping instead of running back to hit again, you'll have the course backed up in no time); Garth looked, dropped, and got on with it. "I'm not playing Royal Aberdeen," he explained from the high herbs off the ninth fairway, "I'm exploring it."

Both refined and bombastic, Royal Aberdeen was a status course with a wild side. It blended the formality of Muirfield with the giddiness of Murcar's dunes next door, and its nine-out, nine-in routing was a steady meal of thinking shots and hopeful strategies. If Garth never golfed another links, he could say he had played one of the true ones. He hit a surplus of shots that day, but none would top the magic of his approach to the final green. Eighteen was an angry par 4 that played upward to a green set directly beside the clubhouse. As Garth stood over his third shot, 5-iron in hand, I eyed the tall glass windows of the clubhouse. *This could be terrible*, I thought. And then I realized, *This could be awesome*. What an extraordinary mark to leave upon the sixth-oldest club in the world. Surely they had insurance.

As his ball rose against the breeze and turned toward the clubhouse and the adjacent practice green where a member was putting, I heard Garth let out the meekest *Fore?* in the history of golf. We both exhaled as the ball dropped safely without making humanly or window-ly contact. Garth had actually hit the green, albeit the practice one, and we watched as his ball rolled up to the member's feet and stopped. The man looked down, wondering where this extra ball had come from, perhaps trying to guess who Dr. Mulligans was. He putted on without a word or even a look our way, and we left Royal Aberdeen with a new understanding that in golf, it isn't always the things you hit but the things you miss that matter.

I had been keeping a number of lists in my evening journal—favorite holes, toughest pars, best par 3s, best short courses—but over the next week, I would start a new list that I enjoyed more than all the others: *Shit Garth Hit*. The first entry was *Practice green at Royal Aberdeen*, but it would grow to include various obstacles and conveyances, both natural and man-made. At the short locals' links of Inverallochy, the list would acquire its most impressive item: *Flagpole*. Not a golf flag, mind you, but a literal flagpole in the parking lot that waved the Scottish standard.

Inverallochy was a cheerful par 66 perched directly atop the cliffs, where Garth greeted me at the first tee with his morning catchphrase: "Hey, Tom, guess what? We get to golf today." I wondered when I would tire of hearing that, but I reminded myself that Garth was right and I was golf-spoiled, and that I should stop hoping that one morning I might hear, *Guess what, Tom? We get to sleep/do crosswords/shuck oysters/juggle fire/scratch our asses today* instead.

The layout was a nice break for Garth—shortish and void of the gorse that crowded Royal Aberdeen. The hospitality in the clubhouse, where they were pleasantly surprised to find Americans had arrived to play their wee track, was surpassed only by the kindness on the course, where a greenskeeper hopped out of his tractor to tell Garth he found his drive two fairways over. It was a morning of majestic views where you could let it fly, and we did. I signed for what was becoming my too-common five over, and Garth flirted with the hundred barrier. He didn't break it, but his ball budget was back in the black as he lost nary a pebble, though he did nearly lose all the cash in both of our wallets.

The first two holes played past the clubhouse, but the third came directly back toward it, the green set next to another terrifying amount of glass. A crowded parking lot was far more frightening than the clubhouse from yesterday, and I imagined Garth engaged in a cliffside wrestling match with the owner of that Audi SUV. As Garth reached for his 5-iron, I decided not to say what I knew we were both thinking, but as we watched his ball bullet toward the cars, I wished that I had. The projectile banked hard and locked in on its shiny target; we braced for impact and let out sighs of *Shiiiiit*. But then came a miraculous *DOING!* The club's thin flagpole was the only barrier between Garth's shot and a sea of windshields, and he somehow managed to hit the sucker dead-on, his ball careening sideways and bouncing through the lot.

Unafraid and unashamed, Garth walked into the parking lot, nodded hello to the family loading into an unblemished Audi, and conspicuously collected his Titleist from beside their tire. My boy had balls, and he left Inverallochy with all of them that morning. And on we went, in search of 99.

At nearby Fraserburgh, the only addition to the Shit Garth Hit list would be a road, which seemed like more of a rite of passage than an error— everybody had hit a road ball and cringed, waiting for the impending smash and tire-screech. Fraserburgh checked in as the seventh-oldest club in the world, yet it held none of the affectations that one might expect at a club of such heritage (Fraserburgh fun fact: It's the oldest club in the world still operating under its original name). It was a sort of second-tier links that touring golfers might skip, and to do so would be a great shame, as Garth and I both adored this wild seaside climb of a course. Laid out by James Braid, whom I was now convinced neither slept nor ate, the course stretched up, over, down, and around a massive hill set in the heart of the links. The first and last holes from and to the clubhouse were sleepy appetizers, but once we took on the mountain at the course's middle, the holes were rambling romps of uneven lies and sneaky turns. It was less manicured than the tour-bus courses, with tiny white flowers dotting the fairways and driving both of us dizzy by the end; hunting for balls camouflaged in the fairway was a nuisance, but it was worth the trouble for the chance to play a course that lived up to the oft-abused label of hidden gem.

As we played our way home on eighteen, we passed a member coming up number one for a few evening holes. Our drives had crisscrossed, so we stopped to say hello. We told him how much we enjoyed his course, and he said, "Happy to hear it. As long as you're having fun, that's all that matters."

It was true, and I wondered whether that was the obvious wisdom I had traveled so far to find. Perhaps it was. I was sure to keep having fun as I closed with a bogey and Garth licked his wounds from his 118 swipes. Two rounds completed, but on this evening, there was still more fun to be had.

With Garth's arrival came the question of shoe-changing etiquette. There was always the debate about whether one could or should change one's shoes in the parking lot or in the clubhouse, or if the clubhouse was open to visitors, or if there was a separate visitors' locker room (there often was) and if we knew the entry code for the door (I often didn't). I avoided such quandaries by wearing golf shoes full-time, but as Garth had some actual sense about driving in spikes, we would pull into a parking lot and have to wonder if bare socks in the car park would be an affront to someone in a red coat. At Rosehearty, a nine-holer just up the coast from Fraserburgh, such concerns were alleviated when we watched a gentleman pull into the parking lot, step to the back of his car, and in a fifty-degree breeze, drop his work trousers and change into golf pants, a process during which he proved that it was not just the French or the Italians but all European men who preferred banana hammocks. In this gentleman's case, the hammock was in fact banana-colored, his bright yellow briefs partly obscured by belly overhang.

I turned to Garth. "I think we're okay to change our shoes in the parking lot."

He agreed.

The small building beside the Rosehearty parking lot was locked. It might have been a clubhouse, but it looked like it was rarely inhabited. I noticed a pub across the street, and I recalled Alan back at the Glen telling me of a course where I was going to have to check in at the bar across the road; he warned me that there were downward steps inside the doorway, and coming from the light into the dark bar was blinding—he ended up going down the steps on his ass the first time. We gave it a shot, and sure enough, we found the steps and the dark bar, where a lone woman tended an empty room.

"You here for the golf?"

We told her we were. She took our money and handed us scorecards, and off we went to play one of the least-fussy courses in Scotland.

Rosehearty was a punishment-void and judgment-free nightcap to Garth's first day. The course was essentially a field with nine holes in it, albeit a lovely, lofted field overlooking the ocean. If it were my local golf escape, I would have been happy enough. Garth broke 100 by forty-eight whole shots, proving what I had always known was the secret to better scoring: playing fewer holes.

It was an hour's drive along the northern coast to our guesthouse in Nairn, where we would be able to unpack for four nights. This stretch of coastline east and north of Inverness was another pocket packed with links offerings, so I had been careful to book us quality accommodations; the four-star Sandown House deserved a fifth. The B&B was large and spotless and a par 5 away from the Nairn links, where we would be playing in a few days. The owner, Liz, was a traveling golfer's angel. Hers was a golfing household, and her two boys had just returned from their semesters in America, where they were both playing college golf. I felt wonderfully at home with this surrogate golfing mother whose breakfasts were so good I actually woke up for them (common practice was to grab as much sleep as possible and shovel a fistful of peanuts into my mouth on the way to the course). She offered club storage and gear drying and end-of-the-day whisky for her clientele. I declined my dram each evening, though she was kind and Scottish enough to keep asking, and her bagpipe-playing neighbor walked over to serenade us one evening with what I believed was the Scottish national anthem. Or it might have been ours. Sounded great either way.

We unpacked, and Liz steered us toward a hotel up the road for a late meal, where I was hungry enough to eat every ounce of my haggis pizza. I was confident that only Americans ordered the haggis pizza, but I embraced my traveler's naiveté. The spicy brown stuff put pepperoni to shame. Ever the golfing actuarial, Garth pored over the math on his scorecards between bites. His 106 at Inverallochy was a tease. I assured him that if he'd given himself the putts and breakfast-balls some golfers did, he might have broken 100 today, but he wanted to do it the right way. *Good on ya, Garth*, I thought. Golf was happy to have him onboard.

He confessed that he had not only never played two rounds in a day but that two rounds in a week was his highest previous tally, so, scores aside, forty-five holes in a day was a total of which to be proud.

"Ready to do it again tomorrow?" I asked.

"Totally ready. Can't wait," he said. "Is that strange? That is strange. What is it about golf? It's addictive. I mean, thirty-six holes a day. I think this qualifies as addictive behavior."

I smiled. He knew my story, and I knew what he was getting at. Perhaps I had traded one dependency for another. I'll admit, the thought was there every time I lifted my absurd stack of an itinerary.

People talk about addiction as a weakness, as a lack of will or character. Maybe they're right, but I imagine such folks would be surprised to know that it's they whom the active addict views as lacking. Lacking the truth. Lacking awareness and emotional sincerity. Lacking any idea as to what life really is and what living it actually feels like. A drunk doesn't drink to feel good; he drinks to not feel like death. They would say an alcoholic wants to drink. They wouldn't have a clue.

Above all other things, addiction is about being unsettled. It's about an unshakable discontentment, and all the fear that comes with it. Those people wouldn't call it a disease; call it a dis-ease, then. The simplest solution for unrest is to seek *more*, to chase *better*, to find the greater and bigger and funner. Settling for pain or, worse, settling for normal is for the weak and foolish. That's how it starts, anyway: trying to level the unsettledness, until it eventually just becomes about getting through the day.

This quest was a dry one, but who knew how sober it was. There was addiction all over it; I was still a chaser, still unsettled. I was grateful that the things I was chasing of late weren't necessarily going to kill me, and hoped it would remain that way until I figured out how to stand still.

In the meantime, I ate haggis on my pizza and fell asleep to snooker on TV, relieved that there was more golf tomorrow, convinced it could be better.

I could smell it in the air at Moray: the talent. It was hanging around the practice green and playing in foursomes of college golf bags. Next to whisky, Scotland's greatest export had to be eighteen-year-old golf hopefuls shipped to American universities, and they were all over Moray, playing second balls and putting not to the pins but to the tees they stuck in tomorrow's hole locations. Practice rounds were under way for the next day's Scottish Open Stroke Championship. Qualification was based on handicaps, and while mine might have snuck me in off the waiting list, the three days it would have stuck me in Lossiemouth was not part of the plan; I had eight courses to explore in that time. But it was helpful to play a course set for championship golf, and I put my mind to playing this round as if my name were on the board and every shot were posted.

The locals referred to the Moray course by its town name, Lossiemouth, but whatever you called it, it was a formidable, gorse-clogged test. There was a St. Andrews feeling about the start and finish of this Tom Morris course, where the clubhouse sat snugly between the ocean and the town. It was a steep forty paces down to the golf course from the street, giving the finish a sunken-stadium vibe. The course also possessed an immovable obstruction I had yet to see anywhere else in golf: landing lights for the nearby Royal Air Force base. You got relief from the wooden towers that were mostly confined to the rough, but it took us a few holes to figure out what they were for. Were they clues to a shortcut to the green, or some sort of elaborate laundry-drying apparatus? When a landing fighter jet nearly knocked off our hats, their purpose became clear.

They came in by the dozen, close enough that Garth's hit list had a chance to go from comical to legendary status. We didn't hit any planes that day, though we got some great pictures of us putting with their landing gear overhead. A plane-strike had apparently happened once, in 1971 when a schoolteacher popped up a drive at Moray that struck a Royal Navy Hawker

Hunter jet. I could only imagine the clubhouse deliberations over that ruling. I didn't recall anything from the Leith rules about Navy jets, but the school-teacher's case was pronounced rub of the green—play it where it lies.

My 75 would have had me playing from the wrong side of the cut line in tomorrow's field of Walker Cup players and future minitour pros, and Garth's 110 would have been a sub-100 round at a gentler track. I was tired at Moray and felt frustration setting in; I was too far along to still be losing balls and making thoughtless doubles the way I did on the second hole. My wipey cuts were not going away; they were getting worse, and I worried that eschewing the driving range in favor of actual play had been a flawed strategy from the start. My swing path needed retuning, but the idea of finding a range to do video work nauseated me. The meal was prepared; it was too late to go back to the mixing bowl. I would have to find a change on the fly and go with the miss I had.

I also had to give myself a break. Back in Philadelphia, Dynda had stressed that golfers who demanded consistency were chasing Bigfoot. Even the best players in the world missed fairways and greens—often, actually—and while on TV it looked like they never missed a putt, the data showed that pros holed less than half their putts beyond eight feet. He believed in golf as a bell curve on either end of which there would always be outlying shots—good and bad—and that while practice might tighten up the curve or shift it forward, the golf ball would always disobey us during a round. Such was its design. How we recovered when it did, and how many putts we made inside of eight feet, was where the money was made, and where the pros separated themselves from the guys shooting 75 in a practice round.

Somewhere along the front nine of Royal Tarlair that afternoon, on my way to an opening 40, it occurred to me that it might not be that I was growing tired but that I was getting weak or strong in the wrong places. I had carried a one-strap bag slung over my right shoulder over some fifty golf courses, and I wondered whether my strengthened right side might have something to do with my expanding misses, grooving me a more over-and-across path that wiped the golf ball and, as I had proven recently, even brought the hosel into play. I understood all of this abstractly, but without drills or a range to rejigger my move, I didn't know what to do about it. So I did something obvious: On number ten at Royal Tarlair, I set my right shoulder back and weakened my grip, stuff they teach you at the junior clinic when you're twelve. I felt the club head dropping inside the ball, and my wipe morphed into a cannon. I made three birdies and shot 33 on the closing nine, and wondered if there were any spots left at Lossiemouth from no-shows tomorrow.

Today's swing fix rarely lasted into tomorrow, and it likely wouldn't be my answer by trip's end at Bruntsfield, by which time I would have worshipped and discarded a half dozen remedies. But the key was to keep looking for one. The fixes didn't last, and the good shots were only as dependable as the bad ones, but if I kept trying to play golf—think, adjust, react—rather than trying to beat it, 33 was not out of the question.

Royal Tarlair was a clifftop course of wild vistas and straightforward holes that might have visitors wondering why they weren't back at Cruden Bay until they arrived at the thirteenth, a par 3 called Clivet that shot to the top of my list of the most dramatic holes in Scotland. At 152 yards off the edge of a rocky precipice, Clivet required you to loft your ball across a crashing sea and down to a saucer of green planted on a stony ocean outcropping far below. It felt like god's version of the seventeenth at Sawgrass, worth the visit just for that signature hole. It might have been a one-hit wonder of a golf course, but as far as one-hit wonders go, Clivet was an absolute Chumbawamba.

Garth's stretch of Scottish golf east of Inverness was crowded with such courses: lots of locals' tracks that didn't shine quite brightly enough to stop the busses but were still classy little jewels, places like Spey Bay and Strathlene and Nairn Dunbar and Buckpool and Hopeman. If your friends wanted solid and unbothered golf, you could plan a nice getaway among the lot, for a tidy little price.

We pulled up to Spey Bay to find campers setting up tents outside the barn of a clubhouse, raising our suspicions about the golf we might find at what looked like a campground from the parking lot. But behind the clubhouse was a genuine out-and-in links stretching along the ocean that had been laid out by Scottish golf legend Ben Sayers, who, as it was explained to us by the manager inside the one-room clubhouse, came up from North Berwick in the early 1900s and laid out the course in one afternoon, using nothing more than two flags. He marked a tee with one and then waved to a lad in the distance until the flag marking the green was where he wanted it.

The topography of Spey Bay showed why Sayers's job was such an easy one. The tides had left dunes that were shaped like long gullies, so some of the holes played like you were skiing through a half-pipe. A bit ragged around the edges (as we heard everywhere, the wet spring had been cruel to courses across the country, and maintenance had yet to really begin), Spey Bay won the competition for best scorecard in my growing collection. Rather than another picture of a golf hole, its cover featured a black-and-white photograph of club member James Ramsay MacDonald, the first Labour prime minister of Great Britain. Word was that he had been kicked out of nearby Moray for opposing Great Britain's involvement in World War I, though our friend in the clubhouse said he was barred from Moray for being of illegitimate birth, and for being a member of the Labour party.

Spey Bay's tunnels were tight and the wind was blowing out to sea, so it took only a few holes before Garth added *ocean* to his list of things hit. But his spirits didn't sag. As we watched his second tee ball chase his first one into the thick gorse on number twelve, he said, "Look at it this way: I've just doubled my chances of finding a ball in there."

It would take all Garth's optimism to make it around Hopeman that afternoon. I had warned him that we had a tournament in our path, but I didn't know until we checked in at the pro shop that it was a stroke-play event. No equitable stroke control, and no blobs or surrenders—it was hack until it's dead.

"You don't have to do this," I told him. "You can just pay and play and say you aren't going to post a score."

"Oh, I'm posting a score," Garth said, unfazed. "I'm in, baby."

We paid at the scorer's table, and they asked for our handicaps for the gross prizes.

"Thirty-eight," Garth proclaimed.

The man looked up from the score sheet, presumably surprised to see a healthy young lad standing before him.

"You'll be a twenty-eight today. Tournament maximum."

I winced, while Garth smiled and said, "Fantastic. Twenty-eight it is."

I couldn't help but fear for my friend, a real-life tournament virgin. I had tournament scabs on top of tournament scars, so maybe he was better off with this being his first stroke-play competition. Ignorance was bliss, especially when they just about chopped your handicap in half.

Luckily for us, it was pissing rain and freezing cold at Hopeman; perhaps the water would wash the numbers off our scorecards or freeze our fingers to the point where we could no longer write them down. Hopeman wasn't particularly long at a par of 68, but the place felt like a gorse nursery wherein they'd cleared a few paths for people to attempt to advance a golf ball. Whether it was the weather or the frustration of having to locate every single one of our threesome's shots, I felt like I was golfing in one giant shrub of thorns, hacking my way through a damp perdition. I jammed a 3-iron to six feet and three-putted. I backhanded a tap-in and missed. I checked out in every possible way. The best shot I hit all day was a chip-in for triple bogey on the fifth after blowing two tee balls into the prickly nevermore, and while Hopeman's signature twelfth was another cliffside downhill par 3 that recalled the joys of Clivet, I played like a petulant toddler, convinced that if I grew angry enough, they wouldn't make me post.

My bitterness about shooting 81 had blinded me to the travails of my friend. I knew that Garth was working on a number of genuine heft, but I barely helped him look for his balls on number five, lamenting my triple instead. When he told his marker his score for the hole—"That would be a fifteen"—I should have stepped in and told him to no-card and just try to enjoy himself. But I think he did, at least partly, because he didn't hesitate to sign his card at the scorer's table, and as names rolled down the digital scoreboard in the bar, it was all laughs and smiles as we watched GARTH R—USA flash onto the board beside a final tally of 130 gross, 102 net: 130 wasn't all that bad with a 15 in the mix. We took a picture in front of the scoreboard with two big thumbs-up and wide, American smiles.

We treated ourselves to Steak Night at the Golf View Hotel in Nairn. From the look of the place, it was a golf traveler's indulgence planted next to the Nairn links, with a spa and a four-star rating. The garden dining room was lovely, though our service proved that there are still curious wrinkles to hospitality in the British Isles. Table service often felt a bit stiff and utilitarian, perhaps the product of the nontipping culture, though 10 percent is welcome, particularly when they know you're a Yank. At Steak Night, our rib eyes came with a free bottle of red wine. When I asked if I might substitute a bottle of sparking water for the wine, the waitress looked at me as if I'd asked for a carafe of rare morning dew. She paused, then said she would have to consult with her manager.

I thought it a simple request and figured I was doing them a favor by substituting a three-dollar thing for the twenty-dollar thing, but when she returned and told me, "I'm sorry, sir. You can only have the wine. We don't allow for substitutions," I had to shake my head.

"Okay. Bring the wine. I'll just dump it in the garden."

"I'm sorry, sir?"

"I'm kidding," I said. I wasn't. "I'll pay for the water." I didn't always feel like the only person in Scotland who wasn't having a drink in the evening, but on Steak Night, I felt a kinship with all the gluten-allergists and anyone who needed the walnuts picked out of their salad.

The steak and chips were lovely, and as I doused my fried potatoes with vinegar, I cataloged for Garth my frustrations at Hopeman. I'd missed three birdies within ten feet on the first three holes and then given up. It was a movie I'd watched before and hated every time, but when I got out on the course, I insisted on playing it again.

"You should learn from today," Garth said. I didn't expect golf advice from a newcomer, and I wasn't sure whether I resented it, but I listened all the same. "Learn from what happened at Hopeman so that it doesn't happen in the qualifier."

I appreciated the input—I think—but it wasn't anything I didn't know. What I did not know was *how* to learn from my mistakes. I'd been beating myself up on the course and checking out in competition since I was a kid.

And why? To punish myself? To teach golf a lesson? I'd learned plenty from my blunders; I just didn't want to do anything about them. What Garth was really telling me, I later understood, was that when it came to my golf, I needed to grow up.

Reworking my swing path or recalibrating my grip were easy, but growing up—now that sounded like work.

I came to Scotland craving some quirky, and experience had taught that seaside short-courses where golf had been squeezed into a tight swath of coastline were the best places to find it. And Scotland did not disappoint when it came to tiny tracks. I hoped Garth had played enough golf to understand that what he was witnessing at Cullen and at Covesea should not be dismissed as too peculiar or diminutive; rather, these two wee treks through the dunes and boulders were condensed genius, veritable golfing muses to fire the imagination of a links golfer for whom all the green and gorse were starting to look the same.

Word around these parts was that the Cullen golfers were nearly invincible in Opens and scooped up trophies by the bushel, because if you could get around Cullen's tight 4,623 yards in a low number, it meant your short game was aces and your irons were grooved on a par-63 course of ten par 3s. A lot of golfers, myself included, treated their 3-through-6-irons like unteachable pupils, misbehavers that we tolerated having in our bags in case of emergency. We fawned over our drivers, wedges, and putters, but Dynda had explained that his friend Sean Foley, Tiger's former coach, believed that mid-irons were the real talent separators. On Tour, proficiency from 180 to 230 yards was a huge statistical divider between the goods and the greats; Cullen required such yardages off most of its tees, so its members owned the elusive two-hundred-yard dart. I also suspected that the Cullen members had a toughness to them that might have intimidated their competition—in the men's locker room, a sign that asked members to remove their trolleys from atop their lockers had been edited with a dissenting opinion scrawled across the bottom: FUCK OFF YE BAMS. I didn't know what a bam was, but I looked forward to referring to most of my friends as such for the foreseeable future.

I finished Cullen at level par, testament to an improved dexterity with my 4-iron, but most likely a result of my not thinking about my score once in my 63 swings. Instead I was thinking about where the pin might be on the handful of blind par 3s or how we were going to get down to those other golf holes two hundred yards below us or if we were really supposed to climb that slope without some sort of lever and pulley system or how these rock formations had come to exist. The lower valley of the course was partitioned by a massive wall of brown stone and was dotted with gigantically phallic stalagmites. At some point this valley had been level with the cliffs, and pre-historic bits of their mass remained, interrupting the fairways with stunning stone sculptures. The same was the case up the road at Covesea, where the turf wasn't as tidy as Cullen's but the quirks spun us around a ravine of heroic golf holes.

At both courses, we played up against washed-out cave walls, through gaps between little buttes and mesas, past gorges and over crags. There was something almost Paleolithic about the courses as we golfed through these tiny Scottish grand canyons. If Fred Flintstone had golfed, these would have been his home fairways.

Cullen was clearly the more established of the two—it dated to 1870, and its original nine was another Old Tom layout (he and Braid were veritable Johnny Appleseeds of UK golf courses). Cullen had a cozy clubhouse and a busy course, and while one might be reluctant to play a track where one was required to buy insurance in the pro shop before teeing off—the standing-room-only layout brought plenty of other golfers' noggins into play—fifty pence was a bargain for the sigh of relief Garth exhaled when he looked down at his Cullen proof of insurance card and said, "Finally."

A half hour west of Cullen, the Covesea course put the *hidden* back in *hidden gem*. We drove past the entrance twice before turning onto a long gravel descent that we inched down as if pulling our mules—*You sure this is the way?*—relieved to at last see golf holes planted between cliffs and beach. Covesea was a recently reborn nine-holer with a modest charm that won me over in every way, from the hand-drawn course map on a homemade scorecard to the sandy greens shaped like skinny amoebas to the fact that on the 238-yard sixth, I hit a tee ball that would sustain my confidence for a good two weeks, rocketing my hybrid through a canyon chute and sticking the ball to two feet (I followed the formality of my playing partner and holed it out properly). But the most charismatic part of Covesea was the welcome from the caretaker of the pro shop, a woman named Angela who was married to the course's designer. She apologized for her muddy boots and offered us candy bars and scorecards stamped with unpretentious advice for visiting golfers: *Don't forget to stop and smell the roses!* We asked about the origins of this links hideout, and she shared with us the story of her husband, Andy Burnett, who was living a golf dream to which this golf dreamer could only aspire.

Andy had built other parkland courses in the region, places I was sorry I hadn't heard of, but it was his vision to own his own track, so he and Angela put together all their pounds and purchased what used to be twelve holes by the sea. They opened a restaurant beside the first tee, a place called the Tee Shack that was busy with locals and tourists at lunchtime. More people came for coffee with a view than for golf, but after a few years of restaurant success, the Tee Shack burned to the ground in the middle of the night. Andy and Angela were left operating the course out of a trailer without the income from their diners, and Covesea suffered from a steep drop-off in play. They worried that people assumed they were closed after the fire, but let the golfing world know that Covesea is open and is a must-play, not just for the vistas and its exuberant golf holes but for the chance to celebrate a course built by the hands of a man who decided he wanted a golf course, grabbed a shovel, and, over the course of a decade of back-busting labor, built himself a damn good one (Angela said that Andy's brother chipped in to help, too).

I didn't meet Andy during our visit, and that was fine, because I wanted to admire him like a kid in awe of an unmet hero. I loved that he risked and toiled and battled the rains and fire for his own slice of links heaven, and in so doing created and sustained a gift for every golfer fortunate enough to stop and smell the roses at Covesea. There were legions of unknown, frontline fighters who risked their finances and their futures to keep a first tee open. I was glad to know the name of one of them now, and I told Angela I would be back someday to meet him. Hopefully the Tee Shack would be back in business by then, and I could raise a cup to Andy Burnett.

On the drive home from dinner that evening, I remembered that I had neglected a duty of genuine importance and hustled back to my laptop for a phone number. My daughter Maggie's ballet recital was the next morning. Her class practiced all year to present four minutes of semiorganized twirling, and when I had first proposed my two months abroad, this was the sole conflict Allyson had mentioned. For a moment, it was enough to sink the whole trip—you have to have a daughter to understand—until the necessary amount of self-righteous rationalizing kicked in, along with a promise that I would send flowers.

One promise, and I had properly fumbled it. I thought my campaign for Father of the Year had to be suspended yet again until I got hold of a 1-800-Somebody who could get flowers to my house in the next ten hours. I judiciously selected the bouquet (*What kind of flowers would you like to send? How about the fifty-dollar kind*) and carefully dictated my note to the salesman on the phone:

"I want it to say, 'Dear Maggie, have a wonderful time dancing in the show today,'" I recited. "'I am so sorry for missing it, and I love you very much. I wish I could be there.'" I stopped myself. This guy on the other end must think I'm shit.

"I'm not a bad dad or anything," I protested to the anonymous flower man. "I'm just away traveling right now . . ."

"I'm sure you're not," he said, uninterested and unconvinced.

My girls couldn't know what I was up to or after; as far as they understood it, Daddy was away golfing, and to them, golf was just the thing they wanted turned off the television. Maybe they would someday play and understand, perhaps visiting these courses on some occasion and being happy that they were following their father's footsteps. And even if they didn't and never took to the game, if they at least read these pages, they would know that they were in every word and every step. Sorry about the recital when you were five, Maggie, but I watched the video, and of all the twirling tulips, no petals spun as beautifully as yours.

"Guess what, Tom? We get to golf today."

It was with real pleasure that, at Nairn, I got to add a phrase to Garth's morning refrain, words I'd never heard spoken on a golf course before: "With the World Speedgolf Champion."

As Garth's week in Scotland drew to a close, the list in my journal had grown crowded with happy memories of extraordinary feats of golf:

Shit Garth Hit

1. Flagpole
2. Parking lot
3. Practice green
4. Road
5. Practice facility (Garth knocked the metal siding at Fraserburgh's driving range with a triumphant *GONG!*)
6. Beach (At Nairn, Garth outsourced his drive to the beach at low tide, then took my dare and went out and played it from eighty yards off the golf course; the picture I took of him in his follow-through on a vast strand without a golf course in sight captured the spirit of golfer versus nature in its purest form.)
7. Ocean
8. Wrong green (On the eighteenth at Buckpool, Garth confessed to fist-pumping as his ball rolled onto the putting surface from 200 yards out, only to look up and find me chipping to a green forty paces to the left.)

Human beings was nearly added to the list when a threesome at Inverallochy came close to getting a physical from Dr. Mulligans, but in fairness to Garth, he also found a lot of fairways and hit every single green. Eventually.

You traveled with golf clubs to play shots and bring home stories, and Garth had been something of a genius in his ability to combine the two goals, hitting more story-worthy golf shots than I might hope to in all my Scottish rounds. Add to his list eighteen holes with a petite young blonde who was in all ways the opposite of every golfer I expected to join me in Scotland and Garth's trip went from memorable to unmatched.

Among my prearranged playing partners, the average age was forty-eight, average weight was *Why are you asking?*, average ability level was *Two sleeves should be enough*, and average playing pace was *What time is dinner?* Gretchen was twentysomething, weighed less than her set of Nike irons, played off near-scratch, and liked to go around eighteen holes in less than an hour.

A friend of a friend put us in touch, knowing she would be golfing her way around the UK that summer, and when the women's World Speedgolf Champion emails you, you write back. I couldn't decline golf with a world champion, even if I didn't know what speedgolf was (it's hit-and-run golf, where your time and total strokes make a cumulative total). Gretchen compared the test of speedgolf to that of the biathlon, that kid-friendly Olympic sport that combines guns and skiing, where the challenge is combining a breathless pace with a precision skill, sprinting your way to a four-foot putt.

I should have expected a speedgolfer to beat us to the tee at Nairn, and Gretchen did. She greeted me with a huggy friendliness that affirmed her West Coast roots—born and raised in Oregon, she now worked for Nike in Amsterdam. She spoke to both of us with an ease that suggested any worries we might have had about uptight golf with a champion were misplaced. Garth warned her that he was relatively new to golf, but as Gretchen planted her tee in the first box, she was nothing but reassuring. "Hey, man, it's all good," she said. "I'm just trying to hit it where the lawnmowers go."

The lawnmowers would need trim only a thin strip down the center of the Nairn links that day for Gretchen. I expected her to go running after her first tee shot, but she casually strolled the fairways beside us on what was one of the most classic-feeling links I had played since the Old Course—an authentic beach-tied, nine-out, nine-in routing unprotected from the sea, teeming with Ice Age–crafted kinks, with the ocean haunting every swing. A detour into the woods held two of the toughest holes in the Highlands, Nairn's thirteenth and fourteenth, a par 4 and a par 3 draped up and down a hillside. It was an unobstructed sort of links where you could see the rest of the course around you and up ahead. I once thought the mark of a great course was being able to see only the hole on which you were playing (an attribute for which golfers commonly praise Pine Valley), but there's something powerful about a view that gives you a sense of a course's whole size and shape and your place upon it. You become aware of your movement through its geography as you consider what lies ahead. Nairn didn't hide from you. It seemed to dare you to fight your way across it, to touch that wall out there on the far end—there literally was an old barn wall at the end of the outward nine—and golf your ball back home.

Gretchen belted it for a golfer of slight stature, a true athlete who annoyingly had taken up golf in her college years and was now considering a run at the turtle's-pace pro circuit, and I surmised that her easy demeanor and true golf addiction would serve her well in that career path. She hopped planes most weekends from Amsterdam, seeking out cheap airfares to golf in the UK, where she played sunup to sundown, often alone—a genuine golf-chaser. She was fiery on her rare mishits; she expected good shots and nearly always produced them, but was otherwise a laid-back playing partner who taught me a Cali-vibe golf expression that I doubted I would ever reuse but had to appreciate for its novelty. As Garth blasted a drive toward the seals, Gretchen called out, "AMF!"

"AMF?"

She smiled and shouldered her bag. "Adios, motherfucker."

She joined us for dinner at a bright place called the Classroom, a spot that proved Nairn to be a bit of a gourmet hub. The dishes were all products of the owner's nearby farm, and my steak and chips was the best steak and chips of the thirty-seven protein-and-potato entrées I had ordered in Scotland to date. Gretchen brought a breath of fresh air to our dining routine, and her energy was a shot of enthusiasm into the trip—she was young and curious, and after a pint of lager, she peppered Garth and me with questions about not just golf but life. What were our best decisions? Our biggest regrets? What did we want to accomplish in life? Be remembered for?

I felt like a worn wanderer speaking to a hopeful wunderkind, my experience meeting her optimism. It was nice to be looked up to for some wisdom, though I had little to offer. I volunteered some hackneyed advice about living without regret and seizing opportunities. Truth was, I learned more from my day with young Gretchen than she probably did from the day with the author whose book she had finished the evening before. On the course, she explained how speedgolf made her regular game sharper. It didn't allow for doubt and pondering—see it, hit it, get on with it. Target and go: it was golf as a sport, and it sounded brilliant. For all the time I'd spent trying to outthink golf, maybe it was the thinking that had to be unthought. It was a tall ask for a player who lived between his ears, but I could at least aspire to play more like this athlete, reacting rather than overplanning and hoping.

Toward the end of our evening, Gretchen confided that she was coming off a breakup and felt a bit disconnected living abroad. She was happy to have had the brief company. I invited her to come back and join me anywhere along the remainder of my trip; she said she would, and I didn't doubt it. Garth and I both left that dinner feeling like we had a new little sister who was searching but couldn't possibly know how fortunate she was for her youth, her talent, and the troubles that, in hindsight, she would come to see as passing breezes.

Gretchen's weekend drop-in had me recalling the things I was doing at her age, how nothing about my life today matched my plans from that time—thank god—and how life had given me so much of something for which I was almost never grateful: experience. I didn't care for calling myself forty, but forty years of experience was valuable. Priceless, really; and forty-one and fifty-one would bring more. I wasn't able to explain to Gretchen that this was why I lived without regret, why I wouldn't trade in any former days, because the good ones were good and the bad ones made them so. She would see it in time. We all get a transcript full of experience, whether we sign up for the classes or not.

. . .

In case I doubted the value of experience or the blessings born of our trials, Garth offered proof of both the next day. Strathlene on Buckie was another solid locals' course where the holes were not quite as memorable as the views or the wind or the climbs. It wasn't a long walk at a par of 69, but heading into a wind that felt as though we had found the tippity-top of Scotland, it felt like hard labor.

Gretchen's inspiration vanished in the amount of time it took to make a double bogey, which was all of two holes. Not even Strathlene's resonant club motto posted above its door—*Far and Sure*—could inspire me to fight for my scorecard. As we slogged along, we were reminded that if you want it to rain in Scotland, simply take off your rain gear. It had yet to fail me, as if I were some sort of weather shaman who could bring water to the crops by zipping off my rain paints. It was a bad morning to be playing the one course in Scotland that perfectly mimicked that moment in a distance race when the half-marathoners finish and split off from the marathoners, crushing the hearts of the latter. Strathlene's fourteenth played right back down to the clubhouse, telling your mind it was time to shake hands and sign cards, but then it sent you back out across the street for four more up a hill. We played them. I think.

Stinging from a heartless morning 77, I sat in my car in the parking lot at Buckpool, the final course of Garth's visit to Scotland, and looked up at the skies and demanded sunshine. I wasn't fucking around—if you want me to keep going, fine, but I'd been wet for a month, and a month was enough. "Enough!" I said aloud to the windshield. Then I stepped out of the car into a rain aimed directly at my earhole. *If Garth says, "We get to golf today,"* I thought, *I'm going to lock him in the trunk and drive us both to the airport.*

Jones had been kind enough to send me one of their Sunday golf bags, which I kept rolled up like a snail shell in the backseat. I'd almost left it at home, but was grateful I didn't on this day when a few ounces off my shoulder might be the lift I needed to reach for another ball. I dropped nine clubs into the bag and headed out onto the Buckpool course, another clifftop links, this one designed by five-time Open champion John Henry Taylor. I couldn't have cared less if the course had been designed by Spongebob Squarepants; I wanted off the links before my feet had even touched it.

I played on, because the edict of golf's ebb and flow, of links' peaks and valleys, was a natural law of the game that I had never seen denied. It worked on its own timetable, and it often broke your spirit as you waited for it to turn, but in my golfing life, the game always found its balance. Front nine 50s followed by back nine 36s. Bogeys begat birdies begat bogeys. Aces followed doubles, sun followed rain, and by the second hole at Buckpool we were warm in our rain pants but didn't dare take them off. Nor did we reach for the sunscreen; I would rather risk a future scalpel than tempt that beaming yellow thing above us to disappear again.

I knew that Garth was playing better, but it was a quiet and warm round at Buckpool where we were happy to soak up the weather in silence, so there was no talk of our scores as we went. Garth had Sharpied a large *G* on all his golf balls as an identifier, and he left plenty around Scotland that week. If you happen to find one, know that what you are holding is not a joke but a trophy. Hold that ball, and recall and revere the 39 handicapper who, after fourteen rounds in six days, through so many soul-testing trials, never quit, and found his number. As he bent down to pluck his final *G* ball out of the final hole—no putts conceded from beginning to end—he wasn't yet upright before he said, "That's ninety-nine."

He texted his wife from the parking lot. A 99 meant more to Garth than most; in some families, the in-laws wanted a suitor to have a career path or a mouth full of teeth, but Garth had married into a family where his father-in-law played 235 rounds a year and his brother-in-law boasted a 2 handicap, so breaking 100 was an initiation beyond the rote stuff of wedding ceremonies. It was a validation for which he had worked hard, so I wasn't surprised when his wife let the whole family know of the 99 via a group text. His brother-in-law's replies were insistent as he demanded to know what Garth shot on the back nine.

On the drive home, sports radio was abuzz with news of Rory's firing an 80 in the Irish Open at Royal County Down, a tournament he was hosting in his home country and was favored to win. Golf was hard. I never delighted in another golfer's struggles, but the news did make me feel a little brighter about the 72 I'd shot with nine clubs. It would be no consolation to Rory, but his 80 wasn't the biggest story in golf that day—99 at Buckpool should have been grabbing the headlines. At the start of Garth's trip, I would have bet money I didn't have on his not sniffing 100 on a Scottish links. So 99 was a reminder: Garth's never quitting, his carding a 130 in competition, his coming on this trip at all—they were all reminders of the idea that had gotten me over here in the first place.

Over the course of the last five weeks, I had become a why man: *Why* is it raining again? *Why* aren't the putts dropping? *Why* are the numbers adding up wrong again? I needed to get back to the notion that had put me on the plane, the inkling that had sold me and my family and my friends on this adventure. The next morning, Garth would be on his way back to the States and I would be on a tiny plane up to a ferry to a drive to the northernmost golf course on the northernmost island in the United Kingdom, because months before I'd believed I might find the secret to golf there. Why? Because if you're after something they say doesn't exist, you have to go to places they haven't been. Maybe—just maybe—the secret was in Shetland. Why? Because my week with a sub-100 golfer had reminded me: *Why not?*

Upward

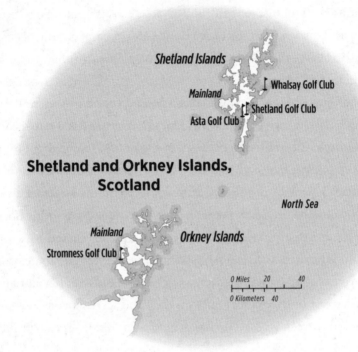

The rental agent was one of three people in the airport when I arrived for my flight—the other two were staffing the small café—and as I returned my keys (I had been instructed to park my rental car anywhere in the lot upon return; there wasn't far to look for it), he inquired about what had brought me to the Orkney Islands with golf clubs.

It was an innocent and polite inquiry, but its unintended weight gave me pause. What the hell *had* I just done with the last thirty hours of my life? My journal noted that I had taken three flights and two ferries, visited four golf courses, and bought two puffin puppets for my girls, but what had really landed me here? If we had a week, I thought, maybe I could offer an explanation.

It would start somewhere around age thirteen, when I emerged from a winter's worth of lessons to the season's first round on Teeth of the Dog in the Dominican Republic—I was a tagalong on one of Dad's business trips—where I banged a first drive, stuck a 5-iron, and dropped a birdie putt, and for an instant, golf was effortless and ideal. From that moment, I was golf—not just a golfer but a person who dreamt golf and loved and resented the game in equal measure, who could abandon it for months or years and still feel it there, binding his foundation. And until I found another birdie like that first birdie, until I again knew effortless and ideal, I would be traveling to places like Kirkwall with this quiver full of arrows.

But I was tired and my phone was in need of charging, so I handed him the keys and told him I was a golf writer here to sample all of Scotland, and had read that the Stromness golf course was worth the trip.

I planted myself next to the only outlet in sight and barricaded myself behind my golf bag. In this one-room terminal, my rolling sack felt like a coffin on wheels. It had barely fit onto the plane that brought me up here, and I had a plea prepared should it raise flags during the next boarding. I would buy another seat for my sticks if need be. I didn't care if they had to move the copilot out and let my clubs ride shotgun: the Mizunos were flying today.

I looked up from my laptop to see the car rental agent standing in front of me, looking relieved to have caught me before takeoff. He had just re-turned from inspecting the car, and I felt myself sliding downward in my seat, wondering if there was room in that coffin for me to hide. We were five minutes from boarding the flight back to Inverness; I had nearly made it, but now I braced myself for news that Kirkwall's inventory of two rental cars had been cut in half. Ours had been a short partnership, but I was certain I'd inflicted a warranty's worth of abuse upon the transmission of my innocent hatchback. An automatic was not on the rental menu in the Orkneys, so I ground my way around the island, expertly shifting from first to fourth, then testing out what reverse felt like at forty miles per hour. The lack of radio stations on this subarctic isle was not a problem; I wouldn't have been able to hear any music over the sound of the moaning gearbox, which, if the agent needed it back, he would likely find in the left lane of traffic about a half mile up the road.

He stood before me with a half smile on his face, his cheeks bronzed by northern life, and I waited for him to hand over a damage report or request a credit card. I'd been careful to ruin the car both inside and out, veering into walls and vegetation as I whiffed at the clutch. I could accept the cost and would willingly pay for whatever alterations he'd located on the Skoda I so thoroughly bushwhacked—not a panel had been spared—but I had yet to decide whether the mounting price of my island jaunt had been worth it.

Aside from postcards of small horses, and the fact that its name sounded very far away, I knew nothing of Shetland. I would learn that it was an ancient archipelago with prehistoric ruins that had been inhabited by Picts, Romans, Vikings, and Norwegians, the former eventually passing along control of the Shetland Isles to Scotland in a dowry deal when the king of Norway's daughter married into Scottish royalty in the 1400s. The unassuming islands played an important role in World War II when a covert Norwegian convoy called the Shetland Bus ran refugees and intelligence between Shetland and Nazi-occupied Norway. Today, the islands' inhabitants made their livings finding fish and petroleum in the northern seas. The largest of these hundred islands was called Mainland (a rather unimaginative title for such an ancient archipelago, I thought), and an hour's flight from Inverness brought me there, to where twenty thousand denizens shared three golf courses for their amusement.

The crush of links awaiting me back in Inverness and the Highlands had shrunken my Shetland island-hopping down to a one-evening stay with a return layover through the Orkneys (another island group halfway between Shetland and the Scottish mainland) to squeeze in Stromness, a course warmly regarded by Gary Sutherland in his island golf book *Golf on the Rocks*. My upward detour from Inverness was the untidiest and most ill-planned portion of the trip, a side jaunt challenged by once-a-day flights, tight ferry timetables, and a thin smattering of places to sleep. I had little idea how I was going to make it from the airport to a golf course, then up to a ferry at the north end of Mainland that would take me out to the isle of Whalsay, home of the northernmost golf course in the UK, and then back to catch the last return ferry to Mainland because wee Whalsay was without accommodation, all with enough time to hustle back down to sample the Shetland Golf Club before setting off to find the lone hotel, with fingers crossed that the lights might still be on in the kitchen.

I expected to be panicked on the morning of my departure, but instead I felt at peace about the day ahead. With no real design to worry about, I was forced to take the next thirty hours as they came. I hoped for the best as I pulled out of the Mainland airport, following signs that had me driving across the runway I'd just landed upon. It seemed I was heading the right way. There was only one road, and only one direction to go—up.

In less than an hour I was pulling into the Asta Golf Club, where I found an empty parking lot just large enough for two foursomes. I was excited to visit this island nine-holer on the banks of Tingwall Loch, where a handful of weary flagsticks were nestled between green and pebbled hillsides. My anticipation had less to do with the course's pedigree—scour the Internet as you might, the tiny course had no real reputation to speak of—than it did with my fascination with its website, which was written entirely in yellow Comic Sans font, a typeface typically reserved for the business cards of birthday party clowns.

I was either about to play Scotland's worst golf course or its biggest surprise; no matter what, it would be worth the hour flight up to Shetland, which I spent wondering how this former four-beers-and-an-Ambien flier had found himself on a budget airline called Flybe in a plane designed to fit neatly inside other planes with a pilot who, I was certain, was up late playing video games in his parents' living room. I imagined the headlines about my demise—surely it would get some coverage in the Highland news—folks shaking their heads at the tragic folly of someone who booked a seat on an airline that sounded like a child's imaginary friend.

Asta was not worth risking one's life for (and I didn't—Flybe turned out to be a smooth and hassle-free conveyor), but it was worth chancing a ferry reservation for the opportunity to walk around its tiny glen of a golf course. The lochside scenery was both stunning and spare, and aside from the road next to the course, there was little reminder of civilization in sight. There was no one in the clubhouse (more like a cabin) when I arrived, but the door was open and visitors were encouraged to drop their greens fees into a box. The scorecard showed a simple map of nine holes—mostly par 3s—with names of both English and unknown origin. The course was mostly a lakeside field with a few vaulted greens and quirky turns, a plot of interesting hillside and waterside grass with a handful of pins inviting you to find your own golf course. Reminiscent of St. Andrews's bygone strategy for managing course wear, Asta's website mentioned that the layout was meant to be played clockwise for two weeks, then counterclockwise for the rest of the month. I had no idea which week I had arrived on, so I played it crisscross-counterclockwise, hitting to whichever flag presented itself and inventing Asta Golf Club as I went.

The fifty-eight-yard seventh hole, Da Neuk, was a quick favorite as I lobbed a ball into a nest of mounds at the edge of the loch, the green sitting below the humps like a lost tomb; yard for yard, it was a clever little treasure. That evening I researched the hole's name. A Dutch translation for *Da Neuk* came back first, and while it would make sense for a golf hole to borrow from Holland, where colf was born, I couldn't understand why they would have dubbed this corker of a hole *That Fuck*. More research revealed that the Scottish translation was *The Corner*—a more fitting moniker, as it sat at the far bend of the course.

As I played my way back to my car along what I guessed was the ninth fairway, I heard what sounded like a waterfall. In the thick grass banks along the edge of the course I found a small gap where a cascading stream was pouring off the neighboring mountain, the water flowing beneath the course on its way to the loch. It looked like a sort of secret and ancient spring, and I couldn't help myself—though I was in a rush to get up to the ferry port, I stopped. I suddenly felt the strongest compulsion to baptize my clubs at the top of the world. I rinsed each of them in the fast-moving water, even giving my putter a splash, hoping that this was where the magic was and that the bogeys might all be cleansed away. I leaned over to take a handful to drink, then thought of the livestock dotting the hills all around me and the centuries of sheep shit in which I had just bathed my clubs. *Lang may yer lum reek*, Asta Golf Club. I found my car in a lot that was still empty and made my way north.

In three weeks' time, I would meet a crowded field of players with proud tournament résumés and world rankings and invitations to events where I could only hope to score a press pass. There were not enough days left in my golfing life to truly become one of them, but as I stood at the top of the home of golf on the edge of the Whalsay Golf Club, a dark ocean separating my feet from the polar ice cap, I realized that I had come this far in search of something I already knew. I thought I had traveled to the northernmost golf course in the UK because none of those players would have. They wouldn't know Asta or the Orkneys, would never have played a round with a muddy four-wheeler for a golf cart or been greeted as I was that afternoon by the club manager, who shook my hand outside the clubhouse and said, "You must really love golf to be all the way up here."

I did, and *that* was why I was here. I could chase the secret to golf and my perfect round until my feet bled (and my crumpled toes did some days), but I would likely find no better answer for this game and what I was chasing than that I loved it. I was here because golf was here. I was a golfer afflicted, always had been, and so were those players down in Edinburgh. In three weeks, it would be nice to walk together.

My ferry ride over to Whalsay was like thirty minutes in an elevator: of the five other cars on the boat, nobody else was getting out, so I sat there as the bridge went up in front of me. We moved. Bridge went down, and there I was on this island off an island. Though I had been disciplined about walking the courses, I was behind schedule for the last ferry back to Mainland. I had also never before had the chance to travel a golf course on a four-wheeler—the only "golf cart" on the property—so I tossed my clubs in the back and we roared toward the first tee. We got to properly play only fifteen or so—plenty enough to get the idea that this was a good golf course any-where, but set on the northernmost cliffs above the fishing boats, it was an absolutely special one.

Like most of the island courses, Whalsay was clay and turf atop rock instead of a sandy-bottomed links, so the wet winter clung to the earth stub-bornly, making for a muddy afternoon between silvery rocks that kept the fairways from sliding into the ocean. You didn't come to a place like this unless you wanted something different, and the course offered that in full, a track of yawning fairways stretched over the crest of a hilltop, calm and cold water all around. Far below the greens, mackerel and scallop boats moved slowly at the top of the world. Some courses felt natural, but at Whalsay, one felt consumed by nature on a track that blended golf and earth on a faraway northern isle. Look for the pin, send your ball after it, chase it down, and mind the sheep and the cliffs as you went.

Graeme, the club captain and my on-course chaperone, hustled me around from one snapshot view to the next, incredibly proud of this place where he and his friends were making golf happen in a land where the sun disappeared for months at a time.

Island life was quiet and hard. People came up here for work, to a world of heavy shoulders and cracked palms where a golf course might feel like an experiment or a desperate diversion. But Whalsay had maintained its tight fair-ways and soft greens for forty years with a handful of holes that any designer would covet; the tee on the cliffside par 4 sixteenth offered an elevated perspec-tive of a soft blue horizon that seemed to wrap around me entirely. The Ryder Cup trophy had visited the year before, and in the pictures from the celebration, it looked as though the whole island had shown up to touch it, with kids waving Scottish flags at the camera. I had come to experience a golf extreme, to follow Scotland's trail of holes to its farthest end, expecting to find a sort of golfing Everest inhabited by off-the-grid hermits. What I found were good people on a great course where running a golf club wasn't a curiosity or a sidenote but a natural part of a peaceful life.

I was sorry to leave Whalsay in such a rush, but the final boat beckoned. From the return ferry, I raced down to the Shetland Golf Club to quickly sample my third track of the day. My morning in Inverness felt like a child-hood memory; I knew the days were long up here, but this one had whole weeks to it. I parked in a lot half full of cars and grabbed a scorecard out of the empty clubhouse. From the first tee I could see a vast inland track below me, treeless holes stretched across a deep valley and dissected by a wander-ing burn. It looked like a fun and proper test, the course dotted with evening threesomes on holes that ran down and then back up the Shetland hillsides. It also looked like too much. For this day, far too much. I ripped a driver off the first tee and took two steps to follow it, then stopped, marked my card with a 1, and dragged my clubs back to the car. I had played Shetland Golf Club—just not quite all of it.

When I got back to the Scalloway Hotel, the bar was shoulder-to-shoulder, a blend of families and fishermen bringing a close to the work week. Men with beards and heavy jackets cast tired stares over tables of foam-lined glasses. Some of them spoke Spanish, visitors in search of mackerel. I found a spot back in the corner next to an old man reading a book and nurs-ing a pint. My fish and chips were lovely and disappeared in a moment, and I surveyed the pub as men and women toasted Friday night. The windows were still bright at 10:00 p.m., giving the tipsy room the feeling of a strangely timed party. It was a place of travelers and laborers and deep-rooted locals all squeezed together as if to check in on one another, demonstrating the cama-raderie of people who shared the joys and hardships of life faraway. I felt at home. I was so fortunate to be a golfer, I thought. I could be in Philadelphia right now, browsing Home Depot for paintbrushes.

I sank into my chair and thought of my friend. Robert would not have cared much for the golf that day—too much work to see more golf beside the water—but he would have made the flight for this pub. It was a room full of conversation-hungry strangers he would never see again; such places were Robert's most beloved milieus, chances to practice his sincerity and see the world as a genuine place. It was like an airport bar, where talk came easy and you could be anyone you chose. For Robert, these settings tingled with pos-sibility, and he would have worked his Yankee accent to its fullest potential, owning the room as he and a table of fishermen cured all the world's ills before sunrise. He would talk of the books he had written and the miles he had traversed; he would win their approval, and not because he could but because he had to. I knew, because I once won that way. Gaining a stranger's appreciation was a panacea above all others, a salve to heal whatever sort of mess our lives presented us the next morning. That evening on Mainland, I missed Robert. I missed the Robert part of me.

I did not miss the hangover the next morning as I departed at dawn to catch a flight down to Kirkwall in the Orkney Islands, where I was stopping off for a few hours to play the Stromness Golf Club. Rain dampened a round I had been anticipating on this 125-year-old layout enveloped by dark sea, with holes woven into an overlapping tapestry. The whole place slanted across a hill that was still soft from the dark months. At the water's edge, concrete World War I bunkers were tucked into the earth of Stromness, and at the far end of the course, a World War II armory sat dormant behind tall barbed-wire fences. The faded green walls and shuttered windows of the long, squat buildings haunted the course in the rain. I thought of soldiers who once crossed these fairways to man a post and await an invasion, and I wondered how I ever could have thought my golfing days were hard. I was so soft, and so fortunate to have the chance to be so.

I took 68 swings (three over) to get around the empty Stromness layout, and for playing quickly, I was rewarded with a rare bounty on this trip: time. So I set off to be a tourist for a few hours before my jump back to Inverness. Whereas Shetland had felt vast and subdued, Orkney was a bustling little destination, its central town of Kirkwall full of bright shops and a busy main street closed to traffic for pedestrians. Perhaps its proximity to the mainland of Scotland made the island a more popular getaway; I was surprised to find backpackers roaming stores whose windows were full of T-shirts and stuffed puffins, all bursting with Orkney pride. It was a place I wanted to return to with the family, with its bright vibe and easy parking. Braver souls might have taken off to cruise the coastline, but once I safely planted my latest stick-shift in town, I opted to rest the clutch and shop for the girls.

I landed back in Inverness late that afternoon, and though I had been gone less than forty-eight hours, I could scarcely recall where I left my car.

It felt as though I'd been puddle-jumping for weeks. I located the station wagon and loaded up my island souvenirs, and later, in my Inverness hotel, I looked at my journal but couldn't bring myself to lift the pen. I was unsure of what I had to say about my northern pilgrimage, other than that I had made a handful of good golf swings on a bumpy island race that had likely sidetracked a focused golf progression.

There was a tee in my pocket sticking into my hip. I took it out and held it in my fingers. It had almost remained in Orkney, but that afternoon, as I sat in the corner of the silent one-room airport, hiding behind my golf bag, the car rental agent approached. I was expecting to hear that I now owned an immobilized Skoda in Kirkwall, but instead he smiled and showed me the tee.

"Glad you're still here. You left this in the car," he explained, handing the tee over to me. And that was it. His inspection of the rental had yielded no issues other than a rogue peg I didn't need. I knew that tees were not throwaways over here, but still—there's honesty and hospitality, and then there's a car rental agent chasing after you to return a tiny white stick.

I think I laughed a little. Where in the world was I? Where did these people come from? Maybe it was my weariness, but I paused at the unnecessary yet undeniable symbolism, as if he were handing off a baton or returning my sword. *Onward*, the insignificant twig in my hand told me. *Carry on*. I was a golfer, and I needed my tee.

We chatted for a moment, and it turned out that he was a golfer as well and played the Stromness course regularly.

"How was your golf?" he asked.

"It was good," I told him. "Really good. A lot different than home."

"That's what you came for, isn't it?" he said.

And it was.

Perspective

Inverness to Wick, Scotland

Wick Golf Club

North Sea

Brora Golf Club

Golspie Golf Club

Royal Dornoch Golf Club

The Carnegie Club at Skibo Castle

Tarbat Golf Club

Tain Golf Club

Fortrose & Rosemarkie Golf Club

Castle Stuart Golf Links

0 Miles   10   20
0 Kilometers   20

She was not a she. She was a he. And he left his footprints—rather, he left his shoes—across the Scottish Highlands.

When I graduated high school, *Cheers* had just wrapped up its long television run, and our valedictorian referenced the final show in his graduation speech, the episode wherein Cliff Clavin divulges to Sam the meaning of life: "Comfortable shoes. If you're not wearing comfortable shoes, life is just chaos."

My FootJoy Casuals had been worthy companions for the six hundred or so miles I had hoofed to that point, keeping me blister-free with a spring in my arches. But Lindsay chose his footwear with a discerning eye for comfort.

When I met him in the northeast town of Tain, I was first surprised to find that he was a man. He was the brother-in-law of a college buddy, Sean, and while we had met years before at Sean's Connecticut wedding, that encounter had gone adrift in my long-term memory (truthfully, my recollection of Sean's Connecticut wedding was beer, a stack of red chips at Mohegan Sun casino, and some beer). So when Sean told me he would be joining me in Scotland and was bringing Lindsay with him, I quietly mourned Sean's marriage to Heather and hoped this Lindsay character was treating him well. It turned out that Lindsay was a ruddy-faced, ginger-hair-going-gray golfing dad in slippers—or at least that's how he first appeared to me outside the hotel in Tain as we met for the drive out to Tarbat.

Lindsay's parents had emigrated from Scotland, and he had been married in a Scottish castle north of Dundee, so I wondered if he wore slippers to showcase his comfort on native soil. Or maybe he was pajama-hungover, unable to locate his clothes or bear to dress in full. Turned out he was neither; on the train up to Tain, Lindsay had donned his slippers for the long, jet-lagged ride, and left his sneakers above him in the luggage rack. They were currently headed back to Edinburgh, so it would be a week of golf shoes and slippers for my new friend, from whom I learned that, when spelled with an *a* in Scotland, Lindsay is a man's name.

As soon as I saw the slippers, I recalled that high school speech. Here I was, searching for a secret, and there it was: comfortable shoes. Being comfortable—on a train, in your slippers, in our own skin—was a key I coveted and knew I lacked. I thought about high school a lot during that week with the lads in the Highlands. The humor was sophomoric, the giggles abundant, and, like those four years, I wanted it to be over without knowing how much I would miss it when it was gone.

My temples throbbed with a heavy island hangover as I made my way north from Inverness. My golf had regressed to a weary, ball-wiping swing and an unwelcome game of approaches played from alternative fairways. My solo trip north had stirred a loneliness that I hadn't felt since the trip's first week. A shrink would diagnose me as an extroverted isolator; I craved attention and approval, but really just wanted to be left the hell alone. Something about being alone at the top of the planet had brought out the latter in me, and I would have been happy to play the next fifty rounds by myself. It was a grace that I was quickly joined by a pack of friends who pulled me out of that little universe and plugged me back into the wide world I was traveling.

Brian and his so-pregnant-our-baby-might-get-Scottish-citizenship wife had arrived the day before Sean and Lindsay. Brian was a year older than me and a close friend from home who, next to Robert, knew my story better than anyone. He was fit and had a good head of brown hair, a decent golfer with a dedication to very short hiking shorts. His wife, Amanda, knew me well, too; she was a pretty triathlete who six months ago had biceps to shame my own but was now training for motherhood. Brian and I had both suggested to/pleaded with her to stay home to be closer to her doctor in her third trimester, but like any good marathoner, she had no ear for apprehension. She got the green light from her doctor and packed her bags. I witnessed pregnancy tension only once during their week in Scotland, when Amanda tried to squeeze herself into the back of their two-door rental as she insisted I have the front seat. Brian had to raise his voice as she climbed in like a tunnel rat, lying sideways across their luggage and propping her belly atop two sets of golf clubs. "Amanda!" was all that needed to be said as we helped pull her back out, her lone concession to the idea that a pregnant woman can't do absolutely everything.

I wanted them to have a memorable week, to make this time in Scotland worth the effort of so much travel to a remote corner of the UK at the most inconvenient of times, and I worried about blending two groups of friends. College and contemporary pals—would they get one another? Would I be myself? Would I divide my attention equally and effectively? Damn—my ego had its own ego. I was convinced that I was the key to the happiness of every cognizant life form. I was relieved and perhaps a bit disappointed to find that this wasn't the case when, three holes into the nine-holer at Tarbat, Lindsay and Brian started exchanging lines from *Family Guy* and laughing like old roommates. At some point on this trip, or maybe years after, I would finally accept that I was being my best when I wasn't trying to be at all.

Brian had received a proper introduction to heavyweight links golf the day before, when we played both Fortrose and Rosemarkie (one course with two names, I was relieved to find) and the esteemed Scottish Open venue Castle Stuart. Situated on a peninsula above Inverness known as the Black Isle, Fortrose & Rosemarkie traced its golfing heritage to 1793—early for the Highlands—and the peninsula took its foreboding name from the fact that snow never stuck there, giving the land a dark appearance while the rest of the Highlands shone white. Concrete posts beside some of the fairways recalled its closings during the World Wars, when it served as a guardhouse during the first and a practice ground for the D-Day invasion during the second. It was a two-way avenue of a course laid along a finger of sand sticking out into Rosemarkie Bay, the holes roaming outward toward a small lighthouse at the turn. With waves left and right, you couldn't find a more wonderfully exposed setting for golf. You felt its age and confidence in the earth it sat upon; it didn't tease or tickle with surprises, but it was a soulful links fit for golf pilgrims in search of a classic.

Across the water, we could see the course we were heading to in the afternoon. If only we'd had a boat, we could have cut an hour off our commute around the Moray Firth and back down to Castle Stuart, a course that was an ideal first-day complement to Brian's morning round. While Fortrose & Rosemarkie was old, natural, and subdued, Castle Stuart tossed us into new, crafted, and audacious. The place glimmered with visitor-friendly luxury, from the flawless fairways and the five-tiered clubhouse meant to look like the helm of an ocean liner cresting over the firth to the dreamy vistas that extended all the way to the men's room—above the urinals, set perfectly at eye level, was a long, thin window with a view of fairways pouring off the property. I felt awkward standing there with camera in hand as I relieved myself—*Please let that door stay shut*—but I needed to capture this proof that when it came to details, Castle Stuart had mastered them all.

I'd met a golf photographer back at Kingsbarns, a lad named Kevin whose new company, Recounter, specialized in nostalgic albums of buddy trips and golf outings, where 20-handicappers were transformed into photobalanced pros. His pictures made golfers into movie stars, so I invited him along to Castle Stuart to see if he could capture my better golfing self. Plus,

I needed a new headshot: my black-and-white photo from age twenty-six was beginning to feel dishonest. The kid in that shot was so full of hope and confidence; what a silly prat.

Kevin's camera worked its magic, but so did Castle Stuart, where the holes slanted sideways along the water's edge, leading you over hills and pushing you down into valleys on a relentless routing of expertly molded drama. The place was pristine and manicured for the eyes of deep-pocketed tourists, and while it looked like an unfair fight at first blush, behind the dunes and beside the water were benevolent fairways and wide greens. The course feigned punishment but offered playability, even if I was still struggling to find the approximate middle of my clubface. Kevin made it all look good as I carded a sloppy 79, capturing me in long follow-through poses, my eyes fixed on an imaginary rocket drive while my actual ball took flight for the firth. I played to the camera and made bad shots look like all-timers. At last, the secret to my best golf: pretending.

The bar at Castle Stuart felt like a pilothouse with 180 degrees of water and fairways hugging us in our booth. As we awaited our lunch before heading out to suck in our guts for the camera, Kevin reminded me that what felt like a never-ending trail of golf holes was actually a very small country. He knew half the faces at Castle Stuart, and our waitress turned out to be an old pal from Edinburgh. I understood roughly a third of their quickly accented conversation, and even learned some local slang: When Kevin said things went *Pete Tong*, it meant they went *tits up*, which meant they went poorly. I felt for this DJ I had never heard of, his name adopted as a rhyming substitute for *a bit wrong*, and was relieved that my last name was rhyme-averse, lest it become slang for shooting 94 in a qualifier for which you had dedicated two years of your life.

I noticed a young man outside stalking a fairway in the distance, snapping photographs and hardly bothering to golf his ball at all. When I inquired about what he was up to, I learned that he was a "shaper," and that such a vocation was an actual thing. Later that afternoon he would let us play through, explaining to us that he worked for Tom Doak and was studying the Castle Stuart contours, an apprentice doing his research.

Perhaps it was the soft state of my game or the fact that our chicken chili didn't arrive in time for our appointment at the first tee, but I took umbrage at this man's occupation. Shapers manufactured a new course's humps and bumps and runoffs, icing a lumpy cake and bulldozing intrigue into the fairways, or they gave facelifts to older courses by pushing earth around—either way, this hands-on notion that a golf course required shaping left me disappointed, even if the courses I loved were the product of their diesel-fueled designs.

For someone who considered himself golf-forward in his thinking and balked at golf's stuffy superciliousness, I could be a curmudgeon when it came to modern design. I preferred course finders versus course designers. Braid, Morris, and, more recently, Eddie Hackett in Ireland—they didn't force layouts onto the landscape. They studied the topography and imagined golf holes and routed them according to the suggestions not of owners or course raters but of the land itself. Hackett's design method was to walk a wild corner of coastline for a few weeks, often taking a daily bus to get there in the days before designers could afford helicopters. Eventually he would emerge from the dunes to tell his clients he had located their golf course (his legendarily meager design fees barely covered all the bus trips). Links were meant to be organic discoveries gifted by nature; that such rare soil now required shaping by people—by us temporary and temperamental people— sucked the soul right out of a golf hole for me.

As precious as rain forest and as rare as the Rockies, links land is a geological miracle shaped by shifting glaciers and receding tides. As the early earth's mantle cooled and ocean floors sank, the waters pulled back to reveal things like, say, Europe, and as seas continued to retreat, they cut valleys and rivulets into coastlines that had once been submerged. The droppings of seabirds fertilized sands that sprouted grasses, and sheep, rabbits, and wool traders did the rest to bring golf to these acres, where a game would help preserve fragile landscapes from holiday cottages. Golf in the dunes was a walk through our primordial past, so the thought of pushing it around to get par up to 72 left me conflicted. I loved these golf courses, new and old, and if I wasn't a golf writer, sculpting fairways from the seat of a bulldozer would be my dream gig. But I was once told that the difference between happiness and joy is the presence of the divine; I can be damn happy on a man-made golf course, but it's on the discovered ones shaped by a mystery that I feel golf joy.

Fortrose and Castle Stuart were the entrées to wee Tarbat's side dish, but as so often happens on a golf trip, memory more fondly recalled the nine-hole layout (with ten greens) of Tarbat for its unexpected fun and quirky authenticity. When we arrived at the cottage-sized clubhouse—some of us in slippers—we found the place empty aside from a few long tables under plastic tablecloths, where a gray-haired man in paint-splattered jeans leaned over a tool box. He looked up at us without so much as a nod.

"Excuse us. Is the manager here?"

He went back to shuffling a small pile of lumber beside the wall. "Better be soon," he said. "He's bringing my breakfast."

We laughed. He didn't. We tried to look natural, four Americans not sure whether they should golf or stay or wait or leave, looking around the Spartan room as if we were genuinely interested in the results from last week's Texas scramble or the condition of the emergency exit sign. Then came a deep rumbling to shake the floor, and—*BANG!*

Brian jumped. Lindsay almost leapt out of his moccasins. Sean shuddered, and I covered my head. *BANG! BANG!* Our hungry friend fired nails into two-by-fours as I followed the boys outside with our ears covered.

"We're going to go play!" I called back to the man over the hum of his compressor. We had wanted to make a proper introduction before teeing it up, but the course felt safer than the clubhouse. At least it did until the manager caught up with us on the first fairway, bouncing down the cart path in a blue pickup truck.

"I'm Tom Coyne, the American . . ." I leaned toward his window, then wondered if we should have waited a little longer to get the green light. He wore sunglasses, and his broad shoulders made the truck's cab look small. The dark steel of a rifle barrel lay across his lap.

"I know who you are," he said, and shook my hand through the truck window. "Sorry I wasn't here when you arrived. Had to get Johnny his breakfast."

He stepped out of his truck and met our foursome, welcoming us to Tarbat with excitement and inquiries about our hometowns. He handed each of us a Tarbat ball marker and pointed out a few spots where the routing got tricky. We were welcome to go around as many times as we liked, he told us, and thanked us for taking the time to visit his course. When he hopped back in his truck, he apologized for being in a rush. "Have to go shoot some rabbits," he said before driving off. We headed back down the fairway, trying to recall where our opening drives had landed and hoping the rabbits were on the back nine. If only there were a back nine.

The schedule decreed we go around Tarbat only once, but we enjoyed it so much that we risked a pellet in the arse and played it again, its short but wavy layout perfect for a foursome of buddies who wanted fun, unbothered golf. Blind shots across twisted slopes on a course enveloped by a charming Scottish village—Tarbat was refreshingly playable. The seventh tee box had us backed up against a cemetery where the yardage was painted on the graveyard wall, and next door I watched schoolchildren play at recess while the group teed off. Lindsay looked over at the children kicking a soccer ball.

"This is a nice life here. Little school, little golf course, everybody knows each other. They do life well here," he said, and I agreed. He knew the place better than the rest of us.

That evening we dined in a pub in Tain where the waitress informed us that they were out of the burrito; I got a polite smile when I sighed and explained that we had come all the way to the Highlands for their burrito. Lindsay ordered curry chicken (a safe bet in the UK), while we all deliberated over ordering the haggis spring rolls. Lindsay said he never touched the stuff. His mother was born and raised in Scotland but had never eaten haggis, and he kept the tradition alive. She didn't eat it, he explained, because there was a time when people *had* to eat it, when sheep heart and lung spiced and minced and wrapped in sheep stomach was all they had. It was Scottish Spam, a food now consumed out of ironic nostalgia but shunned by those who recalled it as a meal of last resort (my mother similarly seemed to deeply resent Spam, a pink remembrance of a lean Scranton childhood). Haggis reminded me of Andouille sausage with a touch of cinnamon that was lovely when fried in pastry or sprinkled over pizza.

In nearly every golf town in Scotland, I found a hotel or B&B called the Golf View and had slept in a handful, but the Golf View House in Tain topped them all. While its view of the Tain links was largely theoretical, the Golf View was a tall stone manor house with manicured grounds and high-ceilinged rooms with old charm and fair prices. When the lady of the house saw me hauling golf clubs toward the front door, she asked if we would mind leaving our clubs in the car or in the foyer. There was a time when such a request would have had me searching town for another room after a Jimmy Chitwood–style protest—*I stay, clubs stay. They go, I go.* But by the time I'd arrived in the Highlands, I was less concerned about my clubs' well-being. It would be no great tragedy if someone touched or even stole them. Maybe I could leave them in the car for a night. Maybe I could leave them outside on the sidewalk, beneath a lamppost, with a large ribbon wrapped around them and a trail of ten-pound notes leading to the door of the nearest pub. Then I would get not just a day's break from golf but a handy excuse for my scores. With borrowed clubs, 82 wasn't a bad number.

Still, I couldn't bring myself to abandon my silver albatrosses, not with the miles we'd covered and those we had yet to traverse together. Besides, a rental bag might be heavier. I explained to our hostess that I couldn't sleep without my sticks, and when we agreed to not use her house towels to clean our clubs like her Canadian visitors had last week, she was fine with them coming upstairs. We assured her that we Americans were exemplary guests compared to our scofflaw neighbors, and with a rainbow outside my window pointing to the fairways of Tain below, I snuggled my Mizuno MP-15s and dreamt of pure contact. I don't often recall my dreams, but I woke the next morning with distinct memories of making a hole in one on a long, links-y par 3—hop, roll, jar. I even recalled the club—my 3-iron hybrid—and my reaction: I threw my club into the sea and walked off the course, hands raised like Rocky, defiant in my triumph.

I liked the Tain links instantly for the unpretentious sign out front that recalled the Highlands of Alaska more than Scotland. *Tain Golf Club* was carved into three tall amber logs beside the driveway, some sort of unexpected Eskimo art beside another log carving of Old Tom Morris, who had designed Tain's original fifteen-hole layout. Called "Old Tom's northern jewel," the course sparkled with class. The holes ranged from solid to outstanding, with the eleventh itself worthy of a Highland haul. Named Alps, its blind approach required you to play over them, parachuting your ball onto a skinny green cupped between dunes and the ocean. The layout was guarded by a tall pine forest on one side, giving us rare safety from the wind as the breezes softened at Tain and finally gave me a chance—a chance to shoot another 41 on the front and make the turn in a fog of frustrated apathy.

I stepped up to the tenth tee with all the focus of a ten-year-old in a water park and took a quick swipe with my driver, barely watching my ball in flight.

"That was pounded," I heard as I picked up my tee. And it was. Launched low and unyielding, it bounded over the humps of the tenth fairway with a devil-may-care, golf-is-easy confidence that I hadn't seen from my ball in a week. It was a ball compressed versus a ball slapped. I knew the small physics behind the titanic difference—a few degrees of swing path, a hundredth of a second of delay in the release of my hands—but as I watched my ball refuse to stop running toward the green, I needed to know what I had done differently, and whether I could do it again. That distracted swing had been shorter for sure, so maybe that would work.

Could it be so simple? Shorten my swing? It seemed an unsatisfying solution; my swing was too profound to be fixed by a back-of-the-cereal-box swing tip. But I tried it on the next hole—boom. And boom again. Boom-bibbity-boom. One shot after another, my ball behaved like a thoroughbred whose jockey had finally let it run.

Golf was neither an impossible game nor a complicated one. It was a simple game for complicated people. And stepping to my ball with one clear idea, no matter whether the notion turned lame tomorrow, I felt hope in my chest. I felt the lift of purpose. There was no purpose without work, and a three-quarter swing was my work for the day at Tain.

And work worked. On the 215-yard seventeenth, a par 3 guarded by a babbling burn that wriggled its way around the green, I didn't see any water. I didn't see the barley left or the bottom half of the pin hidden behind a fuzzy hump. I just saw a chance to try my new three-quarter swing, to keep after what was working. I pulled out my hybrid and took a few cuts at the air, focused by the task—*shorter swing, shorter swing*.

I couldn't see all of the pin, but as I watched my ball rifle toward the stick, I listened for it. It was going to be close.

"I don't see it," Lindsay said. "Dude. I think it went in."

"Fuck you," I said. I'm not sure why.

The four of us hustled toward the green, chins up as we peered over the mound guarding the hole. Do I tell them I dreamed this? Can I see the future? Am I not only golf cured but a golf prophet as well?

"I don't see it," Lindsay said. "I don't see it. I still don't see it." And then, "Oh, there, I see it."

No matter that I would three-putt from twelve feet below the hole; releasing my putter could be tomorrow's work. I knocked a 7-iron to eight feet on eighteen and finished with a birdie. For all the golf I had played, spending an entire summer beside a golf ball, I wanted nothing more than more.

We moved on from Tain with warm memories and pictures of each of us hugging a wooden Tom Morris. As we turned north, Sean and Lindsay were particularly happy about moving up the road to their next stop. While Brian and I had been enjoying our stay at the Golf View, they had made a friend at their hotel in town. At their last three breakfasts, a sweet old lady had inquired as to whether they knew Bob Carpenter, an American whose son was engaged to her daughter and who, according to the stories she would daily repeat to them, was a blend of Arnold Palmer and Bruce Wayne. Each morning, her disbelief at them not knowing Mr. Carpenter grew; she insisted they must be familiar with Bobby C (as we would come to call our unknown luminary), who posted course records at Dornoch and owned homes around the world, who took her to the best restaurants in the UK and rode bareback across the Highlands. Each morning, Sean and Lindsay nodded through their headaches at the legend of Bob Carpenter; it was better than having to hear her story about being locked out of the hotel again. Somebody—we'll call him Lindsay—had returned from the pub and decided to lock the hotel's front door, causing this poor woman to wait outside in the rain for an hour. Lindsay shook his head in outrage at her misfortune. Who would do such a thing? The savage.

Escaping their Bobby C breakfast was a welcome reprieve, but moving to the Golf Links Hotel in Golspie was Christmas morning for Lindsay. He and Sean had checked into the modest hotel beside the golf course that looked like little more than a cottage with a vacancy sign, but as he stepped through its doors, Lindsay, a connoisseur of Scottish whisky, found a sight lovelier than the first tee at the Old. The bar in this anonymous inn was a museum to Scotch, with long rows of glimmering glass jars of brown syrup—over two hundred single-malts—perched on the walls. Lindsay had two nights to sample them all and vowed to do his best, trying a few thirty-year-olds before heading for our tee times at Royal Dornoch.

The wind was blowing the doors off our cars that morning, but Lindsay smiled through the breeze, the pellets of rain evaporating on his red cheeks. *Uisge-beatha*—Scots Gaelic for "water of life" (say *uisge* fast and you'll hear the origin of the Anglicized *whisky*)—ran through his arms and fingers, and while I knew he would be useless by the back nine, I envied his warm stomach and slow-moving glance.

We had arrived in a whisky capital of a whisky country where the word was never spelled with an e; *whiskey* referred to its Irish and American imitations, and ordering either was a transgression in these parts. Distilleries like Glenmorangie and Glen Ord, Dalmore and Clynelish and Balblair outnumbered the golf courses above Inverness, and I had found myself being offered a dram of the local stuff on a daily basis. I came as close to saying yes to a short glass that evening as I would on any day of the trip, but fortunately for me, that night's heady residence already had me feeling drunk before I walked through the door.

I'd been warned that there were two or possibly three courses in Scotland where I would not be able to play, no matter how charming my emails to the club secretary were. One of them was a place called Skibo Castle. A confidential lakeside links played by almost a dozen golfers every year, it had been described as a tee time beyond a visitor's reach, but as I would be passing it on my way up from Tain, I thought a message to the manager was worth the time. A quick reply from their marketing director told me that play was restricted to residents of the estate, and such residency was available only to members of the Carnegie Club. Short the forty-five-thousand-dollar entry fee and annual dues, I felt my chance to play Skibo had vanished, until I opened my last Wonka bar and found a golden ticket: a night's stay in the castle was miraculously suggested. If I could visit on a quiet weeknight, they might be able to sort me a room and a round, so I juggled my Highland itinerary, told the lads I would see them tomorrow as they headed for the whisky bar (Lindsay left his golf shoes in my car, putting him back into slippers for the next twenty-four hours), and headed to a place where I did not belong, but blissfully so.

You know you're headed to an enclave of exclusivity when your GPS can't find an entrance. My nav system piloted me to a green gate with no sign, which I later learned was the maintenance entrance. The gates eventually opened, and I found myself driving a station wagon in the dark through the shaded Skibo golf course. The manor was hard to miss, in the way that the White House is hard to miss from Pennsylvania Avenue, but without a parking lot or any cars in sight, I wondered if I had driven myself into a Victorian vampire noir. After passing through the heavy cathedral doors, I was met by a butler in a kilt who presented me with a silver tray of whisky concoctions, welcoming me to this alternate Skibo universe. That I lamented there being only twelve glasses on his tray and wondered if he might be able to scrounge up some more was a reminder that it was best I take a sparkling water. I was shown to my room by a steward, who was standing by and who greeted me by name.

"My bags, I should go get them from the . . ." I paused, and was told they were being taken to my room.

"But my car, where is the parking . . ." I was told my car would be looked after as well. I was to just hand over the keys and follow him up a set of mahogany stairs wide enough for a light brigade beneath five stained-glass arches befitting a basilica and a bust of Mr. Carnegie on the landing to welcome me to one of the places where *they* lived, people I had never met but suspected existed, people who ran things—things like companies, countries, earths.

My room—rather, my quarters—was paneled in golden wood with a fireplace, three sitting nooks, and a four-poster bed that required a small ladder. Upon it sat a Skibo teddy bear that I could buy downstairs for my kids, if only the place took cash or credit. Luckily for me, the Carnegie Club was nontransactional; you paid your membership, and when you arrived at the castle, you left your wallet in your fast-vanishing car. I had stayed at places that didn't take Amex, but this was my first visit to a place that didn't take money. There was the sort of wealth where you had money, and then there was the sort of wealth where you were above money. This was my first experience of the latter, and I liked it. Very much.

My bathroom was the size of my last hotel's lobby, and while I didn't need two claw-foot tubs in the middle of the room, I began to see how having only one could spoil a vacation or disappoint Madonna's guests—she had married Guy Ritchie here, and a journalist friend told me how the only photog to score wedding shots for the tabloids had hidden out in the bushes at Skibo for a week (he was okay with it; he made enough money to retire). My two dressing tables were covered with silver and jeweled brushes, and my nightstand came with a jar of Skibo Sleeping Pills—ah, so the überwealthy *are* restless and discontented pill-poppers—that turned out to be gorgeous little bricks of salted vanilla fudge. Nearby I found the guide to Skibo etiquette, a multipage brochure with cartoon renderings of various social situations that advised guests on everything from the use of technology (it was banned in public spaces) to appropriate volume levels in the hallways. I was reluctant to step foot in the hallway lest I be discovered as an imposter and escorted out. I was fine remaining in my chambers; I had eighteen hours of life in Downton Abbey, and I wasn't going anywhere.

I soon discovered that I had my own hallway with a side door to my butler's quarters, if only I had remembered to bring him. When I asked the steward for my room key, he couldn't help but smile.

"There are no keys. Your door doesn't lock. Don't worry, it doesn't need to."

I ate room service that I ordered from an imaginary menu—*Just call down to the kitchen and tell them what you would like*—and sat in my room, anxious, wondering if there was such a thing as too much luxury, at least for a golf drifter like me. The sleeping pills lightened my mood, and I was settled by the time turndown service arrived. It took twenty minutes to maneuver the bulk of all the drapes into place, and no, I didn't need them to run me a bath. Or baths. I didn't leave any tip for the maid the next morning, as I was told tipping was forbidden, but she wouldn't mind—I'd never left a hotel room so clean in my life. Aside from an empty jar of fudge, it was like I'd never been there.

The morning spread of smoked fish and pastries and fruit and meats was banquet-sized, though I was the only person who had arrived for breakfast. Butlers in their kilts served me tea while I inquired about the status of my stuff. My bags were already in my car, which was now pulled around front, and my clubs were en route to the golf course. But before golf I was headed off to the spa for a massage; I had been so bold as to ask the marketing director if a massage might be arranged, as eighty rounds of golf had me feeling a bit stiff. I offered to pay any price for it, but soon learned my insistence was unnecessary—there were no prices on the massage menu that I studied under the tutelage of my masseuse, a brunette of Eastern-European accent.

We thoroughly reviewed my health history and aches, after which she administered a comprehensive sniff test in which I inhaled a buffet of aromas from small crystal jars. By identifying my favorite smells, she was able to precisely diagnose my body's deficiencies. My three preferred aromas pointed to my being tired, exhausted, and weary. I wondered if she was just going to send me back to bed, but ninety deep-tissue minutes later, I felt as though I had been freshly cracked from a golden mold. My limbs tingled with life; my stumps sprang with energy. I weighed myself in the locker room to find that I was down thirty-seven pounds from my starting weight, and I studied my oiled frame in the mirror—there were strange lines pressed into my shoulders and chest and stomach. The backs of my thighs and calves were packed hard with something; I felt like a drug mule who had been stuffed with muscles instead of *cocaìna*. I was born anew, a taut, Highland-hardened golfing machine. I was younger. Better. I was Bob Carpenter.

Though my overnight at Skibo was for a party of one, I had been invited to bring a friend along for the golf. Brian's GPS did a better job of finding the Carnegie estate than mine, and we arrived early at the pro shop, where they definitely did take credit cards, at least until the two of us nearly melted ours. I had rarely golf-shopped on this trip, but at a clandestine course like this, neither of us could resist loading up on brag-garb.

Outside, the Skibo rain was of a different sort. Lochside with links features, it wasn't a seaside layout, so the wind sat quietly and let the water soak us in a straight and steady shower. The starter insisted on stuffing two bottles of single-malt into our bags before we teed off—*Take it, take it, man!*—as if it really was the water of life on such a damp, cold morning. Brian took the bottles for his father-in-law, though there was no doubt we both thought about cracking one open by the back nine, where our fingers had turned thin and white as bone.

For all the buildup to our playing an unplayable, my memories of golf at Skibo are a soggy green haze. The course was special, no doubt—as pristine as my room in the castle, with testing lakeside holes and a layout bubbling with contours. It played links-y, even in a downpour. The highest compliment I can pay to Skibo is to say that it was good enough to not stop, even when the routing circled back toward the clubhouse.

At the turn, we found a reminder of why we couldn't quit. In the unmanned halfway hut (again, no prices, just take what you like) a small display case of metal hooks showed bag tags from around the world, where Carnegie Club members had left calling cards from their other courses— Pine Valley, Cypress, Oakmont, and the like. They reminded us that this wasn't a course you wimped out on, even if you were racing your way back to shelter. I couldn't resist adding my own bag tag to the wall, a plastic card stamped with a driver's license photo of my face, gifted to Skibo from the Augusta of Upper Darby, PA—my dear McCall Country Club, a daunting 4,400 yards from the tips, where the membership process was only slightly more involved than joining Costco. It was a damn good little golf course, and as we walked off toward ten, I hoped for my tag's chances beside all those bullies. I gave it a week.

As we soldiered through the eighteenth, our scorecards turned to pulp in our pockets, we were greeted by a young Scottish lass in a tartan kilt standing beside the green. She held a wide umbrella in one hand and a silver tray of hot whiskies on the other. *Where the hell were you five years ago?* I thought to myself. The starter welcomed us into the clubhouse like weary refugees, ushering us into the locker room and insisting we hand over our rain gear— right into the dryer it went while we waited, happily, in no hurry to leave Skibo.

It was a few minutes of another world, a glimpse of life not so much lived as mastered. Every detail sorted, every whim satisfied. I suppose there are more thoughtful, useful ways to spend forty-five thousand dollars than on an annual golf retreat, and the Carnegie name recalled some of them, the philanthropist having once opined, "The man who dies thus rich dies disgraced." I could handle such disgrace, I decided. If it meant I could come back and soak in both of those bathtubs (I would have them draw me one hot, and the other one *really* hot), I would take disgrace with an extra scoop of infamy on top.

Dornoch was the name that drew golfers this far north into Scotland. Tain and Nairn and Castle Stuart were spangled lures, but Royal Dornoch's four hundred years of golf history and its *Golf Digest* ranking as number five in the world pulled the tour busses northward to the hometown of Donald Ross and the course where America's great architect learned his trade. After Lindsay joyfully reunited with his golf shoes (he and Sean had already started plans to market a new invention, the Shoe Leash, to save other travelers from sitting in the pub in socks), we headed out to play Dornoch's Struie course beside the destination championship links. Originally opened 125 years ago as a ladies' course, Struie was its own destination track with a top-fifty UK ranking, fun and fair with some plain holes, but a bright three-hour walk beside the Dornoch Firth. It was vastly overshadowed—and rightly so—by its neighbor course, which, on the next morning, Brian and I would come to know as an uncommon chain of golf holes squeezed along a ridge of dunes between the town and the water.

Royal Dornoch's opening eight played outward along an upper ridge of the dunes, and golfing them downwind, Brian and I felt our muscles expanding beneath our waterproofs. This four-hundred-year-old lion of the North was gorgeous but kind of easy, our balls taking an express on the wind and leaving us short pitches onto the greens. Old Tom laid out nine of the holes, and you didn't have to be a golf-head to notice the inspiration Donald Ross had taken from the crowned greens—his Pinehurst inverted saucers are straight out of Dornoch. From the end of the upper eight holes, the view back along the crescent strand of ribbons of fairway and swirling beach grasses and the spire of Dornoch cathedral—it rivaled Royal County Down's ninth for the best view in golf. It brought chills, which was good preparation for the back nine, where the holes dropped us down along the sand and water and the wind punched us in our souls.

Our day at Dornoch was the best of times and the not-so-best of times. We felt a pull in our guts between the golfer's impulse to cherish one of the game's best walks and the survival instinct to find shelter and higher ground. Above all other subjects—the recent referendum on independence, the upcoming Open at St. Andrews, Liverpool's piss-poor play—weather dominated the conversation as Scotland collectively lamented that their summer had been a week back in April. The country had been beleaguered by a plague of squalls, and smaller clubs were feeling the pinch of diminished rounds. I didn't want to whine about the wind, trying instead to accept the golfing gods' challenge and embrace the kinks in the path laid before me. But this shit was unnatural, even by Scottish standards—by Himalayan standards, these were days to remain indoors. We could see the proof up the road as we pulled into the parking lot of the Golspie Links on a bright Saturday afternoon and found it completely void of cars, and the course entirely empty of golfers.

A lone pro shop employee at Golspie had remained to open the door and check us in for our tee time. Anne didn't know us very well, but she quickly became protective of us as we informed her of our intent to play in the forty-mile-per-hour breezes. She assured us that some of the Golspie course played parkland style, with a few holes ducking into the trees for cover, but commiserated over the conditions. She explained that they had recently lost their fifth green again. It had been washed away in a storm that old-time members called a once-in-a-century weather event, but after they'd rebuilt it, a twice-in-three-years hurricane came along and slid it back into the ocean. We heard her message but were powerless to heed it. Anne plied us with water bottles and energy bars and logo balls, bidding us a bittersweet farewell as we pushed open the pro shop door against the wind, lowered our eyes, and golfed forth into the hereafter.

The wind pushed the sound of the nearby racetrack over to the golf course, and against a backdrop of grinding gears and burning tires (the Scots, Irish, and English loved motor racing in a way that made America's NASCAR devotion feel like a passing interest), we each retreated to gentler places in our minds, far away from the walls of air at Golspie, where four Americans wavered down the fairways like broken kites. Lindsay and Sean imagined two warm stools back at their hotel just over that wall right there, where two hundred bottles of aged warmth danced on the shelves and poured themselves into their glasses. In my head, I was in my office back in Philadelphia with the windows down, dripping from the humidity with a broad smile across my face as my hands shuffled a thick deck of foreign scorecards. And in Brian's mind, he had gone to the blankness. It was a space I knew well, where you lost all sense of place and purpose and moved forward simply because you were too scared to stop. When we arrived at a tee marked ten, he paused.

"This is wrong," he said. "We're on sixteen."

"I don't think so."

"Dude, this isn't ten. There is no way this is fucking ten."

It *was* fucking ten, and by fucking sixteen we were all so wind-drunk that we no longer waited for anyone to hit, slapping our balls and leaning ahead into the air. Sean rocketed one from behind Brian that brushed Brian's sideburns, the ball's quick *zzzzzoom* buzzing his ear like a mosquito.

"That almost killed me!" he laughed without breaking stride or turning around, his eyes wide and delirious.

We all begged for Golspie to end, yet we could tell it was a course you could play daily without getting bored or battered (maybe not so much the latter). It was a strategic blend of bumpy links holes along the water and tall pines to negotiate on the back, another course on a formidable list of tracks—Fraserburgh, Cullen, Fortrose & Rosemarkie—that locals likely took for granted, but if you dropped it somewhere in the States, golfers would line up and fork over hundreds for a tee time. With so much special seaside golf in Scotland, you could forget how special each hole was, and how you'd never seen anything like it before. I tried to relish the gift of every links hole; in a month's time, I would be sweating my way around still and soft courses lined with conifers, returned to level greens and forced carries and balls hopping backward in flat fairways. Scotland was ruining me for golf, but the wind was ruining me for Scotland. I couldn't wait for my track back home; bring on the boredom. After the marathon, how nice it would feel to jog around the block.

On our way back to town that evening, we again passed a hilltop statue that we had asked Anne about back in the pro shop.

"It's a part of our history. Some people want it gone—a few—but the majority would say that it happened, and we shouldn't forget," she told us. "History isn't all happiness."

Through granite eyes, George Granville Leveson-Gower had gazed down upon his county of Sutherland from the peak of Beinn a'Bhragaidh since 1837. The first Duke of Sutherland (a county name dating to the Vikings, when this tip of Scotland was actually *southern land* from their perspective in the Orkneys), Granville Leveson-Gower was wealthy enough for three last names, a British MP who, by marrying a Sutherland, came into control of the largest estate in Europe. His hundred-foot-tall likeness took four years to build, and the locals call it the Mannie, an oddly affectionate label for a monument to an individual who unleashed an ethnic cleansing upon Highland Scots. The Clearances—a term that today still echoes with bitterness and simmers quietly at the root of the independence movement—were most brutal in this region. The Duke's plan was to save subsistence farmers from overcrowding and poverty by forcing them off the land and burning their homes as they went, leaving families to starve and freeze or escape to the coasts and exile abroad. The acres were cleared for more profitable, edible tenants—mainly sheep and deer—and in the matter of a few years, the Highlands went from near overpopulation to being one of the most thinly inhabited corners of Europe.

The Clearances changed everything about Scotland, extinguishing an agrarian way of life, triggering a diaspora of emigrants that lasted generations, muting the native Gaelic tongue, and crushing the remains of the clan system of local governance. Some suggest that the latter was the true driving force behind the mass displacement; the clans had supported the Catholic Stuarts' attempts to regain the throne in the failed Jacobite Risings, and landlords made them pay dearly for backing the wrong side. And for all this, they gave the Duke a statue.

An attempt had been made in 1994 to dynamite the monument and get the last word on the Duke, and from time to time kids would chip away a stone from its base, but the statue stood pat. I admired the perspective of Anne's explanation as to why many of the area residents didn't mind it remaining. The past had power over you only if you hid from it. But the part of me that subsisted upon righteous indignation—that is, all of me— couldn't help but think the Duke deserved a far worse view of the valleys he emptied.

I couldn't fathom a statue of Oliver Cromwell smiling down upon Dublin; if this were that other Celtic isle, the Duke would have been reduced to rubble without protest or surprise. Both countries had been brutalized by English campaigns over the centuries, but Scotland felt more resigned to that past, while portions of Ireland didn't seem quite ready to quit wrestling history. I wondered who had it right. However they handled the past, as an American, I admired them for having it, for their birthright to long memories and ancient acts to either accept or bemoan. Truth was, most of the folks here probably didn't even notice the statue, or saw it as welcome signal that they had returned home to Golspie, or used it as a place marker—*When you see the Mannie on the hill, turn right for the golf course.* Leave it to the visitor to wonder while the people who lived here just got on with their day.

Dornoch is the northern post where many Scotland golf trips touch the wall and turn back home, but some golf explorers who have been this far north will tell you to push on a bit farther. James Braid once did, and what he created has become a shared secret among those who know, who nod and listen as you tell them about your days at Muirfield and Turnberry and Royal Dornoch, then look you in the eye, stare deep into your golfing soul, and ask, *But do you know Brora?*

Home to the headquarters of the international society of Braid's devotees, Brora remains his unaltered vision, where the five-time Open champion popularized a hole shape we take for granted today, the ubiquitous dogleg. You need not know Braid's name to know Brora's class; like all of the most soulful courses, it transcends its architect and hides any hints of being designed at all. I wasn't thinking about James Braid as I hiked its inclines and guessed at what lay behind its sandy bluffs. Rather, I was thinking that if I had to make a case for what made golf along the edges of the British Isles great, Brora would be exhibit A.

Compact at 6,211 yards, Brora possessed everything a course required to top my flight scale: it felt authentically local and pleasantly remote, and its tee times were available and affordable and not booked in blocks by buses of golfers who shared my accent. It was unfussy and undisturbed, a course that found its way through the landscape and let nature create new shots for you. It was tough enough—the beach grasses were cranky at Brora, and the back nine clung to the bends of the strand—but it was scoreable and made for a brisk walk. It had design lineage and homegrown pride and, perhaps most important, it had something you absolutely would not find at home, no matter how randomly you roamed: car batteries. Beside each green, a charger was hooked up to electric wires that surrounded the putting surfaces, protecting them from the resident beasts.

I'd heard that the livestock might join us on this bit of shared pasture, but

I cheered in the parking lot when I saw a bull slowly stride his way across the practice green by the clubhouse. Brora was squeezed between the bay and stretches of crofts, which were parcels of land doled out to crofters by way of an ancient Highland system of dividing property among tenants for grazing and farming. It predated the Clearances, and the grazing rights of crofters were fiercely protected and handed down through generations. Portions of the Brora course were on land regarded as common pasture for crofters to share, so sheep and cattle commingled with golfers, just as they had on golf's original layouts, where sheep laid into hillsides against the wind, wearing grass pits down to their sandy bottoms and sculpting golf's original bunkers. If you ever wonder why links sand traps are so deep, remember that they were originally designed not as punishment but protection; imagine what the wind would do to the bunkers' sands if their walls weren't so upright.

The breezes were just as bold in Brora as they had been in Dornoch, yet I felt the urge to go around the course again; 77 hadn't felt like so much fun in a long time. But the trip was changing again, and ahead of us we each had long miles in different directions. I said good-bye to the group in the parking lot at Brora and watched Sean and Lindsay hop into a taxi back to Inverness. Amanda picked up Brian, who would be a father the next time I saw him. They wished me good fortune and said they would be following me in the qualifier. Lindsay offered to leave his shoes for luck, but I declined the added baggage.

My car turned north as the gang headed south, and while I expected their exit to come with a bit of worry—I would be alone again on the remote edges of Scotland, before ten days of golf with a reader whom I had never met—I felt at peace as I drove up to Wick, the northernmost of Scotland's east-coast links.

The course was quiet and empty and bathed in blessed yellow light when I reached it that afternoon. I met a lone husband and wife drinking tea in the clubhouse who welcomed me and sent me off with a scorecard and some directions to get me around, though it would have been impossible to get lost. Wick was a nine-out, nine-back links, a four-mile avenue of fairway with a towering ridge of dunes serving as the median. Another solid test amid the sand hills; if it were on the way to Dornoch instead of an hour above it, Wick might have seen more visitors, but the place being empty was fine with me. Alone again, I had the chance to get golf-fixated, to stop thinking about where we were all going to get a table for dinner or whether my friends were getting a discount on their tee time. I practiced my shortened swing. I tried new things. I relaxed my hands on my putter, and the ball began releasing dead down its intended line. Relaxed hands—I tried it with the rest of my clubs and could feel a rhythm clicking, my swing slower, smoother, and unpressured—no weather to escape, and nowhere to be but a nearby hotel before dark.

On the back nine at Wick, I started letting it go. My hands, my arms, my shoulders, my head. I stopped forcing. I let the club and my muscles do what they wanted to, which, when I stopped interfering with them, was hit a golf ball toward a target. Birdie, birdie, birdie. Golf was so simple when I stopped telling it what I wanted it to be and just enjoyed it as something I could do.

And I could do it at Wick. I was four under on the back nine, sitting dead center of eighteen when I began to worry about whether there would be enough rooms in St. Andrews for my family and friends and so many fans come to witness my miracle; we would need half the beds in town, and the Open was just a month away. I proceeded to knuckle one into a bunker by the green, where I climbed in and had a boxing match with my ball that I lost in a unanimous decision.

I carried a custom gap wedge that had been engraved with a reminder on the back of the clubface: BE PRESENT. If I was going to find answers in Scotland, I figured I should start by noticing the ones in my own bag.

I wrote for a long time that night in my hotel in the town of Wick, animated by an unusual shot of evening energy. Something about reaching the top of the island had me feeling hopeful and focused; there were many days to go, but the turn toward the finish line made a once interminable quest feel finite. Suddenly, the trip had an end, and I wished I had budgeted for two loops around Scotland, or maybe ten. This life of chase, of heading out every day set on being better, on becoming my best golfing self; there was just not enough time. I regretted ever complaining about the weather or my score-card, and since I was never doing this again, I told myself to slow down and take it easy. Remember Covesea—stop. Smell the roses, no matter if all I saw was yellow budding gorse. They were roses if I looked at them the right way. I had to at least try, because it was all downhill from here.

Promise

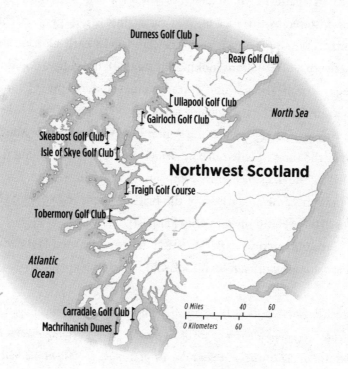

Durness Golf Club
Reay Golf Club
Ullapool Golf Club
Gairloch Golf Club
North Sea
Skeabost Golf Club
Isle of Skye Golf Club
Northwest Scotland
Traigh Golf Course
Tobermory Golf Club
Atlantic
Ocean
Carradale Golf Club
Machrihanish Dunes
0 Miles   40   60
0 Kilometers   60

Fourteen days until the qualifier, and the Colonel was still heavy on my back.

I had imagined this homestretch for months, praying that by now, after so many holes in the home of golf, I would have been shaken by a white-light conversion somewhere along the coastline of Scotland, a golfer who dodged bogeys suddenly reborn as a player who binged on birdies. It had yet to happen. There had been glimpses, but I was still very much my pretty-good golfing self, always looking over my shoulder for traces of Colonel Bogey.

I knew plenty about bogeys; we had been intimate over the years for sure, but it was in researching my visit to the links of Reay that I finally learned the origin of the word. In Scottish legend, a *bogle* was a goblin. The term gave birth to the notion of the bogeyman (Americanized to our boogieman), and a golfer who played like the devil would come to be referred to as one. In order to standardize scorekeeping and allow for handicapped golf, courses adopted "bogey scores," a tally that a good golfer would strive to match. In a game in which match play was the standard, the shift to stroke play was fostered by this idea of "playing against Mr. Bogey" or "chasing the bogeyman." When playing at a service club (many early clubs in the British Isles were born of battalions looking for a game), the golfers couldn't invite a Mr. Bogey to golf—they would outrank him—so the name "Colonel Bogey" was used instead. The Colonel even got his own tune after a British bandmaster was inspired by a whistling golfer. The "Colonel Bogey March" is best known as the tune whistled in *The Bridge on the River Kwai*, but it has been parodied by the likes of Homer Simpson and the students in *The Breakfast Club*, and it became an anthem of the British people in World War II as the tune for "Hitler Has Only Got One [Titleist]."

As I read up on my next destination in Reay, I learned of the influence of this sharpshooting officer. Reay Golf Club's history explained:

> *According to records in 1897, based on a card left by Colonel Bogey, it was decided to adopt a bogey score of 54 for the 12 holes (some reports record this as 50). This was in order to assist in a more consistent method of allocating handicaps to the playing membership.*

As the quality of equipment and play increased, the more ambitious American concept of a par score eventually overtook a bogey score (*par* deriving from the Latin for equal), while the credit for the creation of *birdie* went to a course in my own backyard: at Atlantic City Country Club, Pine Valley creator George Crump was in a match where a playing partner stuffed an approach, to which another partner replied, "That was a bird of a shot," forever tagging a ball holed one stroke below par.

Oh, the sleep I'd lost and the layers of enamel I'd ground away over these words—birdies, pars, bogeys on top of bogeys—that had such accidental provenance, words of no meaning or importance to golf's original linksmen.

They were chance utterances by some golfing forefathers, yet they would come to have such power over not just my mood but my self-worth; birdie, and my world was right. Par, and my world *could have* been right. Bogey, and the world would never be right again, as I commissioned the Colonel to spoil my sunshiniest afternoons.

At Reay, my time with the Colonel began and ended with the club's history page. I went out in some soft, bright air and carded level par over its 5,854 yards. It rivaled Kinghorn for the longest short-course in Scotland, where part of me feels like it's still playing its fifth hole, accurately dubbed the Sahara for its 581 yards played into a North Atlantic breeze, but I liked Reay's signature quirk of beginning and ending with a par 3, and its routing was refreshingly circular, adding variety to the wind. A blend of tough shorties and gentle doglegs, it was another course with James Braid heritage (I was beginning to imagine Braid and Old Tom as immortal golfing Santa Clauses, their work uninhibited by the bounds of real time), and as the northernmost Braid design in Scotland, it was a genuine treat for golfers who found themselves on unchartered Highland soil. Far west of the Inverness trail of courses, things started to feel different as I set out from Reay. They started to look different, too.

Over my years getting to know the links of the world, I'd braved plenty of grumpy correspondence from architecture gurus who disputed my opinion that we lacked genuine links courses in the States. I often humbly conceded to their expertise; I had yet to visit Bandon, Oregon, or the Highland Links nine-holer on Cape Cod, where emails insisted that golf in the dunes was thriving. Before leaving for Scotland, I'd heard that a links had opened on the East Coast of my own continent, and I thought it necessary to investigate before I began receiving complaints from Canada as well. I voyaged northward to Nova Scotia for a forty-eight-hour dunes golf fix, and found everything about the Cabot Links to be as advertised—genuine links set in a far-off town called Inverness, where I wondered if a developer had changed the town's name as a marketing ploy (a Canadian links in a place called Inverness—too perfect), but Scottish names filled Canada's easternmost island of Cape Breton, a first stop for settlers exiled in the

Clearances who came to this edge of Canada and made it a Nova Scotia—a New Scotland.

Perhaps it was the remoteness that recalled Cabot, or the talk of Scots' eviction from these Highlands, but Nova Scotia was on my mind as I set out from my perch atop Scotland and began working my way down its jagged western coast, where the golf courses were far-flung, the roads were medieval, and the scenery grabbed me by the throat.

I thought I'd been seeing Scotland, that I knew the place—water, soft hills, slate roofs, gorse and dunes and sheep. I thought I'd seen the Highlands, but when I got to Scotland's western version of them, I felt like I'd been waiting in the queue for the real ride to begin. In the far northwest, it was a new trip in a new country. It was a nova Scotia.

It was four days of little golf and much driving on my way down from Scotland's summit through the isles of Skye and Mull to the southern tip of Kintyre, but no stretch of the country was burned more deeply into memory than those ninety hours headed south. The landscape was not just scenic, it was preposterous. I climbed granite peaks in my station wagon, scooted along cliffside roads like a timid pack mule, rolled down hillsides, parachuted my car into soft, green glens, and then snaked my way around lochs whose still surfaces were mirrors beneath cloudless skies. I dodged sheep on one-lane roads and scarcely saw a home or another human being, aside from a black Volkswagen following me at a distance.

I didn't know what Penn would bring with him to the Highlands from Georgia. From his emails, I could tell he would be accompanied by wit and good ol' boy charm, but I couldn't have guessed that he would contribute ten days of sunshine, wisdom, and long friendship, and the greatest round of golf in my life.

It started with a thank-you. A person called Penn emailed to say he appreciated my Ireland story, and I thanked him for taking the time to say so. I was surprised when he wrote back and invited me to speak to his golfing buddies on a trip to South Carolina that I regretted not being able to make. I was more surprised when he said he wanted to join me in Scotland, and I was shocked when he actually booked a ticket and forwarded his itinerary. So I don't know why I was still surprised when I heard the door open downstairs at the Aiden House in Durness, the best—and perhaps only—B&B in Scotland's most northwesterly town, and heard a Georgia accent fill the hallways. It was more than a drawl, more than a few soft-tongued expressions. Penn's accent cruised with enthusiasm. His words had colors and shape to them, bright hues and bold configurations.

I laid in my bed in a room where a sign in the bathroom read No Washing Soiled Laundry in the Sink—they must have known I was coming—and knew I couldn't match the energy downstairs. I could only hope to survive it.

Though he had updated me with texts to tell me he was approaching Durness, I still doubted whether Penn would be able to find me up here. If you were tasked with selecting the least convenient rendezvous point on the planet for a traveler from the States, Durness, Scotland, would make your short list. But here he was, all the way from Valdosta, Georgia, an e-persona come to life. It felt strange to meet a new, American face in this yonder corner of the world, to add fresh feet so far into the expedition; Penn was like the explorer who found Dr. Livingstone. I had become a decent double for the Scottish doctor, blistered and bearded and skinny as I was.

"Tom Coyne," he said, embracing me with a big buddy hug. Penn was not tall or fat but he seemed large, a thick frame with paws for hands and brown hair rumpled from a cross-Scotland drive. He was pushing seventy but smiled like a kid; there was literally a sparkle in his eyes. I thought it might have been tears from the seven hours he'd just spent weaving through the Highlands after an overnight flight, but just as the sun would all week, that glint in his smile remained. It was who he was. It was the look of someone who could look at anything and know the good in it.

Durness had little, but it had plenty. It had the Aiden B&B, a restaurant and pub, a golf course, and of all the places to find one, a memorial garden to John Lennon. He had spent his childhood summers vacationing on a family farm in Durness, and years later would even bring Yoko and Julian back to this perfectly unspoiled place at the edge of the UK.

Penn and I headed to the restaurant for a meal shared between two men who knew each other both well and not at all; it was a slightly awkward dinner during which I kept thinking the conversation would be going a lot more smoothly if we took out our phones and started emailing each other. But after two plates of fish and chips, Penn got down to his mission and his charge.

He admitted that he wasn't here just to collect photographs and score-cards; this wasn't a fan's pilgrimage. He believed in what I was doing and was here to assist. He had come because, rather than reading about the result of my links dream quest, he wanted to witness it and help push it toward its proper conclusion. He was a reader who wanted to participate in the story and help write the ending. As a golfer, it felt like welcome support. As a writer, it felt downright postmodern.

"I just want you to love the moment," Penn said, leaning across the table, his eyes gone serious for the first time since we met. "Enjoy it. I'm so excited for you. Everybody is. All of us."

It was news to me that there was an us. I'd sent a message to everyone joining me on the trip about what to bring and what to expect, and from that mass email, a separate chain of chatter among Penn, Duff, Brian, Gretchen, Lindsay, Sean, Scott, and Gramma Billy had apparently kicked off without me. Strangers had all become unlikely friends, and my solo quest was suddenly a team endeavor. I would learn that for weeks they had been exchanging thoughts on how to best get me across the finish line, sharing their excitement for Scotland, and Penn inquiring as to who this Gramma Billy was and if she could dance. She replied that she most certainly could, smiley face and a wink.

I felt a squirm in my gut. There wasn't supposed to be an *us*. *Us* was pressure. In a foursome or a crowd I was carefully alone, and I preferred that comfortable arrangement, because *us* took guts and energy. *Us* was vulnerable; maybe that's why I'd stuck with Robert for so long, a friend without challenge, so safe and staid in his turmoil. It troubled me to think the others weren't just here for some free golf, that they were invested in our friendship, and that I should invest in them in return. But sitting across from Penn and listening to him give a damn, a proper adult who could give without worry,

I thought for a moment that maybe it wasn't the courses that were meant to dispense the epiphanies but the partners.

"Don't think about score, and don't think about your swing," Penn said, his drawl thinned by his sincerity. "Just love the moment. Enjoy it. I can't tell you how great I think what you're doing is. You just gotta enjoy it, man. The moment. And never—no matter what happens at the qualifier—never, never quit."

I asked Penn to tell me all of this again before he left me down in Prestwick, and he promised he would. Prestwick, below Glasgow, felt like it was a continent away from Durness. And in some ways, it was—an audacious land of long drives and short golf, of ferry cruises and shocking meals and odd thrills. As we worked our way down the northwest coast of Scotland in a two-vehicle caravan, Penn and I both confessed to laughing aloud in our cars at what we were seeing through our windshields. It felt as though we were being toyed with; they couldn't put a road on this mountain's edge or lay a loch here beside this canopy of trees shading a winding lane guarded by sentries of sheep and silver rock. But it was all real. And all we could do was chuckle at it.

The northern delights started at the Durness course, where Penn giggled at an opening hole that played like the first stage of an alpine ascent, with a fairway that might have come with carabiners and that breached at a green surrounded by a wire fence. The long winter meant the livestock were still grazing, but they didn't interfere with the fun of Durness, a blissful youth of a golf course. Built in 1988 by and for the local community, it was a nine-holer with a second set of tees allowing for eighteen-hole rounds, and felt far older than its twenty-five years. Durness was a throwback to courses built by shovels versus software, stuffed with quirks you only find at the low-budget builds, places that were forced to make hay instead of resowing the field. What to do about that mountain at the start of the property? Put a fairway on it! And stick a flag on top. The closing par 3 over ocean spray to a green shelved atop black rocks was a stunning finisher, and making two there sent us down the coast from Durness at a gallop.

The ride was a long haul of hairpin turns, lamb roadblocks, and one-lane roads bordered by shoulders marked PASSING PLACE should you get stuck behind a tractor, which seemed the only other vehicle sharing our route. Roaring around a wagon with no eyes on what approached felt more like a PASSING-AWAY PLACE, but we white-knuckled our way down to our next golf at Ullapool, where nine holes along Loch Broom were a chance to peel our fingers off our steering wheels before we continued south to another nine-holer called Gairloch. With so many watery crags poking into Scotland's northwest coast, unless we could find a ferry, my days of straight shots between courses were on hold, giving an area of modest size a feeling of utter vastness.

Gairloch bested Ullapool on that day's sampling of nine-holers, a solid ball-marker course on the velvet-goody-bag-from-the-starter/logo-ball/ball-marker/scorecard-on-the-back-of-a-napkin scale of course fanciness. As I left the shop with my souvenir token, Penn told me of his course back home, where a visitor had once asked if they sold ball markers. "Yup. We sell ball markers. One dollar," the man in the shop said, taking a dollar from the guest and handing him back a dime.

From the compact lunchroom of a clubhouse, Gairloch looked like a wide and tidy bowl of fairway green beside the water, where holes criss-crossed and tee boxes were pushed up into the woods to squeeze every inch out of the property. We hurried our way around on a day that, as I'd studied the map in my office months before, I had pinpointed as the date the trip might drive off a cliff, in any number of ways.

Penn was desperate to dine at a particular Highland restaurant he'd heard about from a waitress at a Georgia bistro. I wasn't surprised to hear that he had gotten to know most of her life story over the course of a dinner—I don't think there were strangers in Penn's world—and when he got to talking about his upcoming trip to Scotland, she insisted that he dine at a place called the Three Chimneys on the Isle of Skye. I was all for accommodating Penn's detour on the itinerary, but shoehorning it into an unforgiving calendar meant we were in for a day that Penn would describe that evening, as we waited for the last table of the night on the Isle of Skye, as golf meets the Le Mans endurance race. Our day had been only slightly more dangerous.

When we arrived at the Skeabost Hotel on Skye that evening after our quick hike around Gairloch, I watched Penn step out of his car slowly. His face was drawn, and his eyes looked downward. I wondered if he had gotten a call from home delivering dire news. He shook his head as if to cast off a vision. "Tommy Coyne," he said, "I just about died back there."

A pang of guilt landed in my stomach. I wasn't aware of my speed as I drove; weeks of wrong-side navigating had me comfortable driving left, and the rental insurance emboldened my pace. Not until I had a car following me did I realize that I was racing my BMW around the bends and making it impossible for a newly arrived guest to follow. In my rearview, Penn's Volkswagen would disappear for a minute, sometimes two, until at one stretch I had to stop and wait for him to catch up. Turned out that while I was zipping ahead, Penn's left front tire had gotten stuck in a roadside rut, pushing him into the trees as he ripped the wheel back to the right.

"I saw how it was going to go," he said. "Slow-motion—here's where you turn the car over, here's where it's going to roll. . . ." His car had rocked and fishtailed across the road until he wrestled it back under control. "If there was a car coming in the other direction . . ." he said with a shudder in his voice. He looked at a blank space between us and shook his head. "Wow. That is how quick it can go."

I owed him a good dinner. Penn insisted on paying for it, but I was going to drive even if it was almost dark when we left with no guarantee of a reservation. I was going to get Penn to his Three Chimneys.

There were any number of inconceivable things about the Three Chimneys. There was the food (we supped on oysters and scallop tartar and rabbit swimming in heaven sauce and lamb loin and sweetbreads that tasted like dreams melting on my tongue), the fact that we got a table (it took all Penn's charm and a little bit of my résumé to score us the last seats of the night—the people dining there that evening had made their reservations over six months ago for this Wednesday dinner), the drive to the restaurant (it was as if the sheep, not having seen a car in months, had commandeered the road for themselves, and as I dodged puffs of white in the pitch darkness on our ride back, I asked Penn if I was really here or asleep back at the hotel and counting these little fuzzy bastards), but nothing was more incredible than the fact that it existed at all. On the side of a hill sat a small cottage with another small cottage of guest rooms next to it, and that was it. Not another marker of civilization in sight. This wasn't the middle of nowhere; we had left the middle of nowhere and driven an hour to get here, where somehow a kitchen had won a Michelin star and was completely booked nearly a year in advance. Where had all these people come from? What was I doing here? How had a waitress in Georgia landed us at some secret gastronomic commune? It was like going to the moon and finding it inhabited by a pack of foodies. I've never been more tired at a dinner where I had to use a fork and knife, but I've also never been more excited for my next plate. And there were many.

We made it home that evening from the best meal either of us had ever consumed, so happy, and even alive. We were blood-bonded by the travails and triumphs of travel; in thirty-six hours, Penn and I had been through and seen more than I shared with people I called dear friends. He emailed the waitress in Georgia and said the happiness of her reply sounded as though she had been in tears while writing it. By listening to her and finding that place that meant so much to her, Penn had made her month. I imagined he did that for people from time to time. Penn knew the good things and lived his life expecting them. And so they came.

I had anticipated the toughest opening drive on this trip to exist in a place called Birkdale or Muirfield or Turnberry; never could I have imagined it would be found a few steps from the lobby of the Skeabost Hotel in Skye. Under renovation by its new owners, the Skeabost was a handsome hunting lodge converted into fourteen guest rooms, but the owner informed me that they also had a golf course, even though no Skeabost golf course had popped up on my map. Penn and I endeavored to sample it that morning, but when the girl at the front desk wasn't entirely sure how to find the first tee—she pointed us in the general direction of the parking lot—I wondered what could possibly await us. We were either about to play the hidden-est of hidden Scottish gems or we were about to go get lost in the woods with our clubs.

Across the parking lot and through some overgrown branches we found a path that led to a wet and tattered green mat. We looked outward toward a small opening in the trees fifty yards ahead and saw what looked like a field that might even hold a flag or two. We hit irons through an opening slightly narrower than the aisle on an Airbus, and in a few paces discovered the golf course. It was a sort of accidental track, seven flags spread around a field with turf mats for tee boxes that some locals played from time to time. The new owner asked my opinion on it and whether I thought the course might be developed into something for the guests. The final two holes had me feeling that it might. The wee par 3s wrapped around the hotel and played along a loch's edge, which could be fun for families or golfers passing through. Penn and I enjoyed our little morning appetizer of a golf course, if for no other reason than we might never meet another golfer who, no matter the miles logged by their club carriers, could say they had played Skeabost. Thousands could brag that they had played Muirfield. Ours was a far more exclusive club, those of us who had found the mat in the woods.

Skeabost hardly cost us an hour, so it was an early start down to the Isle of Skye nine-holer where our caravan would go from one car in my rearview to one and a half. Poor Penn—I was making an effort to drive more leisurely, but the pull of my final rounds down in Ayrshire kept weighing down my foot. Now with the addition of a third car to our train, Penn was stuck in the middle, trying to keep up with me while keeping Scott and his Florida cruise control in view.

A life in and around golf had taught me a few things about dealing with people: don't trust anyone with iron covers; don't prejudge folks with ball retrievers or karma will have you asking them to borrow one; and when the director of golf at a five-star resort that you desperately want to visit emails you out of the blue and says he wants to join you in Scotland, you say *Hell yes* to your new best friend.

Scott was in his late forties, with a clean haircut, a pressed collar, a big smile, and a kind manner; he exuded the positive vibe of a guy who, as a lifetime PGA club pro, had mastered the skill of being nice all the time, or at least faking it. He'd heard me promoting my quest on the radio a few months before and decided I sounded normal enough to spend a few days with on the road. The Florida resort where he was director of golf, Streamsong, was relatively quiet in the summer months, so he could get some time away and add some unusual names to his life's list of golf courses—he literally maintained a spreadsheet of the thousands of tracks he had played since childhood. He even signed up to play in the Open qualifier at Bruntsfield, and for this I was exceedingly grateful. My partners had brought with them camaraderie and jokes and more golf balls, but not all of them brought serious game. Playing beside a PGA pro headed for the same tournament was a real gift to my chances; I knew well from my *Paper Tiger* days that if you want to play good golf, you have to hang around it. All the time.

Like that of most longtime PGA pros, Scott's swing was gorgeous to look at, but not always as perfect in practice; his game had a little office rust, but you could tell there was a real player in his move. It's a common refrain among those in the business that if you want to play a lot of golf, don't make it your living; the life of the club pro is one of long hours near the course but rarely on it—and who wants to spend their rare free hours back at the range where they work? So the next two weeks were about to be the most golf Scott had played since getting his PGA card. We were both the longest of Open long shots, but I felt a little less crazy in my quest with another hopeful around. Here was proof of my sanity, in pro slacks and a Streamsong sweater. I wasn't the only one who thought golf might owe me a miracle.

Isle of Skye Golf Club (called Sconser by locals, after the town) was its own wee miracle, another nine-green course with eighteen tee boxes where our approach shots were framed as beautifully as any of the work by the designers at Scott's resort. The outward holes pointed us to greens on the water's edge, where hills across the bay were our target. Coming in, we worked our way back up a craig and teed off toward a dark stone peak. Out to the water or into a wall of rock, there were shots at the little Skye layout that felt like hitting into forever. I silently kept track of Scott's score as I tallied my own; we traded pars and birdies until he lost a ball on the home stretch, and

I birdied the last and nipped him with a score of one under. A little competition from home was quickly paying dividends with my first round under par since Aberdeen.

That afternoon, three men in three cars arrived safely at the ferry port in Armadale, where we saved a day's drive by crossing from Skye down to Mallaig. Ferries were a way of life on this fractured edge of Scotland where it was all isles and firths, and they would become our routine, with six crossings scheduled in the next five days. They were larger than the boats I'd crossed on up in Whalsay. Some were the size of cruise ships with pubs and cafeterias, and the process was as simple as stepping onto an escalator—drive on, pay the man, snap some selfies on the observation deck, drive off. Reservations were recommended in the summer, and timetables were accurate down to the second. It was all impressively efficient and more fun than driving over a bridge as we slowly watched our next stretch of golfing coastline come into view. We couldn't quite make out Traigh from the ferry deck, but even if we could have, we never would have guessed what it held.

We caravanned down the coast between blue water and green hills and pulled into an ocean cove where tidal pools shimmered and families walked the sand. The *Scotsman* newspaper called Traigh (pronounced *Try*) "the most beautifully sited nine-hole golf course in the world," and it was clear why. We almost forgot to take our eyes off the blissful little beach to find the golf course, which was waiting at our backs.

A one-room white cottage beside the sea seemed an idyllic clubhouse for a nine-holer, and from its door emerged a man with a handful of hats. Roddy, the club captain, introduced himself and told us to put these TRAIGH GC hats on, explaining that ours didn't work here. A stout Scotsman with a sharp wit, Roddy was a welcome guide as we hit from one summit to the next, relying on his wisdom for our lines. When he told me to hit one left and the ball went right, he turned to me and asked, "Did I put you off when I told you to hit it left? I'll be more clear next time."

Traigh's aged dunes sagged and soared through nooks and over valleys to greens sunk into bowls and cratered atop hillsides. Views of the beach followed us as we climbed from one vista to the next, and Scott couldn't help but tell Roddy it was one of the most beautiful little courses he had ever seen.

"We think so, too. God had a trial run with England. Then he got it right with Scotland and put it on top."

Penn's imported sunshine soaked the fairways as we golfed our way back down toward the beach cove of black rocks and sand. I imagined that we were all picturing a life in which we lived in that little cottage by the sea with these holes for our backyard. Some courses impressed you so much that you couldn't wait to return, but the peace and joy of Traigh made it feel like a place you wanted to remain, to drop your anchor and live in simple bliss for a very long time.

We were famished from the day's three-course hustle, and Roddy pointed us toward a restaurant down the road, where I began to wonder if Scottish servers played a running joke on Americans—inexplicably, they were out of the burrito as well. We settled for steaks and burgers, and with our twosome now a group of three, the conversation was light and easy. Penn and Scott quickly began trading stories of courses played and golfing friends in common.

It was unusual to be dining with someone whose golf résumé so dwarfed my own, but in Scott's case, I was sitting next to one of the rarest traveling golfers on the planet. There could be only a handful like him, I imagined; he had played ninety-nine of the tracks on *Golf Digest*'s list of the top one hundred courses in America. The lone holdout? Scott smiled at Penn from Georgia when he said, "Augusta. I've been trying forever, and I haven't been able to make it happen."

Penn looked down at his plate and shook his head, then quietly confessed that he had played Augusta National. His miracle had taken place years before on his company's jet, when a former boss and member at Augusta asked the bank vice president sitting next to Penn if he'd ever played the National. The man replied that he had, and Penn tried to sit still as the CEO's glance turned to him. When asked the same question, Penn replied as calmly as he could, "No, sir, I have not." And with that, the childhood dream of a man who'd attended the Masters for thirty consecutive years came to life in green and gold.

It was the fantasy of every golfer to ever watch a color television, and one I had long ago abandoned. In all my travels, I'd never encountered an Augusta member (at least, none who would admit to it; their membership list is famously unpublished), and while I'd once pitched a magazine story where I would hop the fence in the middle of the night and play the course wearing night-vision goggles (the golf magazines passed; turns out they frowned on commissioning crimes from their freelancers), my days of courting arrest were behind me. I'd accepted that my visits to the Masters practice rounds were as close as I would ever get to the greens at Augusta. I was lucky that I could say I'd been there at all, because as much as Ballybunion and St. Andrews fire the goosebumps, there is no rival to wandering the fields of Augusta National, where the ground feels like clouds underfoot. There might be better golf courses, but there is no golf dream bigger than Augusta, and we golfers need our dreams, especially the unreachable ones. Stalking my perfect round had taken me to so many uncommon places, like Traigh and the Isle of Skye; if I ever got that Augusta rabbit in my teeth, I might stop chasing.

I was sorry to hear that number one hundred was Augusta for Scott's sake, knowing that unless he someday ran the whole PGA, his list was likely to remain incomplete. Unless, of course, Penn proved to have all the Wonka bars.

"I do know a guy," Penn said, in as reserved a tone as I had yet heard from my Georgian friend. He looked down at his empty tumbler in thought, almost afraid to complete his sentence. "He's a good friend. I've known him since high school. It's been years, but . . ."

I looked over at Scott. He was staring at Penn as though he were the one who got that last burrito.

"I could ask," Penn said. I watched as he struggled to swallow all enthusiasm—it didn't suit his persona, but he understood that you don't mess around with Augusta. You don't tease with *I know a guy* unless you really, *really* know a guy. "I can't imagine how often he gets asked, and it would be a long shot," he continued. "But he's a special guy. He might like to hear what you two have been doing, and you never know."

"That would be . . . great?" I said with emotional confusion. It was as if he had told me half the winning lottery numbers. It could be nothing. It could be whisky-induced bluster. Or we might have met our miracle in Penn. Scott and I both thanked him for taking a shot on our behalf at some point down the road, then changed the subject to a less delicate topic. We tried to put his offer in the far back of our minds, discounting it as a pub promise to protect our golfing hearts. *Expect to hear nothing back*, we told ourselves, *but in the meantime, be really nice to Penn.*

After dinner, Scott set off for a few rounds in St. Andrews—we would rendezvous in Machrihanish—while Penn and I headed for the You Must Be Taking the Morning Ferry If You're Staying Here Hotel, which was mostly a pub with rooms upstairs where the bartender couldn't find my reservation. A guy who smelled as though he'd spent much of the spring drinking pints beside the snooker table put down his stick and shuffled over to help us, finding keys for Penn and me. My room came complete with free access to the Internet signal from the neighbors across the street and a complimentary bottle of the previous guest's dandruff shampoo. I felt badly for putting Penn up in such meager and overpriced quarters, but it was the closest bed to our dawn ferry, and not even pillows that felt and smelled like laundry bags could dampen our traveling spirits after the twenty-seven holes we'd just ticked off the list.

We skipped breakfast and were on the Isle of Mull by 8:00 a.m. the next morning to sample a late addition to my list. A woman at the hotel reception in Shetland had told me that my Scottish island-hopping wouldn't be complete without a visit to Mull and the links of Tobermory. She was biased, as it was her hometown course, but Tom Watson himself had signed the guest book, so if I was looking to follow the path of Open greats in search of their answers, I needed to detour through this small western isle on my way down to Kintyre.

The clubhouse was empty at Tobermory when we arrived, so I quickly looked for Watson's name in the guest book (didn't find it; must have been in safekeeping) before signing Penn's and my own and heading out to a first tee that pointed us at a hill of gorse. We trusted the marker post atop the hill, then went scrambling to the top of a plateau in search of our drives. We found neither, but we did find a valley of varying levels that felt like a staircase of fairways, dipping down and back up to a hoisted green. Tobermory's nine holes were crammed with happy quirks and meaty carries over a landscape that shadowed the harbor. There was a theme to the northwestern courses—nine holes, relatively wee, hilltop, rocky, and breathtaking, both for the scenery and the exercise. Tobermory felt like an eighteen-holer for the hauls up and down a hillside where you could imagine county-sized glaciers squeezing these wrinkles into shape.

Penn won our match with a birdie on the closing par 3, nine holes that would henceforth become known as the Tobermory Open when Penn retold the tale of his comeback birdie to Scott, to me, to the waiter at dinner, and to the ticket taker on the ferry that brought us back to Oban and mainland Scotland. We stopped just long enough for Penn to buy some of Oban's namesake whisky, and I tried to take my time on the road down to Machrihanish. The scenery along the edges of Argyll (where the Campbell clan's tartan gave name to your socks) and Loch Fyne was worth a slow drive, but the prospect of dropping anchor for three whole nights had me racing the one-lane leading to the tip of the Kintyre peninsula. As we wound through valleys and around lakes and harbors, I felt my first case of self-induced car sickness coming on, but three hours of coughing back my Snickers breakfast was worth every minute when we arrived at the Ugadale.

When I learned that the Machrie links had been sold and were currently undergoing a rebuild, I was disappointed to miss a course so beloved by links purists and writers like Jim Finegan, one of the great men of the golf writing game, god rest his soul. I wasn't as disappointed to skip a long ferry ride out to Machrie and the Isle of Islay, nor was I too worried about the two free days that dropped into my schedule at precisely a time when I needed to play more and hustle less.

Our accidental Beatles tour continued as we worked our way down to the end of Kintyre along the "Long and Winding Road" that inspired the Beatles tune from *Let It Be* to where Paul McCartney had owned a farm since the 1960s. His 1977 hit with Wings, "Mull of Kintyre," was the bestselling single in UK history at the time, and I have yet to meet an American who's heard it. Our respite couldn't have landed on a more ideal block of my itinerary. A charmed blend of Scottish golf and American hospitality awaited us in Kintyre, and it felt like a retreat from the compromises of life on the road. Our two nights in the Ugadale Hotel, plus an evening in nearby Campbeltown's Royal Hotel, were a trip within a trip where every minute felt like a reward. Menus on which we wanted everything (Penn's experience of Scottish cuisine had been wonderfully skewed; he had eaten better than if he were reviewing restaurants in NYC) and suites that had me choking back tears at the width of my room and the height of my mattress—this was the first place since Skibo where I felt that highest bar being surpassed: It was a place I wanted Allyson to see. There were courses and towns I hoped to revisit, but it was a different thing to walk around a village and plot your return with your family, to sit in the Old Clubhouse pub sharing a plate of haggis nachos and know you would be here doing this a handful more times during the course of your life.

Machrihanish had been special for a long time, since Old Tom had visited to design the original Mach Links that ranked among the best tracks in the world. A local caddie claimed Kintyre's golf legacy reached back centuries further, and that Machrihanish was the true Home of Golf, well predating wool traders and St. Andrews. He described to me a disappeared news story by Scottish golf writing legend S. L. McKinlay in which the origin of golf was credited to ancient Irish monks in Machrihanish who played the Gaelic game of shinty (a predecessor of field hockey, and still beloved in Ireland as the sport of hurling). Shinty sticks did look a lot like early golf clubs, and missionary monks were poking around Scotland's islands well before any suggestion of golf in Scotland was recorded, so we stepped upon Machrihanish's first tee with added reverence for what might have been ground zero for golf on our planet.

The opening tee shot played directly over a cove of public beach and quickly replaced Skeabost as the most stressful opener in Scotland. On the days we played it, the strand was busy with families pushing baby strollers; we did our best to wave them out of the way before teeing off, each of us silently praying to *miss the pram, miss the pram*—and we did, by whole inches. Machrihanish was as good as the top-one-hundred ranking it had earned; Old Tom's layout shot us through tunnels in the dunes and over burns and around corners of sandy purgatory. With each next tee waiting mere paces from the last cratered green, to think the old man found such a routing waiting for him here gave golf at Machrihanish the flavor of the miraculous.

For golfers who had forgotten it was there (as the crow—or the Flybe— flies), it was a short jump over from Glasgow, but the haul up and around and back down to Campbeltown turned a visit into a proper excursion), the area had been made special again by a new neighboring links, the Machrihanish Dunes, plus the addition of the updated Ugadale and Royal hotels, all developed by American David Southworth, whose résumé included Liberty National, the Abaco Club, and Creighton Farms. The new Dunes course had been designed by Scotsman David McLay Kidd of Bandon Dunes fame, making Machrihanish home to courses by both Scotland's oldest and newest architects. It was a heady combination: historic and neo-links, Scottish character and American attention to detail where you wanted it most—namely, in your giant shower.

We checked into the Ugadale weary from a day of double ferries through Mull plus an afternoon eighteen on Mach Old, but when our best friend at Mach Dunes, Kevin Lewis, director of marketing and an American PGA pro, told us his boss was in town and would like to have dinner with us, we put on smiles and clean shirts and prepared for a meal with someone I expected was golf's other Donald.

I would later read that *Forbes* had dubbed David Southworth "The Anti-Trump," and after an evening in his company, it was clear why. While Trump's feather ruffling in Aberdeen was legendary enough to turn most of Scotland against him, Southworth's development in Kintyre was celebrated and subdued. Where Trump's ego was unrivaled among our species, Southworth confessed to me as we made our way into the Royal Hotel's handsome restaurant, with its walls of soft wood and exposed brick, that he often expected someone at his own resorts to tap him on the shoulder and tell him he didn't belong. He was tall, with a quiet countenance; if someone asked you to pick out the millionaire developer at our dinner table, you would have chosen Penn twice before looking to David. He seemed too modest for a man behind PGA Tour venues and golf communities around the world; he asked us questions and listened thoughtfully to our stories and told his own tales of the trials of bringing Mach Dunes to life. He asked if I liked the layout of my suite upstairs, as he had arranged each room himself. By the time dessert arrived, David had changed my entire outlook on deep-pocketed developers and the überwealthy in general, and his links in Machrihanish altered my perspective on the future of golf courses around the world.

Machrihanish Dunes was the first links to be built on Scotland's west coast in a hundred years, and the only course ever built on SSSI—a Site of Special Scientific Interest—as the Kintyre dunes are home to rare and endangered varieties of orchids. Course developers and environmentalists at loggerheads is a familiar headline in the golf biz, and it's the crisis of golf's future: When we force green into our grass via deluges of chemicals and water and jam courses into places where said water does not exist, we're turning what could be environmental sanctuaries into ecological burdens. It's an untenable circumstance for golf, but it doesn't have to be this way—the environmentalist versus developer story had been rewritten at Mach Dunes, a links that, to me, was one of the most important golf courses I'd ever visited.

The key to constructing a course on such fragile soil was that it wasn't actually constructed. The Dunes was a track of nuanced routing and sudden turns and hulking dunes, but more than that, it was a model for golf's future. Kidd took a cue from Morris's course next door. Rather than fighting the powers, he worked with Scottish Natural Heritage to create that rare setting where both conservationists and golfers could raise a toast. Without so much as sticking a shovel into the soil, Kidd identified twenty-three holes already existing in the dunes and picked his eighteen to route for a golf course. No machinery was used in shaping fairways or forcing carries. Tees and greens were hand-cut with push mowers, and sandy patches were left as bunkers, just as they had been on golf's original links. With chemicals banned on the property, greenskeepers composted seaweed from the beach for homemade top-dressing, and they weeded the entire property by hand to control the livestock-poisonous ragwort. While tees and greens were hand-cut, black Orkney sheep were welcomed onto the property to handle the rest of the trimming. Mach Dunes had dug into the past to find its future, and as a reward for doing so, a six-year-old course felt like it had been there for a century.

I heard from a friend who said he didn't care for Machrihanish Dunes's wild layout and untamed greens—too many bad bounces and guessing shots; the place felt too raw to him. I used his missive as an opportunity to grow my character and practice tolerance by saying nothing in response. What a pity: he went around the place entirely unaware of its significance, more interested in safe pars than the gift of golf on an unspoiled yet modern links. As a links devotee, the place was hope and a sort of clemency. When done right, it was okay to want to golf through geography that scientists deemed off-limits. It was a reprieve from the sort of guilt I felt playing Trump Aberdeen, where the landscape and neighbors had so suffered. It was a relief to think that, while great links were washing away, we could find more. Because we didn't need to make them; we could just uncover them, like Morris at Machrihanish and Kidd in the Dunes.

I had a chance to speak with David Kidd some months later about what the Dunes meant to him, as a designer and as a Scotsman with local roots. It was a thrill, he said, to build a golf course here, on hills he had climbed as a child on holiday with his grandparents. They'd told him that the white hotel over there, the Ugadale, was for the rich folks, and Kidd never set foot inside its doors during the summers of his youth. That the Ugadale now boasted a David McLay Kidd suite was something of an American dream come true in Scotland, but the bigger victory for Kidd was that his golf course would preserve the fragile dunes. As he explained to me:

> The most important thing, the thing that I kept driving into anyone who would listen, is that the dunes need purpose, and that purpose is their protection. No one was looking out for those dunes, because they didn't see them having any real purpose. But once you figured out how to golf across

them, now they go from being almost worthless to the crown jewel. If you
said now we want to take a bulldozer in there, bulldoze some areas flat to
make a feed yard for some cattle this winter, people would scream, yet the
farmer could have easily done that once. Not now.

We set out to explore the dunes' new purpose, and enlisted some help for
our tour. The Dunes was a good course for a caddie, and after our first time
around it, when Penn and I played the holes out of order—the routing is a
tad confusing in one spot, and in keeping with its natural vibe, the course is
clean of placards and direction posts—I sprang for a looper named Willie,
who showed us where gulls had built a nest in front of the sixth tee and spoke
of the days when our Navy SEALs would practice their maneuvers on this
beach and then have their tea in the abandoned barracks at the edge of the
course. Surely Willie was having a laugh. US Navy SEALs were *here*? US Navy
SEALs drink tea? But our caddie spoke the truth—Machrihanish Dunes sat
beside a former Royal Air Force base (if you feel like you're lost and have just
pulled into Area 51, you haven't—the first tee is around the corner) where
the SEALs maintained a commando unit, and where the nearby runway was
the longest in Europe and had been certified for emergency space shuttle
landings.

Willie was thin as broth and thirty years my senior, and I felt guilty for
dropping my bag on his shoulder until I struggled to keep up with him. He
told us he was the longtime greenskeeper at the nearby Dunaverty links (no
resemblance to groundskeeper Willie from *The Simpsons*, aside from the accent), just as his father had been. He encouraged us to fit a round in there,
and to also make time for a nine-holer up the coast, Carradale, on our way
to our next ferry. Both suggestions transformed Kintyre from a squeeze-in
before you played Turnberry and Troon into its own destination where you
flew, ferried, or caravanned over from Glasgow and stayed a week, driving
little and wanting for nothing.

Scott rejoined us in time for Dunaverty at the southern tip of Kintyre, in
a town aptly named Southend. Its course dated to 1889, built by local farmers
atop a rock that had once sheltered Robert the Bruce; its jagged headland had

been home to Dunaverty Castle, where in 1647, three hundred men, women, and children were slaughtered when the castle was overrun by an army of Presbyterian Covenanters. The golf course that took the castle's place bore none of those scars; it was an exuberant cliff ride, and an ideal complement to the beefier, stingier courses up in Machrihanish. With a congenial par of 66 stretched over 4,799 wavy yards, it was a tall stroll of deep breaths and unthinkable views. Far in the distance, we could make out the coast of Northern Ireland. I eyed a waterside path I had walked years before and recalled looking at this shard of land on the horizon from a golf course over in Ballycastle, wondering who was there and what the place held. Now I was there—here—a former vision now beneath my feet, and I felt more gratitude at Dunaverty than I thought I possessed.

The American-style hospitality at the Ugadale was nearly outdone by our Scottish welcome at Carradale, where we arrived without a tee time to find the nine-holer packed for a Texas scramble. Meeting Texas in Kintyre had us all smiling with traveler's irony, and the members embraced us like old pals and insisted we enter the tournament. With tee boxes pushed back onto outcroppings and greens tucked into craggy corners, Carradale was all joy as we fumbled our way through the tournament. A PGA pro alongside a scratch handicap not placing in their scramble was a humbling nod to local knowledge; we claimed distraction as our excuse, too taken by harbor views of a peaceful little town shadowed by tall hills of purple rhododendrons. Clocking us as visitors, a woman greeted Penn as he looked for his ball on her fairway and welcomed him to Carradale. When he noted the overwhelming beauty of the place and the color of the hills, she paused from beating us in her scramble and recited a song to him—"The Rhodies of Carradale"—while our groups waited for the two of them up on our greens.

Penn was a romantic with a poet's soul, and the west coast of Scotland had him writing long passages in his own journal at night, trying to capture each day's surprises for his golf buddies at home. But what we had discovered in Kintyre was almost too much for him to put into perspective. He just kept telling me, "I love you, man!" I told him I loved him, too. In his hit song about Kintyre, Paul McCartney sang about wanting to remain here forever.

We didn't know the words or the tune, but in our hearts, we were singing right along.

After weeks spent designing the map of my trip that I was gifting to each course, Tom Young from Ballpark Blueprints decided he couldn't help but explore some of the map firsthand. He had signed up to join us for a day in Machrihanish and then would meet me for eighteen at Askernish, a golf seeker's dying-wish sort of pilgrimage on the far western Hebrides islands. Tom was another partner with whom I had emailed a hundred times yet never met in person, but we seemed bound by our passions for books and beautiful golf, even if Tom's approach to the game felt plucked from the 1950s.

He was easy to identify beside the first tee at Machrihanish Old in billowing blue slacks and a crisp white shirt. He looked like a young Ben Hogan, and wouldn't carry anything in his bag that didn't have Hogan's name stamped on it. I didn't know Hogan made golf balls anymore, but Tom found a way to get his company's logo printed on his. He carried seven clubs, persimmon woods and some hickory shafts, and was so aesthetically obsessed that he eschewed the scorecard and didn't have a handicap. Rather, he wandered the holes with a journal, and on each tee box he jotted his reflections while we scribbled down our scores.

Our foursome of Philadelphia writer, Florida golf pro, Georgia extrovert, and Chicago designer blended like a reunion of college accomplices. Maybe it was the co-conspiratorial nature of this trip's mission, or just the travel itself. I had once read that Mike Keiser of Bandon Dunes in Oregon believed that the remoteness of his courses was an asset instead of a hindrance, that the effort involved in arriving there invested visitors in the experience, and that had felt true since I turned north from Inverness. If getting there was work, then one was predisposed to view *there* as a reward, and we all felt rewarded and invested, old pals pulling for one another and busting chops from that first tee shot at Machrihanish Old.

"You want my driver?" I had to ask as Tom teed up his museum-quality

3-wood, its head slightly smaller than his golf ball. A crowded beach separated Tom's ball from the first fairway. "Don't worry about the stroller," I told him. "Or the baby. That baby is ninety percent air."

The baby survived by whole yards that afternoon—we hoped the family assumed that overhead *whoosh* was a white, round, dimpled dragonfly—and we were off in grand spirits. Our four-ball was accompanied by Tom's wife, Tracy, a hero of a partner whose summer trip to Ireland had been hijacked by her husband's email buddy. Dublin had been swapped out for some place called Askernish, and a long and winding road to Kintyre had made her throw up in the car (curious, there's no mention of gut-sweating motion sickness in the Beatles song about said thruway), but still, she took pictures as we golfed thirty-six and plied us with Kit Kats and cheered Tom's persimmon bunts while we wondered how he made contact with clubheads that looked like they had been shrunken by some sort of Haitian voodoo.

Seeing the station wagon sitting fallow in the Ugadale parking lot as we walked off Machrihanish was like a sublime mirage; my car had collected a glorious sheen of neglect. No driving meant we had time for more haggis nachos and a soccer match on the pub TV. It was the first time this trip felt like a vacation, with time to breathe and talk and relax. We dined in the hotel, where we were joined by the Mach Dunes greenskeepers and our friend Kevin and his wife; we laughed and ate haggis-stuffed chicken and sampled cheeses made in Kintyre, and at meal's end we all made a pact to return here in two years' time to relive the place. It was a strange feeling to make such a plan and believe it would happen. Real friends, toward whom I acted sincerely and in whose presence I felt genuine, were a new addition to my life, and to make three of them in three days' time was Kintyre's gift. We would be back, and I would see them again. I knew well the dubious nature of late-night pub promises. This wasn't one of those.

Lessons

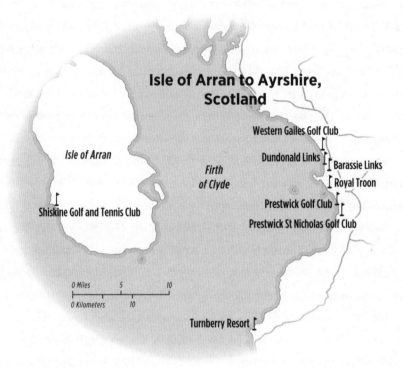

Isle of Arran to Ayrshire, Scotland

Isle of Arran

Firth of Clyde

Western Gailes Golf Club

Dundonald Links

Barassie Links

Royal Troon

Prestwick Golf Club

Prestwick St Nicholas Golf Club

Shiskine Golf and Tennis Club

Turnberry Resort

0 Miles   5   10

0 Kilometers   10

I had identified four or five golf hubs around Scotland that I looked forward to recommending to travelers in search of advice. St. Andrews and East Fife were obvious pockets for a week's trip, not to be outdone by the Golf Coast east of Edinburgh. Aberdeen was another good spot for golfers to rent a flat, and a trip around Inverness and Dornoch held a dozen links within an hour's drive. But the big corner still called to us—Penn, Scott, and I left Machrihanish and caravanned up to the next ferry port, where we sailed for what might be Scotland's preeminent golf belt. Home to Troon and Turnberry and Prestwick and Western Gailes and Dundonald and more, Ayrshire, west of Glasgow, should have had us all tingly with expectation, but I left Kintyre braced for a letdown. After Machrihanish and the Dunes, I expected that Scotland's next chapter could rank as only a mild denouement.

Our route back to the mainland took us through the Isle of Arran to Shiskine Golf and Tennis Club, where Scotland slapped the sour puss off my face. By the third hole, called "Crow's Nest," a tiny par 3 that felt as if we were tossing our balls up into a volcanic crater, I was proclaiming Shiskine the perfect golf course. It was part sporting roller coaster, part geological wonder; it felt like the golfing gods had pounded the place into existence with fire and hammer. I recalled my hike around the Giant's Causeway, there over my shoulder in Northern Ireland—if you laid a golf course across those inexplicable hexagonal rocks, you would get Shiskine, where walls of igneous sills shadowed the greens like the pipes of a giant stone organ.

Three golfers-turned-spelunkers could hardly believe the landscape we were golfing, but Shiskine's real perfection lay in the number of slots on its scorecard. It was my life's first twelve-holer, with a back and front six that seemed the Goldilocks ideal for a round of golf. Nine holes always felt unfinished, but fewer and fewer golfers had time for a full eighteen. Twelve felt just right, and I left with a bag from the pro shop full of my new favorite logo in golf, a simple 1 bisecting a 2, celebrating Shiskine's rare routing. Scott and Penn and I all agreed that we were still on for our two-year rendezvous at Machrihanish but that we would arrive there via the Crow's Nest and the Isle of Arran.

When we arrived at Turnberry, I coughed back my peanut lunch at the site of the fountain in front of the clubhouse. Far more vomitous than any of our ferry trips that morning was the faux-Roman relic plopped onto these hallowed grounds by the new owner. I imagine he could have chosen a statue less relevant to golf and Scotland (Abraham Lincoln? Crazy Horse? Tony the Tiger?), but I couldn't conjure one as I pitied the four stone lions spitting water at a Roman centurion. There were plans for a bigger Roman monolith up at the Turnberry hotel, and I wondered if Trump had read somewhere that Caesar played off scratch. But in fairness to savvy Donald and his second venture in Scotland, wherein he scooped up the Turnberry resort at a fraction of what the previous owners had paid six years before, he had committed to an eagerly anticipated overhaul of Turnberry's championship Ailsa course. As host to four Opens, most famously Nicklaus and Watson's 1977 "Duel in the Sun," Turnberry was a name that needed no adornment, but we couldn't find so much as a ball marker that didn't have *TRUMP* stamped on it in letters twice the size of those in *Turnberry*. Such was the cost of a failing resort's salvation. To the victors go the naming rights.

Trump Turnberry wasn't the acrimonious land-grab bemoaned up in Aberdeen. It seemed a lesson had been learned, and the checks in Ayrshire were written with a gentler, even welcome hand. The place needed cash, and Trump had already redone the famed hotel on the hill to rave reviews, restoring what was once an infirmary during World War II, when the course had been turned into a Royal Air Force base. A dormant runway still dissects the golf course, and a memorial near the ninth hole recalls lost RAF airmen.

Turnberry's Ailsa links was named for the Ailsa Craig, a nearby volcanic plug popping out of the sea that followed golfers around the course, and the site from which the stone signs on the links were chiseled (it's also the source for all the curling stones used in the Olympics—Ailsa granite reigns supreme in the sliding sport). As iconic as the craig and the white hotel were as golfing backdrops, and as omnipresent as the Turnberry lighthouse perched above the birthplace of Robert the Bruce was in links photography, the course was somehow a bit plain. In my golf imagination, the word *Turnberry* was burdened by behemoth expectations and uncommon history; perhaps my estimations were unfair, the reality falling short of my Turnberry fantasies. It was good, but it just didn't seem *Turnberry* good, insofar as I had arrived believing Turnberry meant unrivaled.

The lighthouse had me anticipating Ireland's Old Head, that other lighthouse layout of audacious carries and tee-box vertigo. I was ready for butt-cinching carries and wobbly walks along cliffside paths and shots played with my heels dangling off the edge of the known world, but the Turnberry holes seemed shy and polite. The redesign by renowned architect Martin Ebert (who, along with his partner Tom Mackenzie, has been trusted with the likes of Troon, Hoylake, and Royal St. George's, and was one of the golfing archeologists who uncovered the lost course at Askernish) promised to wring every drop of drama out of its setting, pulling the ocean more into play, and the video rendering of the new course with tees pushed to new edges was eye-popping. The reborn layout all but guaranteed the Open's return to Turnberry, but sadly for Donald, if he spent the £35 million to get his name on the Claret Jug, an R&A official was quoted as saying the site's name would still be engraved as the traditional TURNBERRY, sans the Trump.

My caddie, Jack, was a strapping twentysomething and another collegiate Scottish export studying in the States. I could only imagine the mileage he got out of blond hair and an accent seasoned with Glaswegian wit in North Carolina. When my drive on eighteen struck out to find its own fate, I turned to ask Jack where it went.

"Aye, I don't have a Scooby," he said. I was pleased with myself for decoding his rhyming slang unassisted—*Scooby Doo, clue, he didn't have a clue.* His description of my loose approach shots was more accessible—"You're on the dance floor but nowhere near the band"—and when Penn sent a ball toward unknown parts of Ayrshire, Jack was forthright in his verdict: "We couldn't find that one if it was a football." Caddie commentary aside, I slapped it around and still carded a 75, prompting wonder at what all the Turnberry fuss was about, and I figured Trump was right to pump some theater into the place. I just hoped that the folks who had plotted to blow up the statue in Golspie turned their attention to some fountains down south first.

As the years pass and itineraries accumulate, I won't remember Turnberry for its sculptures or its owner or its lighthouse. I won't recall it for its duel, or for Tom Watson in 2009, or for my scorecard with three circles on holes I cannot recall. Above my desk sits a picture of six friends with arms over each other's shoulders, five men and one woman, each with one finger raised, the windows of the Turnberry Hotel above their heads in the distance. I will remember this photograph, and the faces in it, and why we were holding up a single digit.

I see Penn and Scott, laughter in their smiles, their frames almost hiding wee Gretchen, who had flown back in from Amsterdam to see me off to the qualifier, and I see Duff, who had driven up from London. This trip's first partner had arrived a day early for a lesson from the Turnberry pro, and he's smiling in the picture, even though his palms were bleeding beneath bandages after an evening of hitting balls until dark, desperate for a reliable drive. It meant a lot that Duff was there. He had just returned from Philadelphia, where he'd laid his dad to rest. Duff's father was an old Irishman who loved his Phillies and his golf, a man of genuine Philadelphia grit who owned a small tap room that put his boys through the best schools. When Duff visited his old man in hospice, he wasn't sure if his dad could hear him, but he told him all about the courses we had played down south—two Open tracks in two days—and how much he would have loved it. His father couldn't answer him, but Duff said he smiled.

Beneath his arm in that picture is another friend who had arrived with a gift from home. Beside the Turnberry clubhouse doors, I had found my name stitched across blue Mizuno leather; it was a tour bag from my halcyon *Paper Tiger* days, an accessory befitting an Open qualifier. Just seeing TOM COYNE on a pro bag made my game feel like it had tightened up two shots. But even brighter than the sight of the bag he had somehow exhumed from my basement in Philadelphia was the grin of my good pal Paddy.

I wouldn't have made it around Ireland if it were not for Paddy the Caddie from Philadelphia and then Kinsale. He had been living as an expat in the south of Ireland, watching the kids and caddying at Old Head while his wife pursued her corporate career abroad. He met up with me along the way to lift my spirits and dump writing material into my lap. Paddy was as shy as a Sunday preacher, and his was a steady sermon of ball-breaking commentary delivered with a hint of Philadelphia hoagie-mouth, an accent that whisked me home to where we showed our affections by making strangers laugh at our friend's shortcomings. If he wasn't busting chops, he was connecting friends in common; exile Paddy to a lost Pacific island and he would discover that he had taken the island hermit's cousin to prom. And with a personality as large as his frame, the former college tackle already knew all my travelmates and half the pro shop staff before I arrived.

Paddy played a three-ball with Duff and Gretchen, whom he immediately dubbed G-Money and then the Hottie by the second tee, once he felt he'd known her long enough. She was quickly his surrogate little sister and his audience for eighteen holes of getting under Duff's skin. Better than finding himself at Turnberry, Paddy was thrilled to find himself paired with another Philly guy he could needle—Duff having attended prep school while Paddy was a proud diocesan alum—and it stoked his punch lines. After Duff sent his opening slice toward its final judgment, Paddy proclaimed, "That was a son-in-law."

"A son-in-law?"

"Yeah," Paddy said. "Not exactly what you had in mind."

Little did Duff know that he would spend his day at Turnberry hearing about his elite high school after every wayward shot—"They teach you that at Penn Charter? Charter guys are supposed to be good at golf"—from a former Philadelphia steamfitter who was equally relentless about Duff's college alma mater, singing a modified version of its fight song around the fields of Turnberry: "*Shame, shame on old Notre Dame, they play Army, Navy, and Penn. They play the Polish, Germans, and French, while all the Irish sit on the bench . . .*" After eighteen, Duff looked like he had just spent four hours on hold with customer service, the frustration heavy on his brow. "Jesus." He shook his head, eyes cast off into the distance. "He's just like my friends from home."

By the afternoon round, Duff was firing back at Paddy about the anonymous legacy of Lycoming College football; little did I know, the two had known each other for some months, thanks to the gang's semisecret email chain. Between his inquiries as to whether or not this Gramma Billy character could dance, Penn had exhorted my future partners to engineer a plan for leading me to the secret to golf and the Open. There was no consensus on a golf secret among them, but without knowing it, they had each arrived with answers of their own.

Paddy's pointer was to be Paddy. He cared not what anyone thought of him, a trait I endeavored to practice yet backslid by habit. His shunning of pretense was on display in the Trump Turnberry pro shop, when he approached the register with golf shirt in hand and asked, "You got anything without this wanker's name on it?" The girl behind the counter looked back at him like he had just picked his nose and stuck it on her forehead. He cared not when the steward pulled him a pint to be enjoyed in the Prestwick lobby but instead went looking for a better seat and found himself alone in the members' bar overlooking the eighteenth green. Outside, Duff passed the windows of the room we had been told was off-limits and spied Paddy sprawled across a leather chair, waving to Duff with a pint and a handful of peanuts. That was Paddy—comfortable in the uncomfortable places, and authentically so. Life was too short to give a damn what other people were worrying about. He made such wisdom seem effortless, but for me, it would be work. If I could get there for the qualifier, I had a chance to play my comfortable best.

If Paddy's ticket was being unbothered, Gretchen's was being fearless. She wasn't afraid to hop on a plane for golf with strangers, and didn't worry about traveling alone or making a bogey. Speedgolf? Sure, I'll try that—and maybe I'll win the world championship while I'm at it. I could put my finger on two necessities for playing great golf: First, you had to be good. Second, you had to believe it. Gretchen proved the latter was more important. She hadn't gotten serious about the game until eight years before, but her confidence had her contemplating a run at the pros, and rightly so. On these big-boy courses, she played like an irreverent whipster, unimpressed by their reputations for burly numbers. She carded scores in the low 70s, and at Turnberry her courage could be heard from holes away.

As we made the turn toward Turnberry's back nine, we knew someone had jammed one from the roar up ahead. Later we would hear how at number eleven, Paddy the Caddie told everyone in the group, "Hit 8-iron. I remember this hole in the Open. I was standing right here, and John Daly said, 'I don't give a shit what the wind's doing. It's an 8-iron.' So we're all hitting eight."

Duff and Gretchen looked at their caddie, Sam, wondering whether he was going to offer them a yardage. Sam nodded at Paddy. "He's fuckin' right."

They couldn't see the bottom of the pin from the tee, but as they jogged for the green in pursuit of Gretchen's shot, which had split the pin, Paddy insisted: "I've seen enough golf shots in my life. I'm a looper, I know. That went in. Sam, am I right?"

"He's fuckin' right."

And he was. An ace for G-Money, and later in the pro shop, Paddy dictated the engraving for the trophy. "Make sure it says, 'Hole-in-one by the Hottie. Witnessed by Paddy and Duff.'"

At Kilmarnock Golf Club (also known as Barassie) that afternoon, a muscular links and a worthwhile add to any Ayrshire itinerary, we found the head pro, Gregor—Paddy loved reciting his name, *Gregg-ore*—standing in the pro shop in the dark.

"Power's out," he told us. "Couldn't charge you if I wanted to." Paddy learned that his new buddy was going to have to sleep in the shop; without power to set the alarm, Gregor said he was looking at a night on the floor. Paddy promptly started planning an evening of running beers and food for him—even with fresh acquaintances, Paddy was that kind of pal. And then on the tenth hole, Gregor appeared on a golf cart as though he knew we'd been talking about him.

The Scottish pro pulled up to our group, and I instinctively checked our pace—well ahead of four hours, per usual. But Gregor wasn't here to play marshal; rather, he was bearing gifts in the form of a stack of cups and a clear bottle of expensive-looking brown. He had just made a trip to the western Isle of Jura for this tankard of rare spirits and carefully poured each of us a dram. Even without electricity, word of Gretchen's morning ace had made its way to his pro shop, and Gregor broke out the good stuff and tracked us down to celebrate her. This was why you played places off the published bucket lists, I thought, as Gregor passed the shots around until one landed in my hand and, for just a moment, I completely forgot whose hand I was looking at.

It didn't happen in pubs or at dinner parties, when I knew drinks would be offered and I was prepared to pass gracefully, but in the midst of a round of golf, a glass of rare island hooch proffered by a genuine Scotsman caught me unawares, one of those moments after years without a drink when you realize, *Holy shit, I actually don't drink*. Do I apologize and hand it back? Toss it over my shoulder? Swallow it and pretend? In two seconds my sober years flashed before my eyes as though they had never happened, and looking into my cup of spinning amber, my mind wandered to the state of Scottish emergency rooms, the price of a taxi chauffeur for the remainder of my trip, and the cost and availability of bachelor pads back home. Some drinkers planned for a night on the piss; folks like me foresaw the fortnight. We lifted our cups and toasted Gretchen and Barassie, and as I stood there looking at mine, Paddy took it from my hand and slugged it back without a word. He was that kind of pal.

Scott coughed half of his down and offered the rest to Paddy, who was again happy to help. Scott was another friend who was comfortable in his own frame, and time spent in his company reminded me to savor the journey.

I hung my head the next day as Scott and I walked off Royal Troon. I had just emphatically snapped a string of eleven pars by launching a drive into a pasture of waist-high forget-about-it. It was small consolation to think my ball might be found by a patron when the Open visited next year, because it would take a gallery of hundreds to find it. Aside from that drive and a few untidy opening holes, I had rationed myself more fear for Troon than it required. The Railway Hole was long, but I didn't notice the train tracks for the rain in my face; dumb golf remained the best golf. And the Postage Stamp, Troon's renowned eighth that was a wee par 3 with an even wee-er putting surface guarded by the Coffin Bunker, which did actually look like a pit from which evidence was exhumed yesterday—its green, stuck into the side of a sand hill, stood out for its drama, but it was a hillock of whimsy in an otherwise straightforward golf course.

I arrived at every rota course with a cargo of presumption, expecting each Open track to be an enchanted pathway conjured by potions, its dunes aglow with golfing sorcery. But sometimes they were just golf courses with enough prestige and parking for a major championship. The histories on display in clubhouse photos and trophy cases were all goosebumps stuff, but the golf courses were golf courses—good ones, but void of that aged context, none would stack up to the likes of Cruden Bay or Machrihanish or even Shiskine, not for this golfer. As we loaded our sticks into our cars at Troon, Scott asked how many Open courses that was for me. At that moment, I couldn't tell him; I'd lost count. But Scott knew. "Thirteen. You have one left: Musselburgh."

His awareness struck me. The guy had a checkmark next to ninety-nine of America's best one hundred, plus thousands of other courses populating his spreadsheet back home, yet he still savored every hole, every swing, knowing precisely where he was in each moment. Scott's qualifier at Bruntsfield was a why-not cap to his Scottish adventure; he wasn't missing the fun of each day's golf, fretting over how his final round would end. He reminded me that the best day of this adventure was the one I was in, and whether we qualified or not, we would have played a course called Scotland. And that was something—quite something, and it hadn't all just happened along the way to something else. How I struggled to remember that the along-the-way part *was* the something else.

Duff's wisdom was of a different sort, but his was the most honest and hard-earned. He had bandaged all four of the appendages on his 6-foot-4-inch frame at various times throughout the trip, his skin splitting in protest against two rounds a day. At the fifth hole of Prestwick, where the Open Championship was born as a way to determine Allan Robertson's heir as best golfer on the planet, it nearly took much more than a Band-Aid to save Duff.

He found his tee ball stuck into the slope beneath the green while I moved ahead to summit the blind two-hundred-yard par 3 called Himalayas on the card. I caught my breath on the green and looked over the Prestwick property, perhaps my favorite of the rota destinations for its quirky character and compact routing. Holes overlapped and ran shoulder to shoulder, making for an easy walk and unusual targets—*Take it over that tee box; aim for the pin on that other hole.* It had hosted a staggering twenty-four Opens, including the first dozen, and in the thorough introduction to Prestwick and Open history given us by the club steward, we learned how Prestwick's Open streak was broken only when Tom Morris Jr. won his third in a row in 1870 and got to keep the trophy for good. The cummerbund of red Moroccan leather with the large silver buckle was worth a lot more as collateral than the winner's purse (which, in the beginning, was zilch), and pros of that era—mostly caddies and greenskeepers—liked the Open not for its payout but for all the action they could score in side bets. Golf's most regal event started as something of a horse race in which the players were the thoroughbreds, and it thrived because it gave the leisure class something to bet on (remember this the next time someone tells you they don't like to gamble on the golf course). When Prestwick, the R&A, and the Honourable Company decided to chip in for a new trophy that would become the Claret Jug, it meant Prestwick would have to share the tournament and rotate it among the clubs who had thrown in for the prize.

As I eyed Old Tom's Prestwick masterpiece from the green of Himalayas, I saw a scattering of pins squeezed into a few acres of lumpy sand between the town and the sea; the place seemed an impossible venue for a major championship, and Prestwick's last Open, in 1925, had indeed been a chaotic affair, with players jostling the crowds for room to swing. It had been a while since I'd seen my playing partner on number five—we found his ball below the green before I headed up to the putting surface—but suddenly I heard a loud *pop*, quick and hard as a gunshot. I hustled over to the front edge, where a wall of railroad ties propped up the green like a cake top. I spotted Duff standing tilted on a wall of fescue, his face ashen. On the next tee, he would show me the black tar on his ball from where he had drilled a wedge into the sleepers and sent his Titleist ricocheting back past his ear.

"I almost killed myself," he said, gasping for breath as he reached the green. "I could be dead down there, and nobody would know." I assured Duff that I would have come to look for him—I had a long look at birdie and needed someone to tend the pin.

Duff's Prestwick score ballooned from the day before at Turnberry, and he blamed his struggles, perhaps rightly, on having to golf with me. He was convinced my company brought out the worst in his game; as the blood dried beneath his bandages, he bled golf balls from his bag's deepest pockets. On eighteen, he was rewarded for persevering through our pairing when he found a drive that had been hit farther right than his politics, whacked it toward a hilltop with a 5-iron, and crested the peak to find his ball sitting twenty feet from a pin. I watched as he lifted his fists like a punch-drunk champion, slowly pumping his weary arms at the sky, until he looked left and saw me standing by another pin sixty yards away. He stopped, dropped his bag, and thought for a minute.

I could read the *Fuck it* on his lips as he putted out on a hole we had played half an hour ago, making par on his eighteenth, which was number fourteen on the card, and perhaps becoming the first player in Prestwick's unrivaled history to card a score for seventeen and three-quarters of the golf course.

Duff swore off my company at nearby Prestwick St. Nicholas, where we discovered a cracker of a course that counted Tom Morris as one of its former members. Originally called the Prestwick Mechanics Club, it may have been golf's first effort to grow the game beyond the gentry and the caddying classes; Old Tom had helped found the club as an outlet for working-class golfers, and its members originally shared fairways with his Prestwick links. But playing in the group behind me at St. Nicholas was not enough to cure Duff's allergy to my presence; the mere sight of me standing by the eighteenth green was enough to coax him into the shot golfers fear more than hitting their own forehead. I couldn't help but hang back and watch his final drive toward the clubhouse, his ball peeling right, right—

"Oh no . . ."

And more right.

"Cars."

BA-DING. I couldn't tell which made the *BA* and which the *DING*, the Mercedes or the asphalt, but they had both met Duff's golf ball in an intimate and potentially expensive way.

"Dude," Duff said as he approached, pulling his trolley up into the parking lot, "I saw your ginger head and I knew that shot was coming." His mouth was trying to smile, but his eyes looked like he wanted to stuff his driver down my throat. I put two hands over my mouth—it took both hands to cover the grin overtaking my face. Hitting a parked car with your golf ball is not funny, not at all, yet watching your friend hit a parked car with his golf ball is somehow the height of comedy. What a strange game.

I shot a well-framed and carefully edited video of Duff leaning over the car's hood with its owner, sure to capture the hot crimson of Duff's forehead reflecting off the sedan's yellow finish. I covered the incident like a would-be newsman, establishing the scene and then focusing on the suspect and catching the poignant moment of relief when the gentleman shook Duff's hand, no worries about a thin white smudge he could surely buff out.

"Do not post that," Duff said as we walked back to the clubhouse.

"I think it's too late."

He sighed. "You want to know the secret to golf?" he said. "Here it is: Don't play."

Penn left us after Prestwick St. Nicholas for a drive back to the Edinburgh airport, and though I'd known him for all of nine days, we had bonded like passengers in a lifeboat. Golf made easy friends of most folks, but add wild miles and late dinners and shared scenery that had us both contemplating our insignificance in some grander plan, and we were linked for the long haul. Somehow, a stranger who took the time to email me had taken up a large and welcome residence in my life.

Five years ago, I wouldn't have shared a cup of coffee with Penn from Georgia. I was too bundled up in fear and bravado, a dumbass of unrivaled genius. And I hated coffee. I had spent those intervening years flip-flopping my habits and preconceptions, trying to live as if I didn't know absolutely everything. It had been a scary free fall, but it landed in a generous place. I never felt wiser than when I learned how to not know. Living life without a Scooby was, finally, what I suspected life was supposed to feel like all along: overwhelming, ecstatic, and so fucking vast.

I abhorred golf-is-life aphorisms, but a muscle-pumped lash never sent the ball as far as a breezy pass. Who would have guessed that all the power came from no longer trying to power through life? A mystery, for sure, but embracing mystery had lessened my freight by a load. I had no idea why a person named Penn needed to be on this trip, but something did know why—and it revealed as much when I got an email that evening in Prestwick.

Evening all,

In my room @ the lovely EDI Hilton, rental car turned in, wake-up call for 3:30 tomorrow morning (ugh), already missing my new best friends. I'm sure Paddy will keep you boys & girls in line. I made it here safely even though I was not doing a 24 Hour of Le Mans thing behind a blue BMW station wagon, which I admit felt strange (I love you, Man!).

Anyway, here is my submission for the you-know-what:

1. Never, ever quit.
2. Never let what other people say about you or your game get you down.
3. Forget about the shot you just hit, good or bad; focus on the next one.
4. And when you think you've found The Secret, think again . . . it will be different tomorrow than it was today.

Unbelievable 9 days. Unbelievable! Still trying to digest and take in what we just did. Un-fucking-believable. I'm not sure anyone has ever done that before.

Tom, it was an honor being by your side. Get some rest and get in the zone. Pulling for you, man—but you're already a winner.

Your friend,
Penn

Don't quit. That was it—don't give up. So unsatisfyingly simple, yet perfectly irrefutable. It was a long bed of relief in which I curled up and laid, because not quitting was something I could do. The slings and arrows of eighteen holes had wracked my psyche since grade school, but I could persevere with the best of them—and if that was my task, consider it won. No more *I can't*. That evening, in a room across the street from the Open's first fairways at Prestwick, I drifted off to sleep on *I won't*.

Nowhere in my mind was the other part of Penn's missive, that bit about thinking twice because today's answer would not be tomorrow's. But it should have been.

. . .

I loved G-Money, but our rainy round at Troon was an exercise in opposing molecular properties; her boundless energy seemed to sap life from my every proton. It was a phenomenon I knew well from battling two-year-olds. When they were on the edge of inconsolable, offering positivity and reassurance was guaranteed to push them into arm-flailing fits of snot and scorn. Misery loathes happiness, and Gretchen and I found ourselves on contrary emotional plateaus: while she enthusiastically grilled the assistant pro with whom we were playing with questions about course strategies and life lessons from the golf business, I sank deeper into a blank and isolated funk. *Don't quit* was somehow a distant cliché, powerless against the reality of another morning's rain dripping down my back.

I walked at twice their pace, barely pausing to swing the club, racing for the exit before Gretchen's golf zeal pushed my golf weariness into an outburst I couldn't take back, something along the lines of *Nobody cares if you hit eight or feathered seven because it never stops raining on this godforsaken shingle that millions of happier bastards escaped centuries ago!* I finished up and shook everyone's hand and decided it would be better if I skipped lunch with the gang in the clubhouse. I needed a break, I said, and left without telling them where I was going.

It was not easy escaping golf in Ayrshire. I headed back to our B&B and walked the rainy main street in Prestwick past takeaway curry shops and pale smokers outside the pubs at midday, wondering what my kids were doing right now—probably just waking up and watching cartoons.

I found a barber shop and went inside and sat down. It felt like a small taste of regular life, and reminded me that I would be home soon and wouldn't want to look like a soap-dodger (a favorite bit of British slang I had co-opted) when I got there, so I better get the sideburns tidied up. I had gotten my hair cut abroad before; in Paris, I just sort of pointed to my head and the stylist figured it out, but French was easier to parse than the accent of my Prestwick barber, who must have asked me if I wanted the worst haircut in Scottish history, to which I enthusiastically nodded yes. I left the shop looking like an Amish kid who got invited to a rock show, sides shaved tight with a stiffened poof on top. *Give me a Liverpool jersey and a bacon roll*, I thought, *and I'll cease to be a Yank.*

The haircut did nothing to help the fact that the rest of me looked like I had been locked outside in a storm. For a month. I was shocked by the image looking back at me when I Facetimed the kids, gullies beneath half-shut eyes and bony cheeks and skin flaking off my forehead. I had transformed myself from an Open aspirant into a golfing vagabond. I'd set out to find my best self and force-fill some sort of void, but I ventured too far over the golfing edge. I looked like a clown from a bankrupt circus, and as I drove toward my afternoon tee time, I felt like one. I was the futility of the useless performer.

Bolstered solely by a waning sense of duty to my itinerary and that poster, I sped toward my final eighteen in Ayrshire, hopeful that I would arrive before Paddy and Scott and Gretchen and might play alone. I'd heard Western Gailes described as the genuine hidden gem of this stretch of Scotland. It was a wild and breathtaking links that Scott and G-Money would claim as their favorite of the trip, but I would never know that for myself.

I jogged out to the first tee at Western Gailes, where the starter told me to slow down and catch my breath; I saw a dozen Americans mulling about that first tee and was desperate to get out in front of them. They let me tee off, and I half sprinted to my ball, knocked it onto the green, and raked in a par. I hit my drive down the second, hurried after it, and found a foursome lining up their putts on the green. On the third tee, I could see that half the golf course was clogged with trolleys and rain suits; there was nowhere for a single to go.

Never quit. No matter if the golf is slow and the rain is sideways. Never, ever give up. If the putts are all lips and you're running low on bullets— don't quit. Forget how much you don't want to be there; millions would trade places with you right now and think themselves the luckiest fools on the planet. You do not quit.

I hopped the fence to my right and walked along train tracks back to the parking lot. The walk back in without pausing to hit a shot felt so much longer than the walk out. I put my clubs in the trunk and laid my wet waterproofs on top of them, and my car passed Paddy's as I left Western Gailes and quit.

Askernishing

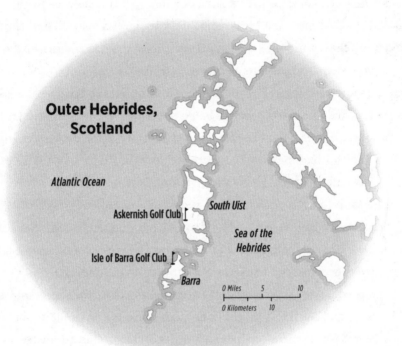

In a small airport on one of Scotland's Outer Hebrides islands, I listened to the loudspeaker and learned of the role fog played in the lives of traveling islanders. Some days you got off the island, and some days you didn't. On this day, the clouds were too low for a landing at the Benbecula Airport, where they turned on the lights for the one daily flight, and then shut them off when told the plane wasn't coming. It wasn't unusual, I was told, and there was a chance I might be fogged in tomorrow as well, which meant I would miss my Open qualifier altogether. A year ago, I would have expected such news to have me selecting five clubs from my bag and swimming for the mainland, but for some reason, that wasn't the case now. I sat in the dark airport contemplating my next move. It only took a moment. I knew precisely where I was headed.

I thought this trip had begun with a text from Julian or a phone call with Robert, but when I arrived in South Uist (pronounced *Oo-ist*, sort of), I remembered that it more likely started six years before, when I read an article in the *New Yorker* that had sent a lot of golf soul-searchers to this same airport in the Outer Hebrides. David Owen's "The Ghost Course" told the story of Gordon Irvine, a course consultant who visited South Uist on a fishing excursion and made a courtesy trip to the island's meager nine-hole golf course. Locals claimed it was a Tom Morris design, pointing to a newspaper clipping in which Old Tom said his South Uist course was "second to none." The accounts of how Morris got to South Uist and what he would have been doing there were dubious. The place was home to a small pocket of Gaelic-speaking crofters, and it was best known to the world for the whisky cargo ship that wrecked on its shores in 1941 and kept the island drunk for weeks, a history celebrated in a black-and-white classic called *Tight Little Island*.

The notion that Morris would have had anything to do with South Uist's cow pasture of a golf course (literally; it was a pasture for livestock) struck Irvine as the stuff of tall island tales. But as he inspected the course, he peeked over the dunes at the southern end and discovered what must have looked like lumps of gold in a muddy pan. Hulking dunes framed overgrown fairways that stretched toward inconspicuous putting surfaces. There was a golf course there, and, judging by the corridors winding through mountains of grassy sand, an extraordinary one at that. Morris *had* designed the links on South Uist; it had just been misplaced by a few hundred yards.

Irvine and the club chairman, Ralph Thompson, enlisted links virtuoso Martin Ebert's help in restoring the course, and it opened in 2008 after numerous battles with local farmers (a legacy of the Clearances was the fact that there was nothing so contentious in Scotland as the usage and potential seizure of land). But eighteen years before that, my friend John Garrity discovered the course for himself on a trip to South Uist. He was poking around Scotland on assignment for *Sports Illustrated*, looking for untold golf stories, and figured a trip to South Uist's nine-holer would yield some quirky adventure. When he went looking for a tee box at the edge of the course, he likewise discovered the unmistakable markings of a meaty links on the other side of the dunes, and with the grass short enough in May, he decided to go play it.

Like the game's original golfers, he hunted for passage between the dunes, putting to rabbit holes and finding tees and greens that convinced him Morris had indeed been there, and had done his greatest work on the isle of South Uist. It was John Garrity who dubbed it "The Ghost Course," and years later he would playfully place it atop his top-fifty list of courses for Golf.com. A phone call reached him in the press tent at the US Open at Oakmont in 2007—it was Ralph Thompson, ecstatic about the top ranking and confused as to how he knew about their golf course when it hadn't even opened to the public yet. Garrity was confused as well—someone else had found it? And it was being restored? Thompson invited Garrity back to be one of the first to play it. When I arrived myself, I recalled Owen's story and looked up Garrity's tale of South Uist, and it occurred to me that I had been looking all over Scotland for golf's secret, and here might be the game's last and greatest one, in a place called Askernish.

A direct flight from Glasgow to Benbecula, just north of the Askernish links, made getting there easier than it was in Morris's day, but I wanted my pilgrimage to feel more earned, to mimic the taxing travels of Old Tom, so I flew into the tiny isle of Barra, a short ferry ride away from South Uist. The flight schedule was contingent on the tides—our fat-tired prop plane was going to land on the sand, the only commercial beach landing in the world. I felt myself earning my Askernish epiphany when the pilot strapped himself into our soda can with wings and turned around with a smile, like he was going to tell us a bedtime story. "Welcome, everyone. You know the routine. Exits are here, there. Weather in Barra is, well, it's not great. Buckle up, please." I surmised that there weren't going to be any pretzels, unless I could fly the plane while he served. Pilots had missed runways before, but it would be hard to miss the whole beach, I told myself as the propellers groaned in my ears.

It was a surprisingly safe and soft landing. Perhaps it was gratitude for surviving my first beach landing, but the rain was cool and soft in Barra, and I felt my Ayrshire hangover washing away. I wasn't worried about the qualifier or lamenting walking off Western Gailes, nor was I berating myself for the quick good-byes I made that morning as I hurried off to the airport. Sore feet and self-pity felt far behind me now, and everything seemed interesting again. It was the traveler's revival: I can't possibly go another foot, but show me something I haven't seen before and I'm two steps ahead of you.

We walked along a path through the dunes and into an airport terminal so small that it would be impossible to leave one's bag unattended, and I found the keys to Barra's rental car waiting for me at a desk. "Just leave the keys in the visor," I was told by the woman at a café that was surprisingly crowded with people who didn't look like they were traveling anywhere. The one-room airport doubled as an island hangout, it seemed, with old ladies sharing tea and men in muddy boots sitting and reading the paper. I drove away from the airport without any worries about getting lost; there was essentially one road around the island, so I was confident I would eventually find the little Barra nine-holer I wanted to sample before sailing for South Uist tomorrow. I was struck by the courtesy of all the drivers on the one-lane road; whenever I approached, they graciously pulled over and waved. It might have been island hospitality, or they might have known—*Here comes the rental car*.

As I sat in the driver's seat of my yellow Ford, I weighed the probability of whether or not I had arrived. A sign marked GOLF had pointed me along an unpaved path, and that path ended here, so while there was no parking lot to speak of, I figured I must be at the course. There was a tattered flagstick atop some gray rocks in the distance, but there was no clubhouse—not even a shed. There was a steel storage container and a fence with a gate, but what made me most doubt my destination was the black bull staring at the hood of my car. It was roughly the size of a dump truck, with a bona fide brass ring hanging from its nostrils (I thought bulls had those things only in cartoons), and I had no doubt that it could flip my hatchback around like a Frisbee if the mood struck. With my eyes fixed on the bull's, I wondered if I could find reverse in this stick-shift should it make a move. I hardly noticed as two gentlemen in caps and jeans approached my window.

I still don't know how Murdoch and Roddy knew I was going to be there at that exact time, but I was relieved to find two Barra members to show me around what was indeed the golf course. They told me I was right to be wary of the bull; he'd been a bit of a problem lately, charging foursomes and busting through the fences protecting the greens. Ravens were actually the bigger problem at Barra, they explained, as they liked to scoop up one's ball and fly it up the mountain and drop it on the rocks, thinking they had snatched an egg.

The course was mostly rock, with patches of moss and turf off which we could play our shots—a local rule gave everyone two club lengths to move their ball everywhere—and we entered each green through an iron turnstile, fences having been put in place to discourage the cattle. There was no missing the cows—or their droppings—at Barra, but for all its ditches and blind shots and hoofprints and rocky caroms, I loved every minute of my two-hour hike along this craigside terrain. I felt like Garrity and Irvine at Askernish, discovering a golf course in hiding. And it was well hidden, even as we played it. Nine concrete tee boxes covered in worn plastic turf would have been impossible to locate without my guides, nor would I have known which fenced ring to aim for without their direction. We traversed ravines and climbed boulders in search of my tee balls. I was too busy minding my next step or taking in views of the beach on which I had just landed to find each shot, but Murdoch was a golf ball clairvoyant. My greatest feat in Barra, grander than if I had won the gold medal at St. Andrews, was that I played the course without losing a single Titleist.

Murdoch and Rory explained that the condition of the course varied depending on members' availability. They themselves pulled mowers out of the metal container I had parked beside and cut the grass, which may have explained why the ninth fairway, all of four feet wide, was the narrowest in Scotland—who had the time to bother broadening it? The members' stake in the course was the best scheme for course ownership I had ever encountered. The club paid rent to a local farmer solely for the square footage of the greens, and the rest of the land they shared with the herds. The greens were like putting on Velcro, but no matter—Barra GC had made golf not just affordable but possible on this improbable stretch of mountainside. And in so doing, they had made a complicated game feel as simple as it should: hit your ball, chase it, mind the cows, and smell the roses. As my shots pinballed off volcanic humps against a backdrop of whitecaps crashing on the beach, I was keenly and gratefully aware that this was a game, and I was playing.

When I teach poetry to my freshmen in English 101—rather, when I implore nineteen business majors to abandon their aversion to verse, because this was going to be on the final—I always go to Billy Collins. Our former poet laureate's work is accessible yet dense with ideas and emotion. The kids know the words, and they feel empowered to interpret them. I also enjoy telling them that Collins is a big golfer, a fun fact I love. I feel like a golfing poet laureate buys me some cred in academia, where not that many other professors have canceled class for a mid-amateur qualifier. Golf has the cadences and emotions and images of good poetry, so why don't all poets golf? Why am I the weird one? A friend who golfs with Collins told me of his passion for links golf in particular, and when I saw the below on Askernish's website, I decided I had to follow the footsteps of not just John Garrity or David Owen or Old Tom but Billy Collins, whose job is knowing beauty, and who does his job very well.

South Uist
There's a handful of reasons to come here.
The salmon's as good as the drinks.
Some like the whisky, some like the beer,
But I'm happiest when out on the links.

It's fine to be a student of genealogy
Busy tracing your family's course,
But the only ghost I need for company
Is the ghost of Old Tom Morris.

The hikers come for the air and the sights,
And the anglers are here for the fishing,
But nothing is better under blue skies
Than when I'm Askernishing.

—Billy Collins
US Poet Laureate 2001–2003

There is *playing golf*, and there is *golfing*; we're familiar with both. But then there is *Askernishing*. Before I had been there, I thought it a clever pub bet of a poem—*Hey, Collins, I bet you can't rhyme Askernish!* But Askernishing was a thing, a genuine experience, and one bigger than a game of plastic balls and iron rods. Askernishing was understanding the indiscernible. It was feeling your own insignificance with joy and with relief. Whether you found it on mountaintops or in magazines or on golf courses or in church, to Askernish was to realize. To be alone yet feel connected. It was good. It was the stuff of poetry.

The first ferry from Barra brought me to the bottom end of South Uist early in the morning. I dropped my bags at my hotel—*the* hotel—on the way up to the course, and by the time I pulled into the field that served as the course parking lot, there were three cars there in the grass ahead of mine, Tom Young's being one of them. I wasn't sure what a found golf course would look like; there were no diggers from where the holes had been unearthed, no archaeologists brushing sand off the tee boxes. There was a lot of grass that looked gray beneath low clouds and thousands of tiny white flowers dotting what seemed to be both fairway and rough. It was all sort of flat, from what I could see, which was only as far as a wall of dunes in the distance.

There was a small teahouse/pro shop where I sat down with Tom and his wife, Tracy, for a cup. There were some Askernish shirts and souvenirs in the back, and up front there were paperbacks spread around the room, as if they wanted to make the writer feel at home. The woman behind the counter made excellent soup and scones, but she also ran an independent press, ThunderPoint Publishing. Not only were they preserving Old Tom's island legacy at Askernish but they were also keeping literary fiction alive in print. The place immediately felt more rare and important; they fought the uphill battles out here on the edges, making things as they figured things ought to be.

Tom and Tracy had arrived the evening before after two nights at the Rusacks Hotel that overlooks St. Andrews's eighteenth—a worthy splurge for the view, never mind the creaky floors. A reader of both Owen and Garrity's accounts, Tom was as eager to visit Askernish as I was, and he had already gone around in the twilight the evening before.

"Well? Is it that good?" I asked him. "Is it worth coming out here for?"

Tracy smothered a laugh. Going from the Ugadale in Kintyre and the Rusacks in St. Andrews to the wee Borrodale Hotel in South Uist was a leap (the latter was actually nicer than I expected, clean with islander charm and a lively pub), and she must have been wondering how her vacation days from work came to be spent trying to find eighteen holes in the rain in the Outer Hebrides of Scotland. She truly loved her guy, and her guy seemed to know why they were there, even if he wasn't letting on.

"You tell me," he said. "I'm not saying anything until you've played it."

So we played. The first three holes behind the teahouse were sleepy and plain, even as they circled us around a field of geographical anomaly known as *machair*, a fertile seaside soil that hugged the dunes and was unique to this corner of the Hebrides. It harbored the rarest of fauna and small wildlife and seemed an appropriately exclusive carpet for the links I hoped did not just top the list but made its own list, on which Askernish was the only entry. But these opening holes, while fair and fun enough if they were the start of my backyard links, had me worried. I hadn't come all this way to find that the miracle of Askernish was simply that it existed, when I expected it to both exist *and* alter my golfing worldview. But the layout mimicked something of Garrity's experience in finding the original course, when he begins his day slowly, then peeks over a hilltop and finds the verse.

The course warms and hints at the drama to come until, at number seven, you ascend the tee, and you have arrived. You have chased Old Tom all this way, to a peak overlooking a valley of deep fairway twisting through towering dunes, and you feel as if you've finally grabbed the old man by the tail of his coat. He turns around to congratulate you and welcome you to the culmination of his work.

The irresistibility of Askernish among design disciples is its time-capsule purity. It's an opportunity to see genuine Old Tom, unaltered by greens committees and updaters. It's unique on the golfing planet as a window into golf's past; academically, Askernish mattered, but I was not here as a professor. I was here to play, and I did so like a child without a curfew.

I've experienced rounds when I didn't want the golf to end, but there was something about the rising action at Askernish that seemed to pull me through the golf course, a pleasure cruise I couldn't depart. When the airport was fogged in the next morning, meaning I would miss my practice round for the qualifier and a long-planned visit to the final rota course at Mussel-burgh, I was thankful for the chance for more Askernish.

Maybe it was the solitude, with nobody on the course save the three of us, and then just me after Tom and Tracy left for their flight to Glasgow. Perhaps it was the remoteness of this edge of the known world, driving golf balls toward Nova Scotia. Maybe it was the holes themselves and the mystery of their sitting unsown for a century, left to the sheep and the wind, waiting to be found again. Maybe it was that there was nothing else to do on the island (I'm sure there was, but I wasn't there to bird-watch). But to me, the ultimate pull of Askernish was in the implications of its deep and unspoiled roots—the place proved the game to be timeless and profound. It validated my golf obsession. First discovered by an old man from St. Andrews and then by a writer from Missouri, Askernish was evidence that there were corners of god's earth, rare and remote, that had been gifted to golfers. It might stretch the bounds of grandiosity to conflate golf and one of its courses with a divine plan, but as I climbed each dune to discover another perfect golf hole that seemed to have no business being there, I couldn't help but feel the providence all over this place. It wasn't heaven on earth—now *that* would be grandiose—but if I make it to heaven someday and find that it isn't Askernish, I fear I might be disappointed.

I'd played with a Scot back on the east coast who had warned me that Askernish was nothing special, a golfer who doubted its connection to Old Tom (*That's a Morris course? Not the course I played. That's a bundle of pish*), and I understood the dichotomy of our reactions. After the time and travel and legends and hype, which I'm presently guilty of inflating myself, Askernish cut two ways: You either felt it in your gut or you kicked yourself for not spending two more days in Ayrshire. The greens are shaggy and severely kinked; the white flower buds dotting the fairways make finding your ball a dizzying endeavor, and you will find dozens of sandy rabbit holes for each one with a flag in it. Askernish won't make everyone on your next Scottish buddy trip smile. But for the open-minded golf soul seekers, they will want to go around again. And again. And did I ever.

My first time around, I was playing golf, snapping pictures, and getting a feel for the place, reconciling what I was seeing with what I had read. After some soup in the teahouse, on my second eighteen I was golfing, my shoulders loose from the morning warm-up and my body trying to shape shots that complemented the landscape. By my third round, I was hungry but unable to stop myself and turn for the car, and by my evening round, after the teahouse was dark for the day, I was Askernishing.

The weariness of flights and ferries and seventy-two holes relaxed my head into a state of mushy mindfulness, and I saw the old man in brown wool climbing the windy dunes ahead of me. He was fit for his age, still swimming every morning in the cold Atlantic waves. I had to hustle to keep up with the white beard in the distance, a test to earn my time on a course he knew they would forget about. It was meant to ripen and age until it was needed. And I felt a tingle in my eyes and a tugging at the top of my throat—I could have cried if I was the crying sort, because a wave of recognition nearly knocked me over. *I* needed Askernish. For a moment, I was entirely convinced that Old Tom made this place for right now, and for me.

I don't know why my parents named me Robert and then decided to call me by my middle name, Thomas. I suspect there was some Irish family secret about my namesakes, but they said I just looked more like a Tom when I was born. I appreciated their reasoning, but if they would have waited a few minutes before filling out my birth certificate, they could have saved me a lifetime of confusion in doctors' offices and with telemarketers (if anyone calls our house asking for Robert, we hang up immediately), and on the first day of class when the teacher asks if anyone has a variation of their name by which they preferred to be called. My profs expected Robert Coyne to say he went by Robby or Bob, but when I asked them to call me Tom, each new semester began with a classroom chuckle, and so was born my college nickname, Robert-Call-Me-Tom.

I knew that traveling the UK for two months on my own was going to stir up warm-bellied memories and old inclinations, but I decided to leave them to a different version of me, and in trying to describe the experience of a life lived in such distinct chapters, I would call that version Robert. Much has changed in four years—so much that I recall many of my yesterdays as belonging to someone else. There were a lot of good times, and then some dark and dire times. Robert was my life of the latter.

I had once dreamed of birdies and bestsellers, but my fantasies changed through those foggy years. I came to long for a nonexistence in which my days might somehow be over before they began. People went to work and shopped and met their friends for laughs and conversation; it all looked impossible while I wandered in life's margin, searching for a way to disappear. I dreamed of normal. I dreamed of not needing a drink before I could steady my feet beside my bed. I dreamed today would be different; when it never was, I dreamed tomorrow might be. I dreamed that I even cared.

Robert joined me and spoke more loudly on some parts of this trip than others, in moments when I wanted to complain or quit or escape. I could have left that side of myself in my notebook, but keeping him quiet requires honesty, and it would have been fiction to leave out the drive behind every swing and every step, to pretend that it really mattered whether I golfed Scotland or qualified for the Open; truth was, that I was now dreaming about either was my life's miracle. I don't suppose I needed all this golf to know it, but it helped remind me that my daily prayer had once been to cease existing, but something still thought that I should. And then I did so. Determinedly.

I don't think I'm special because I made a change in my life, nor do I think booze is the devil's elixir. I loved the stuff, with every atom of my being. Still do. Alcohol wasn't my problem; rather, it was my solution. The problem was that when it stopped being my solution, I couldn't stop drinking it. Ay, the rub, to find the thing that makes your life run smooth and forward, and then find it gives you the shakes and makes your spouse cry at night and sends you to the emergency room, where you flatline three times while your wife and two-year-old daughter are on the other side of the glass.

How a few years later I could find myself standing on a hill on a Scottish island, blood pumping through my muscles, with clear eyes and mind—it was pure mystery, but the soul-affirming kind. It was very much a different life, as distinct as a Robert and a Tom. When I let obsession take over or try to strangle life into coughing out the results I demand, I'm letting him speak for me; but in taking things easy and in small pieces, he goes silent, and so far, so good. That's the daily grind and gift of life today. You have to have dangled your toes out over the abyss to really know it, but no matter whether you can drink with impunity or pig out without consequence or screw around without remorse, I think there are two kinds of people—the chasers and the found. The latter is a rare species. So just because I order club soda these days and eat ice cream by the bucket (there's a lot of sugar in Chardonnay that needs replacing; sobriety comes with a wicked sweet tooth), we're not that different. We're people, programmed to want that which we cannot have, to feel a void that we need to fill with distraction or with purpose, with sadness or joy, with vocations or with drinks. Same problems, different medicines.

My former strategy for living was: Life is uncomfortable, so get comfortable. It was a crap design with an inevitable conclusion, and the new plan has yielded far healthier fruit: Be honest. Try to listen. And try to try. Three simple axioms that got me from dead on a table to Askernishing in South Uist, where there was no room for any Robert part of me on this tight little island. I felt thankful in a way that made me suspect that gratitude wasn't a side effect of good fortune or a condiment to be spread over happiness but the whole damn point in itself. I felt certain that I had found what I'd come for in Askernish, an undeniable answer in the feeling of being truly present. BE PRESENT was engraved on the back of my wedge, but it had taken me forty years to feel it without worry or pretense or distraction, and to feel entirely available to my current circumstances. I suspect it felt like harmony, grace, and joy, but more than anything, it just *felt*.

Now I blasted soaring shots from the bottom of my feet, the contact all middle and the cups wide and hungry. I didn't know which hole I was playing. When you're Askernishing, you're playing now; soon enough, you'll be playing next. As I walked in the shadows of the dunes, my world was a golf course, and I was passing through it in peace. I was walking right. There was nothing uncomfortable about this life, not when you did it properly, and for the first time in all my unsure years, I was sure that I was. Maybe seventy-two holes had given me island fever and forced a softened head into accidental epiphany, but as I folded my fourth scorecard of the day into my pocket and looked out at the light going purple along wavy edges of sand, I knew my Askernish state of mind was no accident.

The course was not forced or orchestrated; rather, it was waiting there to be enjoyed. It wasn't worried about what it was or was not, about where it had been or where it was headed. When I lived my own life that way, it was all answers, and I slept like a child.

So for all my restlessness and roving, I found that the answer was to be present.

Try it.

Present

The Bruntsfield Links, Edinburgh, Scotland

It takes practice.

Alan is waiting for me in the parking lot. It feels like years since I last saw him, my friend who had played nearly every course in Scotland and joined us at Glen back in North Berwick, but it's no surprise that he's kept his promise to caddie for me in the qualifier. With a thick white beard and the sturdy shape of a Scotsman who doesn't pass on a bacon roll, Alan has a fullness to him that, after months traveling its every corner, looks like Scotland to me. Stout, steady, and unbothered—I'm lucky to have him with me. It's a morning I've dreamt of for years, and I had expected to be too nervous to warm up and to spend the hour before my 11:34 tee time in the bathroom trying to decide if I needed to sit or kneel. I feel the nerves—my hands and feet are numb with them—but it's not fear as much as it is anticipation. On my drive in, I pulled over to snap a picture of the parking sign for OPEN QUALIFYING on a placard of that distinctive Open gold I knew from the tournament's scoreboard, and now I photograph the tee markers stamped with the Claret Jug, not worried about looking like a spectator rather than a participant. On the practice tee, I hit a few dozen wedges and 6-irons and drivers off the heart of the clubface, and then we walk to the tee box, where I'm given a sticker with the number 20 on it in British Open font. I stick it on my bag, officially a participant in Game 20. I put an R&A pitch mark tool in my pocket and take a handful of R&A tees, and in a moment I hear, "From the United States, Tom Coyne."

Nobody applauds. Nary a *U-S-A!* chant to be heard. There are just a few of us standing around the tee box, and I'm paired with two journeyman pros from London and Edinburgh who have played this qualifier a half dozen times. They know Bruntsfield well, while I missed my practice round the day before. I missed my tee time at the final rota course, Musselburgh, as well.

Three months before, coming up short by one on my checklist of Open venues would have seemed unforgivable, especially when the miss is a course as seminal as Musselburgh, the Guinness Book of World Records designee as oldest golf course on the planet. Its holes were once shared by some of golf's original clubs, the Honourable Company, Royal Burgess, Royal Mussel-burgh, and Bruntsfield all playing there before outgrowing the seven-holer stretched to nine situated within a horse track. (Next time you curl a putt off the lip, exclaim *Musselburgh!*; the hole-cutter was invented there, and the diminutive dimensions of its greenskeeper's apparatus were adopted as the standard for cup width in 1893.) Skipping Musselburgh seemed antithetical to this entire endeavor, and the idea of playing 109 rounds in preparation for the qualifier and then not even showing up for a practice round on the host track would have made me sick with failure. But it was not a failure. It was fog.

Two days before on South Uist, I left a dark airport after having not traveled anywhere and was forced to put my Askernish epiphany to use. Unless the forecast changed for tomorrow, the flight off the island might be canceled again, and I might miss the qualifier altogether. Three years of my life, lost in the mist.

I considered whom I might call to complain, then briefly contemplated the cost and logistics of commandeering a mackerel boat. And then I decided to settle into my circumstances. Fogged in? *Hard lines*, I thought. If I missed the qualifier at Bruntsfield, it wasn't my doing. What was my doing was getting on with now, which meant asking the rental company to bring that car back and calling the hotel for an extra night. It meant not worrying whether the tee sheet was crowded back at the course I was supposed to play that afternoon, because it never was at Askernish.

The skies cleared and I got off the island the next morning and cruised from Glasgow over to Edinburgh and collected the keys to a carefully researched rental beside the Bruntsfield Links. As I circled the block wondering when the golf course would appear, I felt like Harry Potter searching for platform 9 and 3/4, unsure how they had squeezed eighteen holes between a pub and an alleyway. The signs said Bruntsfield Links, but all I found was a small park covered with the short flags of a pitch 'n' putt. I certainly wouldn't need my driver tomorrow, I thought, and wondered if those folks at the R&A who'd accepted my application months before were having a laugh, and if tomorrow morning a handful of smartly dressed American golfers would be standing in the middle of a city park as caddies wiped away our tears.

My landlord did have a laugh on the phone when I asked her if the Bruntsfield Golf Club was next door—as it turned out, my apartment would have been teeside accommodation if only I were playing a qualifier in 1815 instead of 2015. The Bruntsfield golfers had moved a hundred years ago to a layout some twenty minutes away, though the name of the grassy space they formerly occupied remained the Bruntsfield Links (same for the Leith Links, now a park a few miles north). Between the fog and the treachery of Google Maps, Scotland was not making my final round a simple one, which seemed entirely appropriate.

I'd adjusted my alarm clock for an earlier wake-up—no walking to the course, it seemed—and on the first tee, I'm relaxed. I make a good swing on the opener, my drive running into the edge of the right rough. I knock a 5-iron short of the green, chip up to six feet, and I'm even par in a qualifier for the Open Championship when that putt drops in. I don't recall seeing the line or making the stroke; I give all credit to the ball marker Alan gave me on the first tee, a gold US dollar. "Some luck from home," he told me, and I do feel lucky, even though my limbs feel foreign and I seem to be watching Bruntsfield through someone else's eyes. I'm not sure who this person is who's walking toward a tee box with driver in hand, but I hope like hell he's a stick.

I'm blind to my playing partners and unavailable to distraction. I hand over my scorecard to Alan and ask him to keep the tallies; I want to think of nothing but the next shot, focused and fixed in my present endeavor. I would have done well to soften my concentration a smidge, just enough to notice that my partners, who had each played a practice round, are swinging irons on number two. My drive finds the trees down the right, and I'm in a territory I haven't seen in my two months of a links-only diet—limbs and leaves between me and the flag. I go for the green and clip a branch, and my ball scrambles into a fairway bunker, cozying up against the lip.

"They're supposed to be ninety percent air," I tell Alan.

"What are?"

"Trees. We say that at home. Trees are ninety percent air."

"Aye," he says. "And so is a screen door."

I splash out short of the green, chip well past the hole, and take three strokes to bury my ball, the last of which feels as steady as an old man trying to sip an overfilled cup of tea. My round is racing, and as I pick my ball out of the hole, unable to comprehend triple bogey, I'm unwilling to accept that in the round meant to top so many rounds, I'm three over after two. I've taken two of the most spectacular months of my life and, in twelve minutes, turned them into sheep shit. This isn't how this is supposed to end. Golf has gotten this all terribly wrong.

I don't hear Penn's voice. Instead, I hear my high school football coach blasting Penn's advice, shouting into my ear as I lay in the August mud. *Don't quit.*

It's all I have. All the swing thoughts and scorecards, all the angles and notebooks, all the lessons and wisdom—don't quit is all I can do. It's not an act of courage. If it is, then courage tastes like vomit crawling up your throat. It's an act of get-on-with-it. Scotland has taught me that there is always, *always* the next hole. And my caddie is waiting for me there.

I three-putt two more times before I recall that the goal of golf is to put the ball in the hole, and that my putter's primary function is to assist me in doing so. I wait until the fifth, perhaps the hardest hole yet at 205 yards with a mess of trees and overgrowth guarding the right side of the green, to card another par. Both my partners make bogeys, one of them in spectacular fashion: After hitting into the mess on the right, Calum from Royal Mussel-burgh hits his provisional tee ball to a foot. It's the first time in all my golfing life when a partner demands that nobody look for his ball, even barking, *Please, do not find it!* at one of the spectators following our group. The guy in green wellies can't understand what he's doing wrong, unaware that if he found the ball in the bushes, Calum would have to play it, and bogey from that junk was no guarantee. I've played with a lot of ball-bashing pros, tight dots worn into the centers of all their 6-irons, but this request to not look for a golf ball makes me feel the presence of a true professional. Calum is not quite six feet tall but is sneaky long, with the edge of a young man who plays for his supper and isn't impressed by the Open tee markers or the fancy scoreboard; this is his workplace, and he practices his trade with rote and tidy discipline. He taps in for bogey and leaves his other ball to mystery. Total pro move.

I'm exuberantly over par, but I have the honor on the sixth tee. It doesn't last, as I fail to get up and down, but it feels good to go first, and after a smat-tering of bogeys and pars, I'm going first again on fourteen after making a birdie three on the previous hole, a 455-yard uphill par 4 and the toughest offering on the card. From the fairway, I can tell my ball is close on the green up above, and Calum asks me if I hit six. I tell him I did.

"Damn. I hit seven," he says, lamenting his approach, which failed to reach the crest of the green, and for a moment we're colleagues on a smoke break, commiserating about our daily grind. Alan tells me that last year's medalist at this qualifier was watching from an adjacent tee box as I dropped my ten-footer for a rare birdie on thirteen.

"He must have been wondering who that player is," he says.

I smile. "Him and me both."

I'm even par on the back nine, and a few spectators have joined our group. An old man with a rolled-up copy of the *Scotsman* under his arm has been following us since the second hole. Alan tells me they had a chat and that the man had read the story in the paper that morning about my long Scottish round coming to an end at Bruntsfield that afternoon. I never get a chance to say hello to him myself, though I nearly kill him on seventeen when I step up to the tee, still holding the honor, and blaze one off the butt of my driver.

As a trick shot, the effort is outstanding—the ball nearly shoots between my own legs. But as a drive on a long par 4, it's shit, and dangerously so. The elderly man doesn't move as the ball zips past his feet thirty yards behind me, where he presumed he was standing in a safe position. His expression is blank. He just backs up and doesn't look at me. I want him to laugh or smile or pat me on the back as I pass, shout me some encouragement about golf being a brutal game that gets us all, but his nonreaction burns. It reminds me that this is serious business, and that my shot was not serious at all. He's probably just thinking about what he wants for dinner, but in my head, I've shamed this man's homeland and its game. I hack my ball up to the fairway, embarrassed that the newspaper under his arm has column inches about me but nothing about the real players here battling for one of the seven spots out of ninety-six players. Well, ninety-five, really. The Yank here is just having a laugh.

And a few minutes later, I am. In my gut, I'm shaking with laughter. I could finish this round on hands and knees, nudging my ball across Bruntsfield with my forehead, and I would stand up and smile and feel something that not even the medalist that afternoon would know. His 66 was a rare number, and five under was strange math to me, but in my life's best rounds, on the days when the game felt easy and the course was tilted into the cups, I never felt this.

Six months earlier, back in my shoe box of an office in our row house in Philadelphia, Scottish golf books covering the floor, dolls and My Little Ponies covering the golf books, I stared at a map full of pins without an idea of what they held, knowing only one thing about my plan: I couldn't do it. I had played two rounds in one day less than five times in my forty years; to do it every day, and add an extra round to some of them, was folly. I would do my best and collect some stories and play a lot of golf; when I came up short, I would want to make sure I had good cause, so I stuffed that map with dates and tee times and wondered which was the pin where it would end. So no wonder that I'm smiling on eighteen at Bruntsfield, where my final drive bounds down the center of the fairway and where I pinch a 9-iron to twenty feet. In front of a small gallery, my birdie putt rolls past the edge by the width of a ball, and I tap in for a final par. In the scorer's trailer, while Calum shakes his head at missing the cut by two shots, I don't know whether I should leap or cry or call home. I'm stuffed with this newly acquired emotion, the one I felt at Askernish two days before when I said good-bye to Robert and played on into the dusk. I didn't think I cared for feelings, unsteady and inaccurate as they often were, but this one seems to work; it fills me up. It feels genuine. It feels like plenty.

Scott is there at the eighteenth to snap pictures of my final putt at Bruntsfield, and I hardly recognize myself in that image of me standing over the ball—the missing paunch, the solid posture, the white belt I'd just bought so that I would look like a player—and I do look like a player, just like one of the gang. And more important, as we leave the course that afternoon, I feel like one, too. A nine-over score of 80 is not going to nab me any equipment deals, but it puts me in the company of a few other pros who have them. Not everybody shoots 66 that afternoon, and while I wish one of my low rounds had moved from May to the end of June, I leave feeling my Game 20 sticker was earned. I had even bested Scott by a few strokes, though I wish he would have made it through. I genuinely wished well for a friend and a fellow competitor—how novel—though I'm happy to know dinner is on him.

While the original course at Bruntsfield was gone, replaced by a thirty-six-hole pitch 'n' putt course, I did notice that its clubhouse remained. So when Scott asks where we're going for our celebratory dinner, I know precisely where we're headed.

Dating to 1456, the Golf Tavern in Edinburgh claims status as the oldest clubhouse in the world. Before golf clubs had proper clubhouses, the Golf Tavern—then the Golf Hotel—was used by the Bruntsfield golfers for socializing before the adjoining fields became overrun by traveling fairs and grazing herds and they had to move out to Musselburgh. (Ardglass in Northern Ireland might take issue with their claim to clubhouse fame—the Ardglass castle-turned-clubhouse dates to 1405, but as a clubhouse that was actually utilized by golfers, the Tavern might have the longer tenure.) The Tavern is as dark and cozy a watering hole as one will find in the UK, a room of walnut and leather with horse racing on flatscreens and a sleek menu, the ideal setting for our last supper of haggis balls and a burger topped with a fried biscuit of mac and cheese (I shall commence restoring my belly overhang immediately).

Dinner is mostly quiet, but not unhappy. We're deflating from five hours of focus and three hundred minutes of consequence. Besides, there isn't much left to say. Scott and I have seen it, and we seem to lack the energy to try to recap today and all the days before. I feel strangely immobile sitting there, unsure what to do with myself. There is no more golf to play, no more tee times to chase. The world henceforth will feel strange without a golf club in my hand. I feel lighter without my bag and thirty pounds of Moose Tracks under my belt, but I feel stuck, unsure of my next move. I guess I go pack; maybe watch some TV. I suppose I go home and kiss my girls and go be a dad and a husband with things to think about other than the next shot. I'm not sure how I'll do that, but I'll try it, and take each moment as it comes. As we exhume ourselves from our chairs, Scott smiles and asks me, now that it's over, if I found what I was looking for.

I notice a barrelful of old golf clubs by the door of the pub on our way out, presumably for folks who fancy a few holes in the park across the street. Some college students are chipping their balls around the field when we step out of the tavern and into the light, and we go to our cars and bro-hug our good-byes. I know I'll see Scott soon. Florida friends are easier to keep in touch with than others. He gets into his car and pulls away, while I sit in mine for a moment. I open the door and get out, walk around to the back, and, while I hadn't expected I would touch the grip end of these clubs again for many a month, I slide out my wedge and my putter and walk across the street.

Never, ever quit.

I pitch balls around the park and give myself a lot of putts, too tired to scoop them out of the holes, and I don't bother writing down any of my scores. It might seem a shame to play so many epic layouts and cap the trip with a stroll around a rough trail of sixty-yard offerings, but it's an ideal final round for me. It's proof that I still love this game, and a relief that I haven't exhausted its possibilities. And it's an answer to Scott's question: Not yet.

Lifetime

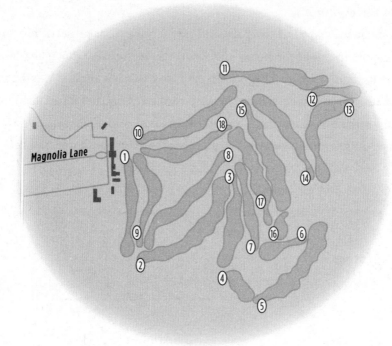

Magnolia Lane

I dreamed about the call. I imagined it coming via the rattling bell of a red rotary phone, even though nobody owned those anymore. But back when I started dreaming of playing there, back when I was a kid, they still did. As years went by and my golf world expanded, I accepted that all my travels hadn't made the call any more likely. I consoled myself with the lie that going there would spoil the dream and ruin April for me, that it was better to appreciate it from beneath its pedestal than to poke around its corners and find it wanting. So I didn't want the call, not until I got it, and when it came, I was unsure how to feel, how to act, unwilling to trust the words I was hearing. What do you do when the impossible dream comes true? Well, now I know:

You text every person in your contact list who has ever heard of golf, and some who haven't, *THE AUGUSTA NATIONAL.* Smiley face.

In Scotland, I had set out to find the round of my life. What I discovered there was the friend who would take me to it. I designed a trip that began in the southeast corner of England and ended in Edinburgh, but there was another plot unfurling, and these pilgrims had farther to journey. My itinerary, it turned out, had been too modest; I needed a map large enough for a Scottish golf trip that ended in Georgia.

Penn came through in a way that, in the long history of games, few sportsmen have been able to triumph. Jordan, Jeter, Flutie, and Woods had nothing on Penn when it came to clutch. He reached out to a close friend whose close friend was a member of Augusta National, and suddenly Scott and I were booking plane tickets on a week's notice, temporarily immune to all notions of cost and calendar conflicts. Penn even planned to go off and play another course during our visit, sacrificing his spot at Augusta for the two other members of his Scottish Highlands caravan. Doing so would allow Scott to put his one-hundredth golf ball on the wall and finish his life's list, and would teach me something about the people with whom you connect and the things you do for them as your lives roll forward.

Under bright-blue Southern skies, we make a left turn that I cannot quite believe, pulling our tires up to a gatehouse where we're told we will be granted passage on this Wednesday in late October. A very serious security guard lowers tank-deflecting ramparts into the pavement, and we turtle our way down Magnolia Lane. If there was ever a stretch of road that required no speed limit, this was it, the famed aisle leading to Augusta's white church of a clubhouse. I film the whole drive, the footage nearly ruined by the giggles of an off-camera dork who can't stop saying, "Wow," and "Wow," and "Dude, wow." That dork is me, professor turned linguistic imbecile by the sanctity of my surroundings.

In the parking lot, we meet our host, whom I resist hugging, and the day quickly becomes an exercise in restraint—restraining myself from scooping up range balls for Christmas gifts (unblemished Augusta ProV1s), resisting leaving the pro shop shelves bare, holding myself back from trying on that green jacket hanging there in my host's locker, mere inches from my fingertips. I keep it together through our morning trip around the par 3 course, through lunch in the clubhouse where two other members are dining with their guests (a sign by the entrance denotes which members are on the property—a total of three on the day we visited), to our afternoon round on the big course, where I try to catalog every swing and step. I've met design pundits who think Augusta is an overrated layout, and I pray for their darkened and irredeemable souls. My gut is a hurricane of nerves and memories as I walk the center of each fairway, whether my ball is there or not. I know I can stalk the edges with the patrons every April, so I make sure to enjoy the view from the middle and remember as I go.

I expect I'll be asked about favorite holes or my performance on Amen Corner, so I note that the descent on ten to a ball in the fairway, a hole that takes you from the tips of the pine trees down to their roots, has to be one of the best walks in sports. On eleven, I make a snazzy par from the right side of the green, and on twelve, the famed par 3 guarded by a dream-crushing creek, I make par when my tee shot hangs beautifully on the bank. Scott takes my picture as I climb the half-moon of Hogan Bridge in my golden Nicklaus golf shirt (Criquet Shirts named it "The '86" for Nicklaus's Masters miracle, and it made my wardrobe selection surprisingly easy), my arms raised like a champion as I trail behind my caddie in his crisp white jumpsuit. On thirteen, I make bogey with a smile after chunking a wedge into the tributary of Rae's Creek, and I hit it over the back of fifteen in two, managing a meek par 5 from there.

I have a half dozen birdie putts inside ten feet. I don't make one, and I don't stop grinning until I'm well off the property. As I swipe through the photographs of the day, my smiles make me look like I'm about to giggle out a secret, as if I'm trying to hide from the camera the fact that I'm surreptitiously shit-faced. My eyes look a little crazy in the shot of me reclining in a wicker chair on the patio; same for the photo in which I'm posed beside the Masters trophy, a giant silver rendering of the clubhouse of which the annual winner receives a replica. And for good reason, because I felt crazy. How could I not, after being given a tour of the champions' locker room, where winners now have to share lockers (Jordan Spieth and Arnold Palmer seemed the standout locker pairing); and grabbing a pack of Augusta National matches from the Crow's Nest, where they still have ashtrays and a rotary phone; and taking pictures of Eisenhower's desk overlooking the course, untouched, the framed black-and-white of his wife angled toward his chair; and going down into the cellar, where the fallen tree they named after him has been crafted into a wide table for wine tastings, next to where Bobby Jones and Cliff Roberts's favorite bottles still sit in storage, their names penciled on the labels under a thin film of dust? It's just too much. I feel unhinged, in the most wonderful possible way.

On a day that exceeds impossible expectations, it seems appropriate that I sign for a score of 80, the same tally from both Bruntsfield and my first round at Littlestone. It's a reminder of where this round really began, and how I found my way to Georgia by sticking pins into a map of Scotland.

It was a long road and an endless round, the sort of journey on which you expect to learn who you are. I haven't—not yet, and that's fine. There are plenty of miles left to try, and I am trying. But, better than knowing something as capricious and uncertain as *who* I am, I know *where* I am. I'm not at the Augusta National, behind the clubhouse, standing beneath a centuries-old oak with thick arms bowing toward tight green grass, a storied meeting spot where friends have found one another since the Masters began—*I'll see you at the old oak tree*. I'm not here, in Georgia. I'm not in Scotland. I'm not on the links. I'm not jabbing my fingers at a keyboard in a white-walled office in Philadelphia with scorecards scattered across a desk, where two little girls on the other side of the door argue over who gets to pick dessert. I'm not in any of these places, because I am where I know that I have always been, and where I hope to remain for the rest of my hours, safe and well in the lap of the Gods.

The Scores

COURSE	YARDS	PAR	SCORE
Littlestone Golf Club	6,632	71	80
Royal Cinque Ports	7,245	71	81
Prince's Golf Club	7,228	72	78
Royal St. George's Golf Club	7,204	70	80
Mullion Golf Club	6,053	70	74
Perranporth Golf Club	6,296	72	76
Trevose Golf & Country Club	7,112	72	76
Royal North Devon Golf Club	7,045	72	74
St. Enodoc Golf Club	6,547	69	75
Holyhead Golf Club	6,090	71	78
Bull Bay Golf Club	6,276	70	76
Conwy (Caernarvonshire) Golf Club	6,936	72	75
Wallasey Golf Club	6,588	72	76
Royal Liverpool Golf Club Hoylake	6,933	72	76
Royal Lytham & St. Annes Golf Club	180	36	35
Royal Birkdale Golf Club	7,156	70	79
Blackpool North Shore Golf Club	6,444	71	77
Eyemouth Golf Club	6,404	72	70
Dunbar Golf Club	6,560	71	76
Glen Golf Club	6,275	70	76
North Berwick Golf Club	6,506	71	82

COURSE	YARDS	PAR	SCORE
Archerfield, Dirleton Links	6,946	72	73
Muirfield	7,245	71	81
Gullane Golf Club, No. 2	6,385	71	69
Renaissance Club	7,303	71	79
Kilspindie Golf Club	5,502	69	72
Kingarrock Hickory Golf	2,022	32	39
Craigielaw Golf Club	6,601	71	74
St. Andrews Links, Eden Course	6,250	70	78
St. Andrews Links, Strathtyrum Course	5,620	69	74
Burntisland Golf House Club	5,993	70	74
Kinghorn Golf Club	5,141	65	74
Lundin Golf Club	6,371	71	74
Leven Links Golf Course	6,551	71	75
The Golf House Club, Elie	6,273	70	73
St. Andrews Links, Jubilee Course	6,742	72	74
Anstruther Golf Club	2,345	31	33
Crail Golfing Society, Balcomie Links	5,861	69	70
Crail Golfing Society, Craighead Links	6,651	72	81
St. Andrews Links, New Course	6,625	71	80
Kingsbarns Golf Links	7,224	72	78
St. Andrews Links, Castle Course	6,759	71	75
Scotscraig Golf Club	6,669	71	73
St. Andrews Links, Old Course	6,721	72	82
St. Andrews Links, Old Course	6,721	72	79
Monifieth Golf Club	6,655	71	74
Carnoustie Golf Club	6,948	72	81
Montrose Golf Links	6,585	71	75
Stonehaven Golf Club	5,103	66	70
Royal Aberdeen Golf Club	6,861	71	77
Murcar Links Golf Club	6,516	71	77
Newburgh on Ythan Golf Club	6,423	72	73
Trump International Golf Links	7,428	72	77

COURSE	YARDS	PAR	SCORE
Cruden Bay Golf Club	6,263	70	76
Peterhead Golf Club, Craigewan Links	6,173	70	81
Inverallochy Golf Club	5,436	67	71
Fraserburgh Golf Club	6,308	70	76
Rosehearty Golf Club	2,075	31	33
Royal Tarlair Golf Club	5,894	71	74
Cullen Golf Club	4,623	63	63
Strathlene Buckie Golf Club	5,977	69	77
Buckpool Golf Club	6,169	70	72
Spey Bay Golf Club	6,209	70	75
Moray Golf Club	6,572	71	77
Hopeman Golf Club	5,624	68	81
Covesea Links	2,026	31	31
Nairn Dunbar Golf Club	6,765	72	77
Nairn Golf Club	6,774	72	74
Asta Golf Club	2,251	31	31
Shetland Golf Club	5,562	68	1
Whalsay Golf Club	6,171	71	75
Stromness Golf Club	4,804	65	68
Castle Stuart Golf Links	7,009	72	83
Fortrose & Rosemarkie Golf Club	6,085	71	81
Tarbat Golf Club*	5,298	68	74
Tain Golf Club	6,404	70	74
The Carnegie Club at Skibo Castle	6,833	71	77
Golspie Golf Club	6,021	70	80
Royal Dornoch Golf Club, Championship	6,748	70	82
Royal Dornoch Golf Club, Struie	6,265	71	78
Brora Golf Club	6,211	70	77
Wick Golf Club	6,123	69	74
Reay Golf Club	5,854	69	71
Durness Golf Club*	5,555	70	72
Ullapool Golf Club*	5,281	70	73

COURSE	YARDS	PAR	SCORE
Gairloch Golf Club*	4,534	63	64
Skeabost Golf Club*	3,114	62	62
Isle of Skye Golf Club*	4,776	67	66
Traigh Golf Course *	4,912	68	70
Tobermory Golf Club*	4,912	64	67
Carradale Golf Club*	3,920	65	61
Machrihanish Dunes	7,082	72	77
Machrihanish Dunes	7,082	72	82
Machrihanish Golf Club	6,462	70	77
Machrihanish Golf Club	6,462	70	81
Dunaverty Golf Club	4,799	66	75
Shiskine Golf and Tennis Club	2,996	42	44
Trump Turnberry Resort, Ailsa Course	6,725	70	75
Prestwick St. Nicholas Golf Club	6,044	69	74
Prestwick Golf Club	6,908	71	77
Royal Troon	7,208	71	81
Barassie Links	6,852	72	78
Western Gailes Golf Club	7,014	71	5
Dundonald Links	7,100	72	75
Isle of Barra Golf Course	2,462	34	37
Askernish Golf Club	6,259	72	79
Askernish Golf Club	6,259	72	74
Askernish Golf Club	6,259	72	76
Askernish Golf Club	6,259	72	77
Bruntsfield Links (Open Qualifier)	6,437	70	80
The Original Bruntsfield Links	500	27	27

* Denotes nine-hole course played twice or with two balls.

Total Yards: 657,450   Total Rounds: 111

Total Days: 57   Holes per day: 33.4

Total Holes: 1,908   Total Score: 7,858 (542 over par)

The Lists

My Top-of-the-Pops, I'd-Change-My-Flight-to-Play-It-Tomorrow Courses

1. Askernish
2. Cruden Bay
3. St. Enodoc
4. Shiskine
5. Machrihanish Old
6. Machrihanish Dunes
7. Old Course
8. Brora
9. Murcar
10. Nairn

My Top Open Rota Experiences

1. Old Course
2. Prestwick
3. Royal Birkdale
4. Royal St. George's
5. Carnoustie
6. Royal Cinque Ports
7. Muirfield
8. Troon
9. Turnberry
10. Prince's

My I'm-Only-Doing-Scotland-Once Courses

1. Old Course
2. North Berwick
3. Royal Dornoch
4. Kingsbarns
5. Cruden Bay
6. Machrihanish Old
7. Carnoustie
8. Prestwick
9. Castle Stuart
10. Royal Aberdeen

My But-I-Already-Played-Those-Courses Courses

1. Brora
2. Glen
3. Dunbar
4. Lundin
5. Crail Balcomie
6. Elie
7. Fraserburgh
8. Gullane
9. Castle Course, St. Andrews
10. Western Gailes

My True-Wanderer Tracks

1. Askernish
2. Shiskine
3. Durness
4. Dunaverty
5. Reay
6. Wick
7. Whalsay
8. Tain
9. Isle of Barra
10. Skeabost

My Best Wee Ones (Short Walks and Nine-Holers)

1. Shiskine
2. Anstruther
3. Cullen
4. Covesea
5. Traigh
6. Carradale
7. Isle of Skye
8. Tobermory
9. Tarbat
10. Rosehearty

My Top Courses of England and Wales

1. St. Enodoc
2. Wallasey
3. Royal Birkdale
4. Royal St. George's
5. Perranporth
6. Conwy
7. Bull Bay
8. Royal Cinque Ports
9. Holyhead
10. Trevose

My Loves-That-Didn't-Make-a-List

1. Kilspindie
2. Burntisland
3. Stonehaven
4. Newburgh on Ythan
5. Kinghorn
6. Golspie
7. Spey Bay
8. Dundonald
9. Barassie
10. Kingarrock

My Top Nineteenth Holes

1. Muirfield
2. St. Andrews (the Dunvegan)
3. Machrihanish Dunes
4. Castle Stuart
5. North Berwick
6. Skibo
7. Kingsbarns
8. Trevose (England)
9. Bull Bay (Wales)
10. Rosehearty (the Mason Arms)

My Top Golf Accommodations

1. The Ugadale Hotel, Machrihanish
2. The Royal Hotel, Campbeltown
3. The Sandown House, Nairn
4. Renaissance Club, Clubhouse, North Berwick
5. Milleur House, North Berwick
6. Golf View Guest House, Prestwick
7. Meldrum House, Aberdeen
8. Kilmarnock Arms, Cruden Bay
9. Number One B&B, Deal, England
10. Number Fifteen B&B, Hoylake, England

My Top Scotland Itineraries

1. **The Golf Coast**—Play: North Berwick, Glen, Dunbar, Muirfield, Gullane, Kilspindie, Craigielaw, Luffness, Archerfield, Renaissance. Stay: Milleur House, Renaissance Clubhouse, Craigielaw Clubhouse, Marine Hotel, or rent a home from NorthBerwickHolidayHomes.co.uk.

2. **East Fife**—Play: St. Andrews (Old, New, Castle, Jubilee), Crail, Kingsbarns, Anstruther, Elie, Lundin, Leven, Burntisland, Panmure, Carnoustie. Stay: Rusacks Hotel, or rent in St. Andrews from FifeCottages.co.uk or East Fife Letting Company.

3. **Aberdeen**—Play: Cruden Bay, Royal Aberdeen, Murcar, Fraserburgh, Stonehaven, Newburgh on Ythan. Stay: Meldrum House.

4. **Inverness and the Highlands**—Play: Nairn, Cullen, Covesea, Castle Stuart, Fortrose & Rosemarkie, Moray, Tain, Royal Dornoch, Golspie, Brora. Stay: Sandown House in Nairn, or Links House in Dornoch.

5. **Western Getaway**—Ferry to play Shiskine, then ferry to play Machrihanish Old, Machrihanish Dunes, Dunaverty, Carradale. Stay: The Ugadale Hotel.

6. **Ayrshire**—Play: Prestwick, Prestwick St. Nicholas, Troon, Turnberry, Western Gailes, Glasgow Gailes, Dundonald, Barassie. Stay: Golf View Guest House, Prestwick.

My Top Reasons to Go

1. Golf
2. Sea
3. Links
4. Scotland
5. From where you're sitting right now, you can get only some of the above, and none of it touches the feeling of following your ball across the dunes at twilight.

Acknowledgments

My gratitude for this adventure begins with Jofie Ferrari-Adler at Simon & Schuster, a sage editor and trusted ally, and a damn fine golfer. Jofie provided me space to wander and unwavering support; he gave me far more than the chance to write this book. And aside from my family, nobody has stood by me more than my agent, Dan Mandel, a friend who changed my life the day I met him.

The arrangement of this trip took a confluence of good fortune and good people, and some of the best include: At Visit Scotland, Malcolm Roughead, Alan Grant, Euan Munsie, Adam Couper, and especially David Connor, who helped piece together an itinerary I'm sure they hope is never again attempted. At Golf Tourism England, Andrew Cooke was of great insight and support, and at Visit Wales, Claire Sanders was a valuable advocate. And many thanks to the members of Belleair Country Club in Florida and the McCall and Meadowlands clubs in Philadelphia for your generous tee sheets, and for waving this single through.

Much credit goes to the books that augmented my links education: *True Links* by George Peper and Malcolm Campbell and *The Story of Golf* by George Peper; Paul Daley's *Links Golf*; Gary Sutherland's *Golf on the Rocks*; and everything by the late Jim Finegan, an irreplaceable gentleman of the game. Many thanks to Neil Laird and his ScottishGolfHistory.org, an utterly addictive website that reads with the depth and intrigue of a good novel.

Old friends at Mizuno and Titleist/FootJoy were again there for me when I came calling for gear: Bill Price at Mizuno fit me with clubs better than I deserved, and Bill Lacy, Joe Games, Chris Garrett, and June Medeiros kept my feet well and dry and my ball supply healthy. And new friends at Seamus Golf, Criquet Shirts, and Jones Golf had me outfitted as the player I aspired to become.

Many thanks to Thomas Young at Ballpark Blueprints for painstaking work on the poster I gifted around the UK, and to Kevin Kirk at Recounter Photography for images I only half believe are me. Julianna Haubner and Benjamin Holmes at Simon & Schuster made this a much better book, and to Jonathan Karp, Jerry Quinlan, Tom Casey, Jim Slattery, Mike Dynda, Dr. Jim Suttie, John Boyne, Gordon Murray, Scott Pauli, Mike Doyle, Claire Bruce, Graham Lane, Sarah Turner, Laurie Watson, Kevin Friend, Bob Schroeder, Cristin Luck, Ru Macdonald, Lee Wybranski, Billy Collins, Ralph Thompson, Anna Bedney, Joshua Evenson, and Archie Baird: your wisdom and talents all added a great deal to a trip I will relive as long as memory allows.

To the friends who joined me and became a part of these pages: I cannot adequately thank you for your friendship, your insights, and your genuine selves. And to Allyson and my girls, my search for a miracle need never have left home.

About the Author

TOM COYNE is the author of the *New York Times* bestseller *A Course Called Ireland*, *Paper Tiger*, and the novel *A Gentleman's Game*, named one of the best twenty-five sports books of all time by the *Philadelphia Daily News* and adapted into a motion picture starring Gary Sinise. He has written for *Golf Magazine*, *Sports Illustrated*, *The Golfer's Journal*, and numerous other publications. He earned an MFA in fiction writing from the University of Notre Dame, where he won the William Mitchell Award for distinguished achievement. He lives outside Philadelphia with his wife and two daughters, and he is an associate professor of English at Saint Joseph's University.